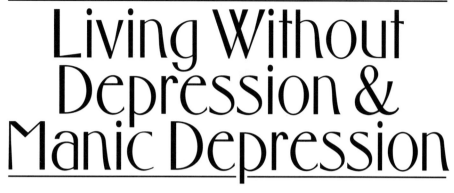

Living Without Depression & Manic Depression

A Workbook for Maintaining Mood Stability

MARY ELLEN COPELAND, M.S.

NEW HARBINGER PUBLICATIONS, INC.

Publishers Note

This publication is designed to provide accurate and authoritative information in regard to the subject matter covered. It is sold with the understanding that the publisher is not engaged in rendering psychological, financial, legal, or other professional services. If expert assistance or counseling is needed, the services of a competent professional should be sought.

Warning: Anyone who experiences depression and/or manic depression needs to be under the care of expert health care professionals. Depression and mania are dangerous and can be life-threatening. The treatment strategies described in this book do not replace on-going treatment. Do not abruptly stop other treatments in deference to the ones described in this book. Modify your treatment only after you have carefully considered it and discussed it with trusted health care professionals, and have put appropriate monitoring and support systems in place.

Cover design by SHELBY DESIGNS & ILLUSTRATES
Text design by Tracy Marie Powell
Author photo by Robert McClintock

Distributed in U.S.A. by Publishers Group West; in Canada by Raincoast Books; in Great Britain by Airlift Book Company, Ltd.; in South Africa by Real Books, Ltd.; in Australia by Boobook; in New Zealand by Tandem Press.

Library of Congress Catalog Number: 94-067047
ISBN 1-879237-74-1 Paperback

00

10   9

In loving memory of Kathryne Strouse Copeland
January 7, 1912–April 5, 1994

This book is dedicated to the memory of my mother, *Kathryne Strouse Copeland,* my guide, inspiration, and support, who has shown me and thousands of others that there is hope, that we can take back our lives, that there is light at the end of the tunnel. Because of her, "hopeless" means "hope," and "incurably insane" means "That's what *you* think." Her courage and strength have paved the way for each of us.

In 1949, she was hospitalized in a state mental hospital for major depression. For eight long years she lived in that hospital as her moods alternated from deep depression to extreme mania. We were told to forget her, that she would never get well.

My mother got well. The extreme moods ceased. She came home. She spent the rest of her life, 37 years, living to the fullest—working as a dietitian in the New Haven, Connecticut school system for 20 years, babysitting for her grandchildren and great-grandchildren, cooking for everyone, supporting her family and friends. She became a highly-respected and much loved member of the community.

She has a huge network of family, friends, and people she has inspired. We will all miss her, but her message of courage and hope will never be forgotten.

Contents

Part IV   Addressing Specific Issues

Foreword

A few days ago, as I was watching the news on television (something I don't recommend for a depressed person), the commentator mentioned it was the anniversary of a historic event. I vividly recalled the event, where I was living, what I was doing, and what I was feeling at the time. I was one of several people who, because of their disabilities, were living in a housing complex for the elderly. So there I was, at the age of 47, living in a high-rise apartment building where the other residents were on average at least several decades older than me.

My brain felt like it was filled with sticky, gauzy cobwebs. If someone asked me a question, I couldn't remember it long enough to answer. The simplest mathematics problem, like adding two months' phone bills, had me stumped. I moved slowly, managing to accomplish in a day the bare minimum of tasks to get by. I was overweight. My hair and skin were coarse and dry. My connections with the world were minimal, limited to a few close friends who had stayed the course and to persistent family members. I spent a lot of time watching mindless programs on television while wishing for an end to the horror my life had become. I was in the midst of another deep winter depression.

I had experienced mood swings for as long as I could remember, but had always managed to get by. In 1986, these mood swings became overpowering, taking over my life. They alternated from months of severe out-of-control mania with spending sprees, bizarre behavior, and impulsive and destructive decision-making and actions, to deep depression, where I was unable to think or to feel, where I felt dead inside. The swings persisted in spite of several hospitalizations, doctors who searched diligently for the right combination of medications, and counselors who were supportive and persistent through one crisis after another.

It was during this time that I asked my doctor how people diagnosed with affective disorders—mine was called manic depression, or bipolar disorder—get by on a day-to-day basis.

He said he would get me that information. I looked forward with anticipation to our next visit. When I asked for the information, he said there wasn't any.

I explained my dilemma to a vocational rehabilitation counselor, and with her support I slowly began my study of how people with depressive disorders get by on a day-to-day basis. There were 120 people in my first study. When their responses to my questionnaire started pouring into my mailbox, I felt overwhelmed. The mood swings were still overpowering my life and I had no idea how I was ever going to take this goldmine of information and assemble it into a useful document, much less put any of the suggestions into practice in my own life.

It was at that time, when I felt I had really hit the bottom (meaning I knew I had lots of good work to do and no energy or enthusiasm to do it), that, thankfully, things started to change.

First, several doctors suggested I try light therapy to treat my horrible but predictable winter depressions. I bought an inexpensive shop light fixture, replaced the fluorescent bulbs with full spectrum light bulbs, and set it on the table to light my living room while I watched TV and made furtive efforts to compile the study data. I noticed that I started to feel better. My mind began to clear. I could work on the data for longer periods of time. I found this interesting and even a little exciting. I decided to buy two more shop light fixtures and four more full spectrum bulbs, talked my son into mounting them on a piece of plywood, and I had myself a primitive but effective light box. The more I used it the better I felt.

This new energy gave me the spark I needed to incorporate into my life some of the strategies suggested in the study, and which I later described in my first book, *The Depression Workbook: A Guide for Living With Depression and Manic Depression*. My mood stability continued to improve and I felt healthier.

While making these changes, a doctor encouraged me to see an endocrinologist because he felt my puffy appearance, dry skin and hair, slow movement, and inability to tolerate cold indicated that I might have a thyroid disorder. The endocrinologist found that I did indeed have severe hypothyroidism. With treatment of that condition and the resulting increases in energy, stamina, and concentration, I not only began to feel that there was a light at the end of the tunnel but that my life, as I used to know it, was not over as I had feared—a fear my family members and friends shared.

My healing and recovery have continued. I still have mornings where I want to stay in bed curled up in a fetal position with the covers over my head, but these mornings are fewer and fewer, and the work I have to do and the promises I have to keep get me up and going. There are other days when I feel as if I am going so fast that my feet aren't touching the floor, my heart is pounding, and ideas are whirling around in my head faster than the speed of sound. That's when I know I have to curtail my activities, decrease the stimulation, calm myself down, do some relaxation exercises, and take a slow walk in the woods.

Is it easy? Never. I have to meet the challenge of keeping myself balanced on a daily basis. I have to use every ounce of my creativity to find coping mechanisms and solutions that keep me stable. Some days I feel as if I am climbing a 1500-foot vertical cliff on a hot, muggy day, searching for crevices for my hands and feet so that I can make my way to the shelter at the top before the encroaching lightning storm sends me crashing into the abyss. Other days, it's like walking barefoot across a field of gently undulating sand dunes on a warm, sunny spring day.

In the past two years I have experienced several of the most traumatic events of my entire life, events that threatened to tear away the very underpinnings of my soul. I keep going, one moment at a time, one foot firmly planted in front of the other.

Could I have made it without the safety net provided by my ever-growing circle of close friends and family? No way. This mutually supportive network is now pleasantly supplemented for me by a phone call or letter from someone somewhere in the country who has been touched by my work. I, in turn, am moved when they tell me:

> Recently, I purchased a copy of *The Depression Workbook*. I am very impressed by all the compassionate, hard work that has gone into this publication, as well as the considerable knowledge regarding depression. I believe this workbook would be very helpful to the many patients that I and my colleagues work with on the psychiatric unit . . .

> What a *great job!* I can easily see that you put a *ton* of work into this project. Thank you for sharing the results with us.

> What a wonderful workshop! The clients and I learned so much.

> Too bad you didn't have hours to talk and an hour to answer questions.

> So great to have an authority on mood disorders who has had her own mood disorder and shared her own experience.

> You are a very empathetic, empowering speaker.

In the years since I first set that shop light fixture on my living room table, I have completed two major research projects, written and published two books, and co-produced a video tape and an audio tape. I have given numerous presentations to thousands of people all around the country. I have led all-day and half-day workshops at national and statewide conferences, and to groups of people who live with mood instability on a day-to-day basis, their families, and their supporters. I have made presentations to hospital and mental health center staffs on what information people with mood disorders really need from health care providers. I have completed the work for my second master's degree in my new field, counseling psychology. I not only have my life back, but the possibilities seem endless.

In addition, I have made many significant changes in lifestyle and attitude, too many to mention here. The key changes include:

- I now live in a bright, cheery, comfortable, easy-to-maintain space where I have privacy.

- I limit the time that I spend working on serious (and potentially depressing) life issues—such as the effects of childhood abuse and low self-esteem caused by years of mental illness labeling—to my weekly counseling and peer counseling sessions. I have chosen to focus the rest of the time on my work, the things I enjoy doing, and the things I appreciate about being alive. I would rather spend my time reading a good book or going cross-country skiing.

- I have given up my workaholic style. I understand that I have the right to have fun and plan some pleasurable activity in every day.

- I take good care of myself. I watch my diet carefully, exercise almost daily, use my light box whenever the days are dark and dreary, and reach out for assistance to a team of health care experts whenever I have health problems that are difficult to solve.

- My new career, which I have developed myself, has a flexible schedule and makes optimum use of my abilities and talents.

- For the first time in my life I feel closely connected to, and loved by, many wonderful people. I have a strong support network within my family and community. In addition, I am blessed by the support of a broader network of people from all of the country.

The most important change of all is that, for the first time in my life, I want to live. I treasure this wonderful life I have made for myself. Each day is a new adventure. My outlook on the future is bright and clear.

Preface

"I'm so afraid you'll become weary and exasperated with me, Mary Liz. I feel like I am such a burden."

"I hear your fear and despair, Mary Ellen."

"You must wish I'd just drop into a hole and disappear."

"No, that's not how I feel."

"Well . . . perhaps you wish I would be well again."

Yes, I did. With all my being, I wished you well again, Mary Ellen. But hopes had been dashed so often over the years, I hardly dared believe it was possible.

However, in the six years since you made those wistful remarks, I have watched with cautious yet mounting excitement as you took each step along the way to becoming a full participant in your own life—as a grandmother, daughter, and mother; as confidante and counselor; leader and author; lover and friend.

Ever the skeptical Yankee daughter of a pragmatic Scotsman that I am, I was not completely convinced that you'd made it back until one day when the familiar dragons of depression came gamboling out of their caves and you felt the old cords tighten around your ankles and pull you down. Mustering all the strength and wisdom you'd gained on the long journey back to wellness, you called in your support network of friends, assessed your situation with competent, trusted professionals, adjusted your priorities so you could nurture yourself, took charge of your recovery, and proved the efficacy of your own strategy as described in *The Depression Workbook*.

In fact, recently when I was in great need of support myself, you were one of the friends to whom I turned for help. I'd just sold my house, stored all my possessions, packed a few suitcases, and was about to leave for the West after a lifetime in New England. I was exhausted and overwhelmed by all the details of this move, so you took me out for walks through the fall foliage, giving me my last chance to be nourished by the unique brilliance of the Vermont sugar maples. I was also quite frightened. Had I done the right thing? Too late now . . . all I had left of my old life was a cat and a six-foot walking staff (neither of which the airline was too pleased about transporting!). One cold night before I left, you took me in, gave me warm tea and strong affirmations and sent me on my way. I was so thankful you hadn't "fallen into a hole and disappeared" six years ago. Welcome home, Mary Ellen . . . it sure is good to have you back.

Now you travel all over the country (even in airplanes, which were once an impossible nightmare for you), speaking before large groups, sharing your life and your wisdom through your workshops, videos, and books. I must tell you, however, that this last trip to Alaska in the depths of winter does not point to the highest level of sanity!

Mary Ellen, you're not the same whirlwind superwoman I first met 33 years ago. Thank goodness for that! You have fewer illusions about perfection these days and a deeper understanding of boundaries and flexibility. You've learned to listen for what needs balance in your life and to say "no" as easily as you say "yes." You show me that wellness is not simply the absence of disease or disability—rather, it's about balance and resilience and courage.

Ah, my friend, not in our wildest dreams could we ever have known it would come to this. I rejoice in the knowledge that you are indeed "well again."

—Mary Liz Riddle
Boulder, Colorado
January 14, 1994

Acknowledgments

I wish to thank the following people for their assistance and support in this project: Irene Alexa, Kathryne Copeland, Rupa Cousins, Wells Cunningham, Laura Evans, Tim Field, Janet Foner, Neil Friedman, Dr. John Glick, Ellen Goldfarb, Dr. Herman Goldfarb, Norma Goldfarb, Tim Hamilton, David Hilton, Harvey Jackins, Karen Kamenetsky, Sonja Kjear, Mary Lawler, Dr. Wayne London, Mary Moller, Barbara Peller, Nancy Post, Patti Smith, Bev White, Iva Wood, Karen Young, and all the people who have so willingly taken part in my studies. You made this possible!

Introduction

About This Book

Recurring episodes of deep depression interspersed with occasional mania began when I was in elementary school. As a child, I didn't understand why sometimes I didn't speak to anyone unless asked a question, why I spent my recess and lunch hours standing alone against a cold brick wall. At other times I was the "life of the party," a high achieving, popular leader in school activities. As an adult, these episodes of mood instability increased in frequency and intensity, eventually leading me to seek medical and psychiatric help. While the medications and hospitalizations were somewhat helpful, I was anxious to find out how others with mood swings like mine got by on a day-to-day basis. My search for such information was fruitless. Confused and frustrated, I began, with the help of vocational rehabilitation services, a study of 120 volunteers who experience depression or manic depression. As strategies and ideas poured in, I began compiling the data into a step-by-step format and implementing many of the techniques in my own life. These strategies, along with discovery and treatment for severe hypothyroidism, have been responsible for five years of wellness and success. As I realized how valuable these techniques were, I began sharing them through workshops and writings. They were so successful that I developed my first book, *The Depression Workbook: A Guide for Living With Depression and Manic Depression.*

Since then, I have traveled extensively around the country presenting workshops and giving lectures to thousands of people, including those who support others with mood disorders. In the process, I have met many outstanding people who have been diagnosed with severe mental or psychiatric disorders, but who no longer experience symptoms that are severe enough to have a significant impact on their lives. They work, take care of family responsibilities, and do the things they enjoy without being hampered by depression or mania.

This intrigued me. I wanted to find out how they got well and have stayed well. And I wanted to share this information with others who are searching for answers. No one should have to live with mood instability, which frequently leads to invalidation, unemployment, low self-esteem, limited support, and severed connections. Nor should the disorder keep people from being who they want to be, doing what they want to do, and reaching their life goals.

Who Will Benefit From Using This Book

This book was written for anyone who experiences depression or manic depression, and for those people who love and support them. It contains recommendations and ideas from people who have experienced extreme depression and manic depression. I gathered this information through my ongoing study of the coping skills and wellness strategies used by people who experience extreme high and low moods. These strategies are well-tested, safe, and often effective. I hope you will find many of them helpful.

Living Without Depression and Manic Depression emphasizes strategies that are:

- Safe. You can use the strategies in this book without fear of harm. It is a good idea, however, to let your health care professionals know that you are using this book. They can provide additional information and support, and help you monitor your symptoms.

- Complementary. The strategies in this book are designed to *enhance,* rather than *replace,* your current treatment program. *Do not abruptly stop your current treatments because you are learning about new ones in this book.* You should never discontinue treatment without first carefully considering the issue in consultation with your health care professionals. Also make sure that you will be monitored and provided with appropriate support, should you decide to discontinue a treatment.

- Economical. Most of the strategies in this book are inexpensive or free. It costs nothing to do relaxation exercises, physical exercise, peer counseling, or institute lifestyle changes. Support groups are also often free. On the other end of the spectrum is counseling, which can cost up to $125 an hour. Check to see whether your counselor offers a sliding scale fee if your insurance plan provides limited coverage of mental health care.

- Simple. By simple, I don't mean to imply that they are easy. Journaling, focusing, and peer counseling may seem simplistic, for instance, but they really do help keep extreme moods under control. It takes dedication, consistency, and persistence to incorporate these practices into your life on a regular basis. That's the hard part. It's all too easy to slip out of positive new habits and revert to old, deeply ingrained ones that interfere with your balance. Some of these techniques can help you keep on course.

- Effective over the long term. I emphasize the long term, because few methods of healing can create a profound and immediate or a short-term change for someone with mood instability. This does happen on occasion, however. For some people, a day or two of light therapy can make an amazing difference. More often, therapies bring gradual improvement. People notice that they are having fewer bad days and that mood stability is getting to be less and less an issue in their lives. Be satisfied when you find yourself taking small steps toward a lifestyle that enhances wellness and stability. Every step counts.

The best time to familiarize yourself with these strategies is when you are well. When you are in the throes of an episode, it may be difficult or impossible to learn the techniques and take the recommended action. Wait instead for periods of remission, when symptoms are not an issue. Take advantage of these windows of opportunity. Then you will know what action to take when you are unstable.

How To Use This Book

This book was written in workbook style to give you the opportunity to explore more intensively the various ideas presented. Many people have told me that completing the exercises in my first book, *The Depression Workbook: A Guide for Living With Depression and Manic Depression,* was very helpful. You may choose not to do the exercises or to do only those that you feel are appropriate for you. It's your choice. Whatever you feel will work best is the right thing to do.

Remember, this is your book. It may comfort you to know that most people are inhibited by writing exercises. It reminds them of elementary school workbooks, where everything had to be neat, tidy, and spelled correctly. That's *not* the case here. Forget the old rules. Write whatever you feel like, any way it comes out.

All the exercises within have been designed with safety in mind. That's one of the reasons why the approaches in this book, like those in *The Depression Workbook,* have won the endorsement of educational and support groups.

This book is meant to be used in its entirety. However, each chapter stands on its own. Cross-references in the chapters that direct you to related information in other chapters, and a list at the end of each chapter provides additional resources. I suggest that you read the book through and then return to the chapters you feel are more suited to your needs. For example, people who have thoroughly explored the medical issues, but who have yet to focus on resolving the life issues that are related to their episodes, may want to skip ahead to the chapters on that subject.

What This Book Covers

If depression or manic depression interferes with your life, and you are determined to get your moods under control, you may find it helpful to consider several paths to healing. There is the medical path, the lifestyle path, and the life issues path. You can follow these one at a time or pursue several at once. You may need to focus specifically on addressing symptoms as they come up, or discover that what is most important right now is to learn how to stand up for yourself and get what you need. This workbook will guide you each step of the way.

This book begins with the most important chapter, "How To Advocate Effectively for Yourself." Before you can do anything, you have to take responsibility for your own health and be willing and able to advocate effectively for yourself. Next, in chapter 2, you'll learn how to enlist others to support you in that process.

If you suspect that an underlying medical condition may be giving rise to your symptoms, read chapter 3, "Eliminating the Physical Causes of Mood Disorders." In chapter 4, you'll find a thorough discussion on how to use medication safely.

Part II begins with a chapter explaining how to develop and then fine-tune a lifestyle that promotes health—from getting your daily dose of light to the key areas of diet, exercise, sleep, and your living space. Chapter 6 offers some suggestions for making sure that you don't overlook the healing power of life's pleasurable moments. Chapter 7, "Creating a Career That Works," contains strategies for finding fulfilling work that meets your needs.

Part III covers life issues, beginning with chapter 8, "Minimizing Negative Influences From the Past." The material there will assist you in exploring your life history and discovering any unresolved issues from the past that are *still* interfering with your wellness. Chapters 9 through 14 introduce you to practical strategies you can use to complete your healing around these issues, including resolving trauma, choosing the best counselor and making the most of counseling, exploring thoughts and feelings, and restoring self-esteem.

The final four chapters show you how to take preventive action when you first experience symptoms indicative of depression or mania. In these last chapters, you'll have a chance to pull together strategies you have learned in the previous chapters into a detailed plan for taking a proactive role on your own behalf.

What's This Book Does *Not* Cover

Detailed information about various psychiatric drugs and other medical treatments is beyond the scope of this book. There are many excellent books, written by expert authors, that address these topics. If you are considering the use of medication or specific medical therapies, you need to be under the care of a qualified health care professional who has the expertise you need.

Other information can be obtained by reading the pharmaceutical insert that comes with the medication, attending informational sessions and support groups, and by doing research at general libraries, medical libraries, and libraries at psychiatric facilities. If you are unable to do the research yourself, ask someone you trust to do it for you.

You will find information on how to use medication safely and how to minimize side effects in chapter 4.

This book also does not address the very controversial issue of the origin of depression and manic depression. Scientists are still debating whether the source of these is genetic, biological, physiological, environmental, or some combination. There are many excellent books on this topic. For my purposes, however, the origin of depression or manic depression is not significant. I have chosen to focus on how to reduce and eliminate the symptoms, and to present opportunities that will enhance your life.

Another Resource

You will notice that my first book, *The Depression Workbook: A Guide for Living With Depression and Manic Depression,* is listed in the resource section of many chapters of this book. Based on my original study of 120 people who have been diagnosed with major depression or manic depression, it contains a step-by-step program for breaking free of the bonds of depression and manic depression. You may want to use it to supplement your work in this book. It can be purchased in bookstores or ordered from New Harbinger Publications, 5674 Shattuck Avenue, Oakland, CA 94609 (1-800-748-6273).

PART I

Taking Charge

1

How To Advocate
Effectively for Yourself

It wasn't until I realized that it was up to me to get my moods under control, that there was no magic cure, that I began to turn the corner on the road to wellness.

If you suffer from mood instability, you may feel as if you have lost control over your own life, and lost the ability and right to effectively advocate for yourself. It is also common for people with mood disorders to have very low self-esteem. The way to regain your sense of control and with it the hope and self-esteem necessary to stability and wellness is to successfully advocate for yourself. This chapter will teach you how.

In my studies, I have met many remarkable people who spent years completely debilitated by severe depression or manic depression and who have learned to be their own best advocate. They are now strong advocates for appropriate treatment and services for others. Many have become national leaders in the movement to get equal insurance coverage and other benefits for psychiatric disorders on par with the benefits available for other medical illnesses. You may have seen some of them testifying at the televised senate hearings. Others have taken leadership and supporting roles in a wide variety of fields.

Tim Field of Seattle, Washington, is an excellent example. Founder and editor of a Washington State client/consumer mental health newsletter, "The Sentinel," Tim has suffered major episodes of depression for years. He has found that being a strong advocate for himself and others is essential if he wants to feel in control of his life and his depression. "People need to know and demand their rights in all types of situations," he says. "Empowerment and recovery start from the inside when you begin to take charge of all the aspects of your life. People must always remember that there is hope."

Tim adds:

To me, self-advocacy is part of empowerment, and empowerment is nothing more than learning to take care of yourself every single day, every single hour. Easy to say but hard to do. For me, empowerment has two parts: involvement and insight.

Involvement means taking an *active* role in everything you do or that happens to you. This is especially true when dealing with problems such as depression. Since depression is a life-threatening problem that may continue to periodically rear its head, it is only prudent to learn as much as you can about it, the same as you would if you had cancer or diabetes. It's not like a broken arm, where you can be passively "repaired" by a doctor. Depression is a different kind of problem, in the sense that you can't expect a doctor or therapist to "fix" you. There is no "cure," though your life is still at stake.

It took me over 15 years of periodic visits to hell to figure this out. So I have set out to learn as much as I can about depression and to integrate this knowledge into knowledge about myself, with a goal of finding what works for me. But I couldn't start doing this until I stopped denying what was happening to me. This was the beginning of insight, and it has helped me grow and mature. I decided that if I had these problems, I needed to find out what exacerbated them and what I needed to avoid. I also needed to learn what is good for me and truly important. Learning *that* is very much a spiritual endeavor for me. Having come so close to death has changed my perspective about many things. The career path, material wealth, and other measures of "success" that many people feel are so important I no longer care very much about. I am letting go of these things that used to seem so crucial to me but really just added to my stress and unhappiness. Finding what works for me means exploring new avenues to discern what has the most positive effect on me. In this way I have discovered how powerful and positive the support groups, new and *safe* friends, and new places to live and ways of doing things can be. All of these aids help me avoid becoming dormant and isolated.

Another person in my most recent study said, "I came out of the closet and could say the name of my illness when I started to facilitate a support group. Since then I've been on the radio, local television, have gone to two National Alternatives conferences, and spend much of my time volunteering, advocating, educating, and getting educated on mental health issues. Learning new things, helping others, and meeting new people all help to keep me interested in mental health issues."

Ten Steps To Being an Effective Self-Advocate

1. Believe in Yourself

You are unique, valuable, and worth the effort it takes to advocate for yourself and protect your rights. You can do it! But you may need to work on raising your self-esteem so you can become your own best advocate.

Accurate assessment and self-acceptance are necessary first steps. Which statement best describes you?

☐ *I already believe in myself. I am going to continue the work of becoming my own best advocate.*

☑ *I need to work on raising my self-esteem to become my own best advocate.*

See chapter 14 on "Raising Your Self-Esteem" and the resources listed at the end of this chapter to identify some strategies that you can use to begin working on your self-esteem. The following affirmation can also help. Try repeating it over and over again:

☐ *I am a unique and valuable person. I am worth the effort it takes to advocate for myself and protect my rights.*

2. Know Your Rights

Everyone is entitled to equality under the law. Some people who have episodes of depression and manic depression erroneously believe that they do not have the same rights as others. I believed this for a while. I allowed people I did not know well and did not trust to make decisions for me and take control of my life. I now have systems in place so if I am not able to make good decisions for myself, others will make them for me. You can do that, too, if you haven't already done so.

You can start taking action by making a commitment to learn what your rights are.

☐ *I am committed to learning what my rights are. I will contact my state agency of protection and advocacy to get this information. I will keep a file of my rights in my mental health file.*

If you do not have systems in place for your treatment decisions, place a checkmark in the following box and follow through by completing the treatment preference document at the end of this chapter.

☑ *I am committed to putting systems in place so that if I am not able to make good decisions for myself, others of my choice will make them for me.*

3. Decide What You Want

Clarify for yourself exactly what you need. This helps you set goals and be clear to others.

Your needs may be in the area of treatment. This is often the first area where individuals gain experience in advocating for themselves. Perhaps you need to insist on a complete thyroid examination. Maybe you need to demand sick leave when you experience an episode of depression. Perhaps you need to contact your legislator about health care programs that do not treat depression and manic depression the same as other medical conditions. Chapter 3 on "Eliminating the Physical Causes of Mood Disorders" and chapter 4 on "Taking Medication Safely" raise a number of treatment issues that you should consider in setting goals for yourself and making them clear to others.

Don't overlook the lifestyle issues covered in section II and the strategies for exploring your life history and focusing on your current feelings covered in section III. Chapters in both of these sections are designed to present alternatives that can help you clarify what you need and want for yourself.

4. Get the Facts

When you advocate for yourself you need to be sure that your information is accurate. For instance, when advocating for a complete thyroid test, go to your doctor's appointment armed with references such as *Medical Mimics of Psychiatric Disorders* (see the resources list in chapter 3). If advocating for sick leave when you are feeling depressed, contact your state agency of protection and advocacy, or your attorney, to find out what your rights are.

As you work through the chapters of this book, you'll find that many of them contain resources for collecting information. Writing down the information you gather and keeping it where you can find it helps. Develop a mental health file of your own and keep it updated and in good order.

5. Strategize

You'll always find it useful to write down what you think will work and the steps necessary to achieve your goals. Think of several ways to provide for the needs you've identified. Ask supporters for suggestions. Get feedback on your ideas. Then choose the one that feels right. Be sure to let the person or agency know how it helps them to help you.

6. Gather Support

Work together with friends. Help each other and be mutually supportive. Nothing helps self-advocacy more than supportive friends. Join groups with common concerns. If necessary, call your protection and advocacy organization for additional support. Keep track of this data by writing it down.

Chapter 2 on "Creating a Support Network" is designed to help you make the most of this crucial resource.

7. Target Your Efforts

Ask yourself what person, persons, or organization can take action on the issues you've identified. Talk directly with the individual who can best assist you. It may take a few phone calls to discover which organization or person can help, or who is in charge, but it is worth the effort. Keep trying until you find the right person. Maybe the right person is your spouse or another family member.

8. Express Yourself Clearly

Good communication skills are vital for effective self-advocacy. Learn to say directly what you mean. Be brief and stick to the point. Don't allow yourself to ramble on with unimportant details. State your concern and specify what you want. Good communication is a skill that does not receive the attention it deserves in our educational institutions. If you feel you have a hard time communicating effectively, work on this with a counselor or supporter, read related publications (ask your librarian for ideas), or take an adult education or community college class on improving communication skills, public speaking, or assertiveness training. Then practice these skills with supporters.

Later sections in this chapter provide some specific pointers on communicating effectively in person, in writing, or over the telephone.

9. Assert Yourself Calmly

If someone gives you a hard time, stay cool. Don't lose your temper and lash out at the other person, their character, or the organization. Instead, speak out, and listen. Respect the rights of others, but don't let them put you down or walk all over you.

Repeat these affirmations over and over until they are easy and comfortable for you:

☐ *When I advocate for myself, I am calm. I know this increases my effectiveness.*

☐ *I speak out with ease and also respect the rights of others and listen to what they have to say.*

☐ *When I advocate for myself, I am brief, clear, and to the point. I expect people to respect me.*

10. Be Firm and Persistent

Don't give up! Keep after what you want. Always follow through on what you say. Commit yourself to getting what you need for yourself.

Repeat the following affirmation to facilitate this process:

☑ *I am firm and persistent. I persist until I get what I need for myself.*

Meeting in Person

Speaking to someone in person is the most effective way to advocate for yourself. Make an appointment. Don't just show up. Here are some additional pointers:

1. **Plan what you are going to say and the points you need to make.** Practice with the help of friends, tape recorders, or mirrors if you feel unsure of yourself.

2. **Dress neatly for the appointment.** This gives the person the message that this is an important meeting.

3. **Be on time.** If you aren't respectful of someone's time, they may be less inclined to be receptive to your needs.

4. **Look the person in the eye and shake hands firmly in greeting.** Call the person by name. Use positive body language.

5. **Tell them why it is in their best interest to respond to your request.** Speak loudly enough to be heard without shouting.

6. **State your message clearly and simply.** Tell the person exactly what it is that you want.

7. **Explain why you need it.** Remember that how you say something often makes a greater impression than what you say.

8. **Expect a positive response.** Don't capitulate if you sense some initial resistance. Be firm.

9. **Listen in a relaxed way to what the other person is saying.** If you don't understand, ask questions for clarification. If you feel you are not getting anywhere, tell the other

person that you wish to pursue your issues further and ask to speak to the person's supervisor.

10. **At the end of the meeting, restate any action that has been decided upon so you both understand each other clearly.** For instance, you might say, "As a result of this meeting, you are going to order a thyroid test for me." Or "As a result of this meeting, I understand you are going to change my status to active." Thank the person for his or her time and assistance.

11. **Send a follow-up note thanking them for meeting with you and summarizing any agreed upon action.** It is a nice gesture. It also acts as a reminder and provides assurance that you both have the same understanding about the result of the meeting. Here's an example of a thank you note you might use:

Dear Ms. Gretsky:

Thank you for meeting with me last Wednesday morning. I appreciate your attention to my housing situation. I look forward to hearing from you next week, after you have contacted Mr. Stiglios.

Very sincerely,
Jane Drew

Getting Action Through Letter Writing

Writing is a useful way to request information, present facts, express your opinion, or to ask for what you need. Make the letter short, simple, and clear. One page is best. Long letters may not be read, and it is likely that you'll have trouble sticking to the point.

It is acceptable to write the letter by hand if you don't have access to a typewriter or computer. Ask a supporter if it is clearly readable, understandable, and legible. Typing services are inexpensive and might be worth the cost.

If appropriate, send copies of your letter to others you want to inform such as your legislator or advocacy agency. Put "cc" (which means copies circulated) at the bottom of the letter with a list of others to whom you are sending copies.

Keep a copy of the letter in your file for future reference. It's a good idea to follow up a letter with a phone call to make sure the person got the letter and to discuss the situation further.

Advocating for Yourself by Phone

Letters and visits may be initiated or followed with phone calls if appropriate. The telephone is useful to gather information, to keep track of what's going on, and to let people know what you want. Before you call, write down the essential points of what you want to say.

When calling:

1. **Identify yourself.** Ask for the name and position of the person speaking with you.

2. **Briefly describe the situation and ask if they are the right person to handle such a request**. If they are not the right person, ask to be transferred to the appropriate

person. If that person is not available, ask that they return your call. If you have not heard from them by the next day, call back. Don't be put off or give up because your call is not returned. Keep calling until you reach the person who can help you.

3. **Once you have reached the appropriate person, make your request for action brief and clear.**

4. **If the person cannot respond to your request immediately, ask when they will get back to you and the date on which you can expect action.**

5. **Thank the person for being helpful, if that's the case.**

6. **Send a thank you card.** In cases when a person has been particularly helpful, this is a good idea, since it opens the door for further contact on related issues.

7. **Keep a written record of your calls in your file.** Include the date of your call, who you spoke to, issues addressed, and promised action.

8. **If you do not hear back from the person when expected, or if the promised action is not taken, or the situation is not resolved, call them back.** Persist until you achieve your objectives.

Making Arrangements for Times When You Can't Make Decisions for Yourself

Of course you hope that each episode of mood instability will be your last. Even with your best intentions and efforts, however, this may not be the case. While the episodes may get less frequent or lessen in intensity as you learn how to better manage them, they may continue to be an issue. That's why it's important to use that window of opportunity between episodes to develop a document that describes the care you want for yourself if you have another episode and are not capable of making your own decisions. When you are in the midst of a deep depressive episode or an out-of-control mania and you have not prepared in advance for this eventuality, the decisions made on your behalf may not be decisions you would make for yourself.

Like you, I hope I never have another severe episode of mania or depression. In mania, I do things that are damaging to my relationships, destroy my reputation, and cause me to take action contrary to my ethical and moral standards. Depressions are terribly painful and disabling. I am afraid that another deep depression might end in suicide. Therefore, I have developed a document to be used if my moods get out of control.

Before you develop your document, carefully research all treatment options, using the resources listed in this book. Include in your study information that expresses a variety of viewpoints. Discuss treatment options with your physician and other health care professionals. It is much easier to do this when you are well than when you are in the midst of an episode.

Don't expect your treatment plan to be like anyone else's. You are unique physiologically, respond differently than the next person, and have your own feelings about the appropriateness of specific treatments. You have the right to be treated as an individual who has unique needs and concerns. Be sure your document of treatment preference addresses the issues specifically of concern to you.

Also make sure that your document will hold up in court. Laws about such documents and their legality differ from state to state. Check with your attorney to see what kind of a document is legal in your state. Even if the document is not legal in your state, it will be a helpful guide to your chosen supporters.

At the end of this chapter is a sample of such a document.There is also a blank copy for your use. Store your copy of this document in your mental health file. Give a copy to each of the five people listed and to your attorney. Discuss the document with them to be sure everyone is clear about your intent.

Hospitalization Rights

The rights of a person who is hospitalized, especially a person who is hospitalized against his or her will (this generally only happens if a person is a danger to himself or others), vary from state to state. Many people who suffer from mood disorders feel that they have been neglected or harshly or inappropriately treated in hospitals and that they have not received the same quality of care as people with other medical illnesses. Situations like these are wrong.

You have a right to expect the following, at the very least, in any health care facility. Give copies of this list to supporters so they can advocate for you if you cannot advocate for yourself.

You have the right to:

1. Communicate in person, by sending and receiving mail and by reasonable access to telephones, with the people of your choice.

2. Wear your own clothing.

3. Keep personal possessions, including toilet articles.

4. Practice religious freedom.

5. Use a private storage area to which you have free access.

6. Take care of personal hygiene needs in privacy.

7. Be furnished with a reasonable supply of writing materials and stamps.

8. Receive a written treatment plan that is updated as your condition or treatment changes.

9. Be represented by counsel whenever your rights may be affected.

10. Not be required to perform routine labor tasks of the facility except those essential for treatment.

11. Refuse any unusual or potentially hazardous treatment procedures.

12. Be accorded the same civil rights, respect, dignity, and compassion, and be treated in the same manner and with the same effects, as a person not in such a facility.

Resources

Copeland, M. (1992) *The Depression Workbook: A Guide for Living With Depression and Manic Depression*. Oakland, CA: New Harbinger Publications.

The self-help techniques in this book are helpful in raising self-esteem and learning self-advocacy.

Garson, S. (1986) *Out of Our Minds.* Buffalo, NY: Prometheus.

> Part IV, "Coping: Rights and Responsibilities," of this handbook is an excellent source of information of patient and family rights.

Ilardo, J. (1992) *Risk-Taking for Personal Growth: A Step-by-Step Workbook.* Oakland, CA: New Harbinger Publications.

> This book will provide valuable assistance as you make life changes.

McKay, M., and P. Fanning. (1992) *Self Esteem.* Oakland, CA: New Harbinger Publications.

> This is the best book I have seen on raising self-esteem. I recommend it highly. Many people who have gotten well and stayed well have found this book to be a valuable resource.

McKay, M., M. Davis, and P. Fanning. (1981) *Thoughts and Feelings: The Art of Cognitive Stress Intervention.* Oakland, CA: New Harbinger Publications.

> This widely used resource helps you overcome negative thought patterns that get in the way of taking positive action on your own behalf.

Spaniol, L., and M. Koehler. (1994) *The Experience of Recovery.* Boston: Center for Psychosocial Rehabilitation.

> This is a compilation of educational and affirming writings by people who have recovered from psychiatric disabilities.

Spaniol, L., M. Koehler and D. Hutchinson. (1994) *The Recovery Workbook.* Boston: Center for Psychosocial Rehabilitation.

> This is a highly recommended self-help resource for anyone who has experienced psychiatric symptoms.

Zinman, S., and H. Harp. (1994) *Reaching Across II.* Sacramento, CA: California Network of Mental Health Clients.

> An excellent self-help resource filled with resources and information for anyone who has ever been involved in the mental health system. For your own copy, write to:
> California Network of Mental Health Clients
> 1722 J Street, Suite 324
> Sacramento, CA 95814

Organizations

Depression & Related Disorders Association
> Meyer 4-181
> 600 N. Wolfe St.
> Baltimore, MD 21205

National Alliance for the Mentally Ill
> 2101 Wilson Blvd, Suite 302
> Arlington, VA 22201
> (703) 524-7600
> 1-800-950-6264
> *Information, advocacy and support for family members and people with psychiatric symptoms.*

National Association for Rights, Protection, and Advocacy

c/o Mental Health Association of Minnesota
2021 E. Hennepin, Suite 412
Minneapolis, MN 55413

National Association of Protection and Advocacy Systems (NAPAS)

900 2nd St. NE Suite 211
Washington D.C. 20002
(202) 408-9514
FAX (202) 408-9520
TTD (202) 408-9521
Call for phone numbers of protection and advocacy agencies anywhere in the United States.

National Depression and Manic Depressive Association

730 North Franklin Suite 501
Chicago, ILL 60610
1-800-82-NDMDA
Numerous support groups around the country, national and regional conferences, mail order bookstore, information.

National Empowerment Center

20 Ballard Road
Lawrence, MA 1843-1018
1-800-POWER-2-U
Information, education, resources, and support.

Information

National Foundation for Depressive Illness

PO Box 2257
New York, NY 10116
Call 1-800-248-4344 to find out how to get more information on depressive illnesses. Write for informational newsletter and physician referral listings by state.

National Institute of Mental Health

Depression Awareness, Recognition and Treatment (D/ART)
1-800-421-4211

National Mental Health Association Information Center

1021 Prince St.
Alexandria, VA 22314-297
(703) 684-7722

National Mental Health Selp-Help Clearinghouse

311 South Juniper St. Suite 1000
Philadelphia, PA 19107
1-800-553-4KEY
Educational resources.

Support Coalition International
David Oaks
PO Box 11284
Eugene, OR 97440-3484
A network of advocacy organizations of psychiatric survivors and allies in the US and Canada.

Document of Treatment Preference

I, *Sally Henderson*, in the event that I become incapable of making decisions for myself, which means I am exhibiting any of the following symptoms:

- *depression with suicidal ideation*
- *agitation*
- *psychosis*
- *extreme risk taking*
- *bizarre behavior*

give the following people the power to make decisions in my behalf:

Thomas Henderson

Sarah Muldoon

Ann Reardon

Nancy James

Polly Suserf

I would like three of the above people to agree on my treatment.

I am willing to take the following medications:

Medication	To be taken under these circumstances
Tegretol	*For severe mood instability*
Valproate	*If Tegretol doesn't work*
Paxil	*For depression*

I am not willing to take the following medications:

Medication	Reason to avoid
lithium	*Previous allergic reactions*
tricyclic antidepressants	*Do not work for me*
neuroleptics	*Severe side effects*

I am not willing to have electroshock treatment.

I am willing to be admitted to the following facilities:

Facility	Reason this facility is acceptable
Midtown Medical Center	*Good care, variety of treatment options*
Northern Medical Center	*Have heard they provide good care and treatment*

I am not willing to be admitted to the following facilities:

Facility	Reason this facility is not acceptable
Eastside Hospital	*Bad reputation*
Uptown Medical Center	*Lack of treatment options*

My health care professionals are:

Name	Phone number	Area of expertise
Dr. Sara Kener	*901-234-5678*	*General medical, endocrinology*
Dr. Jean Helter	*901-787-4345*	*Psychiatry*
Dr. Jill Tomer	*901-923-1234*	*Naturopathy*
Coner Enepo	*804-987-3456*	*Psychotherapy*

Health care professionals that I do not want involved in my treatment:

Name	Reason why
Dr. Sam Hill	*Bad reputation*
Dr. George Whiter	*Lack of expertise in this area*

Additional instructions:

Please take away my car keys, credit cards and check books in the event that I am spending large amounts of money indiscriminately.

My attorney is:
Patilda Derickey
422 East Elm St., Bay City
(901) 234-8765

Signed: *Sally Henderson*
Date: *March 23, 1994*

Document of Treatment Preference

I, Leigha Bowen , in the event that I become incapable of making decisions for myself, which means I am exhibiting any other following symptoms:

Depression with suicidal thoughts
Siverly agressive, Destructive behavior,

give the following people the power to make decisions in my behalf:

Cathy Bowen
Carolyn Bowen

I would like (number) N/A of the above people to agree on my treatment.
I am willing to take the following medications:

Medication	To be taken under these circumstances

What ever the Dr. thinks is needed
for my treatment! Except for the
meds. Wrote down below!

I am not willing to take the following medications:

Medication	Reason to avoid

Prozac, Paxel — Made Me Suicidal
Abilafy — Made Voices & Hallousanation worse
Welbutrin, Depacoat > Don't work!
Zoloft,

☒ I am   ☐ am not willing to have electroshock treatment.
(If you are willing, under what circumstances?)

My mother has to be there to supervise
& agree & ok the treatment! I have to
to be knocked out for procidure!

I am willing to be admitted to the following facilities:

Facility   **Reason this facility is acceptable**

Hotel Hope
Elahan place   Heard to be careing
Salmon Creek Lagacy / Kind & Gental!

I am *not* willing to be admitted to the following facilities:

Facility   **Reason this facility is not acceptable**

SWW Medical Center - Not a good hospital
don't Know what there
Doing poor bedside
manner!

My health care professionals are:

Name and phone number   **Area of expertise**

Dr. Kerber   Nurse Practishaner!

Health care professionals that I do not want involved in my treatment:

Name   **Reason why**

Additional instructions:

Do Not Keep me from my mother or
my Kids! Don't treat me like a broken
idiot!

My attorney is:

Name _____

Address _____ Phone _____

Signed: *Leigha Bowen*   Date 6-19-2010

2

Creating a Support Network

My support team is absolutely crucial to my wellness. I maintain good relationships with supporters through honest communication—trying not to "burden" anyone.

Having caring people you can lean on when necessary is important to everyone's well-being, but it is especially critical for people who struggle to keep their moods under control. A network of supporters can literally mean the difference between staying well or backsliding. In my study of the experiences of 120 depressives and manic depressives, three-fourths of the people who have gotten well and stayed well are in support groups.

This is why it's essential to develop a support plan and stick to it. While the journey to stability is yours alone, you need others to pave the way, monitor your passage, enrich your life, and counter the feelings of loneliness and isolation that so often accompany mood instability. You must also do the same for them. The aid you give, in turn, can help you feel good about yourself.

A woman in the study said:

My support team is absolutely essential to my long-term wellness. I never really think about "giving up" anymore. They are always willing to listen to both my joys and my sorrows. I maintain close relationships with them through regular phone calls.

Another woman commented:

I keep good relationships with the members of my support team by keeping appointments, being in touch, being honest, and not taking on more than I can handle.

At minimum, you need five good friends or supporters you can call on when you need them; these are people who can count on you as well. Don't worry if you don't have five such people in your life now. You can build your network gradually using the strategies outlined in this chapter. You'll learn how to identify good candidates for your support network, establish relationships with them, and maintain those relationships over time.

How many supporters can you identify now? Include family members, friends, and health care professionals. Who are they?

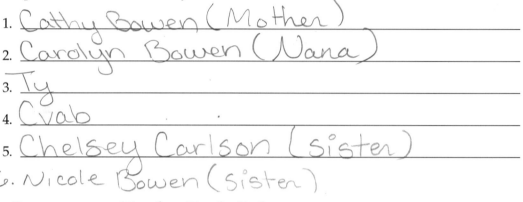

1. Cathy Bowen (Mother)
2. Carolyn Bowen (Nana)
3. Ty
4. Crab
5. Chelsey Carlson (Sister)
6. Nicole Bowen (Sister)

What Supporters Do for Each Other

Caring, supportive friends listen to each other and let the other express feelings freely without judging or criticizing. Few people are used to listening to another without making some comment of their own. Most feel they need to respond to what you say by agreeing or disagreeing, or telling you what you should do. This does not help.

Let your supporters know that you just want them to listen, unless you specifically ask for their advice and feedback. You can make this clear each time you get together. For instance, you might say, "Today I just need you to listen to me while I express my feelings and figure out this situation for myself." Another time you might say, "I'd like some feedback and advice." Being clear is the best way to get what you need and want for yourself.

These relationships need to be reciprocal. You too must be willing to spend time and just listen, without judging or criticizing your supporters. One way to make sure you both get equal time is to use the peer counseling approach. See chapter 11 on "Peer Counseling."

Supporters can also see to it that your wishes are carried out when you cannot make decisions or take action on your own behalf. To ensure this, provide them with a copy of your document of treatment preference from chapter 1 and any specific plans you have made to avoid episodes. See chapter 15, "Preventing Depression," and chapter 17, "Preventing Mania." Talk with them to make sure they are clear about what treatments are acceptable to you, what works for you, and which approaches have not worked for you in the past. Be sure to ask them how you can support them during the times they are incapable of acting in their own best interest.

Some of those interviewed from my study had this to say about how they educate their supporters and prepare ahead for crises:

> I share reading material and other pertinent information with my supporters.
> They also share information with me.

The more I find out about my illness, the more I share these insights with others on my support team.

You can also arrange meetings between your key supporters and health care professionals when you are well so that if they need to contact each other when you are having difficulty, they will already be acquainted. Let supporters know who your health care professionals are, what role they play, and how they can be contacted. This makes it easier for them to get help for you.

Another individual in my study said:

I appreciate my friends and family encouraging me when I decide to get medical help for depression. I have asked those close to me to encourage me to see medical help when I am "stuck" and not functioning.

How To Find People for Your Support Network

Support groups for people with depression or manic depression are wonderful places to make new, understanding friends. So are groups for people who are working to overcome addictions or who are dealing with issues such as weight, sexuality, and parenting.

Such groups counter the social isolation so many people experience. They provide you with the opportunity to be with people who are grappling with similar health concerns and the comfort of knowing that you are not alone. Because of what you have in common, communication tends to be easier in such groups. When things seem particularly bleak, group members who have issues similar to yours and who are doing well can offer you hope. Such people are likely to be far more understanding about your mood swings than people who don't know much about depression or manic depression.

A woman who has had episodes of manic depression for many years says:

I am in a support group of about fifteen people. In the group, people talk about how they are managing their lives. If they request it, they can receive feedback from others in the group. It is very helpful. You can talk with others who have similar symptoms [but] who see things from a different perspective. The supportive atmosphere helps a lot.

Another study participant said:

The support group helps me to know that I am not alone with this illness, to get along better with others, understand people and listen to others, and have others listen to me.

A man who is in a support group said:

We treat each other as equals. We talk and listen to each other. We go on some outings together. We meet once a week. It is very helpful to me, providing me with a social life.

There are numerous support groups available. They are generally listed in the community calendar section of the newspaper. Mental health agencies and organizations also can refer you to support groups. Be sure to attend a support group several times before deciding whether it is right for you. Every group can have an off night when things just don't "gel."

If you can't find a group that suits you, however, consider starting your own. Get together with several friends, ask them to come to a meeting, and encourage them to invite other friends as well. As a group you can decide how often you'd like to meet and whether you want to focus on any particular issue. Often, such groups are strictly social and simply provide an opportunity to get out and be with people who can be counted on to be understanding and supportive.

A woman who started a very successful support group says:

> The support group rules insist on confidentiality, no vulgarity. Meetings are non-confrontational, and no one can monopolize the conversation. Although there are educational programs sometimes, the most important thing is *sharing*. It has taught me not to get too involved in other people's problems. If they ask for help, I suggest something. If they don't follow my advice, I have no problem. I am not one to say, "I told you so."

Do you belong to a support group? How has it been useful to you? Have you met people at the support group who are now your supporters?

_____

_____

_____

☐   *I am going to locate and join a support group. Here's how I plan to locate a group:*

_____

_____

_____

Here are some other ways to make new friends:

Volunteer. There are many agencies that could use your help. Inquire at churches, schools, hospitals, youth agencies, soup kitchens, the Red Cross, and so on. Many communities have volunteer referral organizations, which are a good resource when you are looking for just the right place to volunteer. Volunteering provides you with the opportunity to meet others with similar interests while you are doing something you enjoy. Regular contact encourages the development of supportive relationships.

Are you a volunteer? How has volunteering been useful for you? Have you met fellow volunteers who are now your supporters?

_____

_____

_____

☐ *I am going to locate a volunteer position by doing the following:*

_____

_____

_____

Join community activities and special interest groups.   Many communities offer a broad range of activities and special interest and action groups. These activities not only bring new supporters, but they also enrich your life. Use your local newspaper to find these groups. Make a note of those activities and events that interest you. Then follow through and attend. Make it your goal to attend one or several community activities on a regular basis. When you see the same person several times, start a conversation. Again, if a person seems interesting, pursue the friendship.

Do you already go to community activities and events that interest you? How have these events been useful? Have you met people who are now your supporters?

_____

_____

_____

☐ *I am going to start attending community events on regular basis. I am going to locate such events in my areas of interest by doing the following:*

_____

_____

_____

Take a class.   Is there something you'd like to learn? Take a class in a foreign language, in computer science, bird watching, knitting, wood carving, literature, pottery, or whatever interests you. Many such classes are inexpensive. Scholarship aid may be available. The classes are an excellent place to meet new people who share your interests. Check your newspaper for offerings and times.

Do you already take classes that interest you?

☐ *I am going to start attending a class. I am going to locate classes in my areas of interest by doing the following:*

_____

_____

_____

How To Approach Potential Supporters

When you meet people you enjoy, invite them out for tea or lunch or to share an activity. Be sure to set a date for your next get-together before you part company. Take the time to get to know them slowly and consider whether they're someone you want on your support team. When you feel you have identified individuals who meet *all* of your criteria for a supporter:

- Ask them if they are willing to be your supporter. Explain to them exactly what you want and need from them.

- Tell them that you will be their supporter, too, and provide the same for them. Make it clear that you are not looking for a one-way relationship.

- Explain that you have several supporters, which means that it is not necessary for them to be available at all times. Tell them that if they are unavailable to you when you call, they should tell you, so you can contact another person on your list. Work responsibilities, family responsibilities, illness, or previously made plans such as a vacation can render someone temporarily unavailable. If a person says they are unavailable, you must respect that and find another person to meet your needs. This keeps your supporters from getting "burned out" and keeps you from interfering with their lives.

When I asked my friend Bev to be a supporter, I told her that meant I would call her if I needed support and assistance and that we would keep in contact on a regular basis, either through a phone call or an activity. I said that what I wanted most was someone to listen and share activities (something we were already doing). I explained that she was one of several people I was asking to be my supporter, and that there might be times when I would ask for feedback and advice and times when she might be needed to consult with other supporters and take action on my behalf when I couldn't do that myself. I told her that I would provide her with the same kind of support.

If you feel uncomfortable asking someone to be your supporter, practice by role playing with your counselor a family member or a supporter.

☐   *I feel uncomfortable asking someone to be my supporter. I am going to practice role playing with:*

_____

_____

_____

Why It May Be Difficult To Ask for Support

Many people who have had episodes of mood instability for years, and who feel they have not reached their goals or others' expectations of them, may also feel they are not deserving of support. Some of you have been told by loved ones or your health care professionals that you will never amount to anything. This may cause you to minimize your achievements and feel that you don't measure up to people whose moods are more stable. Or you may feel unloved and unlovable.

Either way, such self-perceptions make it hard for you to reach out for the support, attention, and love you deserve. People who feel this way often think, "Why would anyone want to offer their caring to someone as unworthy as me? Why risk rejection since *that* will hurt me more than if I had never reached out?"

In truth, you are as valuable as anyone else and as deserving of attention, respect, and love. If you don't believe this deep down, use the following affirmation:

I am a lovable person and I deserve support, attention, respect, and love.

Repeat this again and again, and before long you will know this to be true. Knowing that you are lovable and deserving will make it easier for you to build and maintain a support team. If you can reach out to others and give them the same quality attention, respect, and love they give you, you will find that you have many strong supporters.

How To Let Other People In

People who have experienced mood instability for years, and the accompanying feelings of loss and rejection, may find it difficult to accept the fact that another person likes them, accepts them as they are, and wants to spend time with them. If this is true for you, there are several things you can do to get past this barrier:

- Ask the other person to spend five minutes telling you why they like you. (Use a timer.) Then do the same for them. They can repeat the same thing over and over, such as saying , "You are a warm, friendly, interesting person." Repeat this exercise often! You will find that repeating the same affirmation is very useful.

- Develop a positive rebuttal to the negative thought: *No one likes me*. Change it to: *Many people like me*. Repeat over and over to yourself or to your supporter, "*Many people like me.*" Repeat it when you are stuck in traffic, washing the dishes, waiting in the doctor's office, before you fall asleep at night—whenever you have empty time to fill. Take a moment to focus on what it feels like in your body to know that people like you. Before long, you will know that many people like you.

- Make a list of people who like you. Make copies. Then hang them in prominent places around your house to act as constant reminders. Add names to the list as new people come into your life.

How To Build Supportive Relationships

Build relationships with supporters by spending lots of quality time together and sharing activities you both enjoy. You may want to go on long walks together, share a meal, listen to music, play music together, or see a movie. Potluck suppers are another great activity. The work is shared and there's a good variety of tasty food. A friend whose family is less accessible found it helpful to have a series of potluck suppers at her home.

Just be sure to spend most of your time socializing and enjoying each other, rather than dealing with emotions or heavy issues. You often meet supporters because you have interests in common. As the relationships proceed, don't forget to make time for the activities and interests that brought you together. This works best if you suggest and initiate activities sometimes, and your friend does likewise.

☐ *I am committed to spending quality time with my supporters.*

Keep regular contact with members of your support team even when things are going well, no matter how busy you are. Make a commitment to yourself that you will have weekly contact. If time is really tight, even a phone call will suffice.

A woman in the study said:

I meet once a week with my supporters. I know I can talk about anything with them and they aren't going to make fun of me or think I am losing it! The best way to maintain these relationships is by being myself and being supportive to them.

☐ *I am committed to having at least one contact with each member of my support team every week.*

Spend time listening and supporting each other. You may find it useful to set aside a specific time each week to meet. For instance, every Friday afternoon from 1:00 p.m. to 2 p.m., I meet with my friend Laura for a shared listening session. An appointment book will help you keep track of such meetings.

☐ *I am going to set up regular contact with the following supporters:*

Name _____ How often? _____

Name _____ How often? _____

Name _____ How often? _____

How To Keep Supporters

Spending quality time with your supporters on a regular basis is important. But that is not all there is to maintaining these relationships. You must be considerate of each other. Here are some issues to address:

Neediness. During severe mania or depression, people can become very needy and draining. During these periods, don't depend on only one or two people, or ask for help without giving support in kind. If you do, the person you lean on heavily may quickly tire and quietly, or sometimes loudly, disappear.

One study volunteer said:

Over the years, there have been various friends who have helped, but the intensity and chronic nature of my illness seemed to "wear them out as friends."

Avoid this difficult situation by following these guidelines:

- Have many close supporters so you don't wear anyone out.
- Give them the same kind of support, attention, respect, and love they give you, so the relationship is about fifty-fifty.

Mood instability. Because of your history of mood instability, the people closest to you may feel that they never know what to expect from you. In the past, you may have been so high that it was uncomfortable to be with you, or so down that they felt dragged down, too. You can minimize their discomfort by educating your supporters about depression and manic depression. You also need to do everything you can to keep your moods as stable as possible, using the strategies you have learned from this and other resource books. This is a gift to you and your supporters.

Inappropriate behavior. Inappropriate behavior can embarrass others, turn them off and quickly sour your friendship. People who have had up and down moods all of their lives may have never learned socially acceptable ways to relate. Inappropriate behaviors include:

- Talking incessantly without giving anyone else a chance to talk.
- Not paying attention when others are talking.
- Being very demanding.
- Not being sensitive to the needs of others.
- Being inappropriately loud and boisterous in public places.
- Being inappropriately affectionate.
- Interrupting when others are talking.
- Excessive borrowing from people.
- Not keeping up personal hygiene.

Ask health care professionals and others you respect and trust if you have any social habits or behaviors that others find offensive. Listen to what they have to say without getting angry or defensive. Ask others to verify these opinions. Then work with your health care professionals and friends to get rid of such habits. Admitting to others that you are working on eliminating irksome habits may be difficult, but it helps. Then work at it. Allow yourself to be supported while you do it.

Do you have any inappropriate social skills? What are they?

_____

_____

_____

☐   *I am going to work with _____ to change these habits to more appropriate ones.*

Nine Ways To Make the Most of Your Support System

Clearly, a social support network is essential to your continued well-being. It is well worth the time and care it takes to develop supportive relationships and to nurture and maintain them. You now know the specific steps you need to take to do this. Here are key recommendations that will allow you to get the maximum benefit from the support team you've built.

1. **Do everything you can to keep yourself well and stable.** Make your wellness your highest priority.

2. **Work on developing appropriate social skills if this is an issue for you.** Address this in counseling or peer counseling sessions or in discussions with supporters.

3. **Be an active member of a support group.**

4. **Be mutually supportive.** This means being there for others when they need you just as you expect them to be there for you when you need them.

5. **Be careful not to lean on any one friend too much.** Turn to someone else instead. Being considerate of other people's needs is to your mutual benefit.

6. **Educate your supporters about depression and manic depression so they will know what to expect and how to deal with problems if they come up.**

7. **You may want to have everyone in your support group meet and exchange phone numbers.** Let supporters know who your health care professionals are, what roles they play, and how they can be contacted. One such meeting may suffice. Some people, however, feel more comfortable with ongoing meetings scheduled once a month or every two or three months.

   ☐ *I am going to arrange meetings between my support team and my health care professionals.*

I am on several support teams and have gone to several such meetings. One was a festive lunch at a Chinese restaurant. We spent only a short time talking about the support needs of our friend and the rest of the time getting to know each other and having fun.

   ☐ *I am going to set up a meeting of my supporters.*

When? _____ **Where?** _____

8. **Peer or exchange counsel with a supporter.** Set up a regular time, such as 2:00 p.m. every Tuesday, to get together. Divide the time in half. During the first half, one person gets to talk, share, cry, or whatever, with the full attention of the other person. Then reverse the roles. This method tends to deepen relationships, helps people feel better about themselves, and may even help them sort out the answers to pressing problems. See chapter 11 on "Peer Counseling."

   ☐ *I am going to try peer counseling.*

When? _____ **With whom?** _____

9. **Make a list of your support team members with phone numbers.** Strive for at least five people on your support team. As you implement the above strategies and enlist new supporters, update your list. It's difficult to remember who your supporters are when you need them most. Keep copies of this list by your phones, on your bedside table, and in your purse or pocket.

Resources

Copeland, M. (1992) The Depression Workbook: *A Guide for Living With Depression and Manic Depression*. Oakland, CA: New Harbinger Publications.
   This book iscludes a chapter on developing and keeping a strong support team and support groups.

Spaniol, L. and M. Koehler. (1994) *The Experience of Recovery.* Boston: Center for Psychosocial Rehabilitation.
   This highly recommended self-help resource book is for anyone who has experienced psychiatric symptoms.

Tallard, J. (1988) *Hidden Victims.* New York: Doubleday.
   This book contains excellent, easy-to-read section on starting your own self-help group.

Support Team Members

Support Team Members	Phone Numbers
1. _____	
2. _____	
3. _____	
4. _____	
5. _____	
6. _____	
7. _____	
8. _____	
9. _____	
10. _____	

3

Eliminating the Physical Causes of Mood Disorders

Severe episodes of depression and mania were, for many years, an overwhelming part of my life. I assumed that during my numerous hospitalizations I had been given a complete medical checkup. Yet, it wasn't until I was referred to an endocrinologist and treated for hypothyroidism that my mind cleared and my moods stabilized. Now that I am treating my thyroid disorder and using a variety of self-help strategies, I finally have my life back.

An underlying physiological illness can cause, or aggravate, a mood disorder. In some cases, treating the illness eliminates the depression or manic depression entirely. Consider the case of one woman who suffered from severe, agitated depression for years. Drug therapy and lifestyle changes did little to help. Finally, a CAT scan revealed the presence of a brain tumor. Once surgeons removed the tumor, her depression ended.

Another woman, an alcoholic who has had unstable moods for seven years, was diagnosed with a hormone imbalance, a sluggish thyroid, and endometriosis. She found that she needed to take medication to treat her thyroid and balance her hormones before she could make any significant progress toward wellness.

In my own case, I found that treating an underlying thyroid disorder reduced my symptoms somewhat and made it easier for me to address the remaining symptoms. This is not uncommon. In fact, there are many accounts of people whose mood stability has improved dramatically when they were treated for hypothyroidism or hyperthyroidism. Hypothyroidism, which is what I have, is when the thyroid gland is too sluggish. Hyperthyroidism results from an overactive thyroid. The hormonal changes that accompany puberty and menopause can also instigate mood swings. So can many common medications.

These are not problems you can diagnose yourself. You need a skilled medical diagnostician. This chapter will give you some criteria for selecting one, tell you what you can expect from your examination, and how to make the most of your health care team.

Reasons To Make an Immediate Appointment

I urge you to get a comprehensive medical evaluation right away, if you or someone you support is experiencing any of these conditions:

1. Depression that persists longer than two weeks, or is interfering with your quality of life or family or career responsibilities. (Sometimes depression stems from a major loss or life change and you simply need time to heal. If the depression persists, however, the stress may have caused a physical condition which needs to be treated.)

2. Agitated depression (depression accompanied by desperate, repetitive movement, words, and crying, and accompanied by feelings of anxiety, anguish, or panic) or deep, suicidal depression.

3. Moods that alternate from high to low and interfere with your quality of life and with career and family responsibilities.

4. Manic episodes that include bizarre and reckless behavior, flight of ideas, inability to sleep or stay still, aggression, overcommitment, and pressured speech.

If anything on this list applies to you, get a medical examination now. The cost of such an examination is well-justified when you consider that depression and manic depression interfere with your ability to enjoy a normal and healthy life.

Mood changes and instability have many different causes. If only the symptoms of depression or mood instability are treated and there are underlying physical causes that need treatment, the treatment may be ineffective, and health issues that need immediate attention may be dangerously overlooked. Medications such as insulin, sleeping pills, pain medications and prescriptions used to treat various gastrointestinal disorders for other health problems may also affect mood. Puberty, menopause, and other age-related passages may also be causing mood instability.

Don't wait until you have physical symptoms to see your doctor. There is no reason to be embarrassed about discussing with your doctor symptoms you consider "emotional" or psychological. A sensitive physician will not make you feel that it is *your* fault that you feel the way you do. Physicians today are more and more willing to acknowledge that body and mind affect each other and that all illnesses have a physiological and psychological component. Blushing, for instance, is a clear example of how an emotional reaction causes a physiological change.

There may be a physiological component to your mood disorder. Below are some possible causes of depression and mood instability. Do any apply to you? If so, make a copy of the page, check off the categories that apply to you, and bring this copy with you when you go for your comprehensive medical evaluation.

Be aware, however, that this list is not all-inclusive. (That would take a book in itself.) Tim Fields, who has experienced episodes of major depression for years, prepared it. He decided to investigate every possible cause of depression, in the hope that he would come up with the best treatment for himself.

Some Possible Medical Causes of Mood Disorders

Adrenal Gland Disorders

☐ Addison's disease (may cause severe depression).

☐ Cushing's syndrome (may cause serious, usually "agitated" depression.)

☐ Diabetes mellitus (especially chronic, sub-clinical, left untreated, it may cause severe depression).

Other Endocrine System Disorders

☐ Pheochromocytoma

☐ Premenstrual syndrome (PMS) in women

☐ Testicular failure

☐ Thyroid imbalance

☐ Panhypopituitarism

☐ Estrogen deficiency in women (especially at menopause)

☐ Pituitary gland disorder

☐ Viral infection (such as Epstein-Barr, mononucleosis, mumps, herpes simplex)

☐ Hypoparathyroidism

☐ Ovarian failure

☐ Hyperparathyroidism

Allergies

Central Nervous System Disorders

☐ Alzheimer's disease

☐ Post-concussion syndrome

☐ Narcolepsy

☐ Parkinson's disease

☐ Normal pressure hydrocephalus

☐ Multiple sclerosis

☐ Binswanger's disease

☐ Temporal lobe seizures

Other Diseases

☐ Ataxia telangiectasia

☐ Syphilis

☐ Tuberculosis

☐ Viral encephalitis

☐ Brucella

☐ Cancer and carcinoid syndrome

☐ Heart disease

☐ Lupus

Chronic Poisoning

- ☐ Carbon monoxide
- ☐ Lead, manganese, or mercury
- ☐ Insecticides
- ☐ Volatile substances

Drug Interactions or Intoxication

- ☐ Aspirin
- ☐ Ibuprofen (Advil, Motrin, etc.)
- ☐ Blood pressure medications
- ☐ Corticosteroids
- ☐ Over-the-counter cough or cold medication
- ☐ Antiparkinson's drugs
- ☐ Birth control pills
- ☐ Arthritis medications (NSAID drugs)
- ☐ Anticonvulsants
- ☐ Psychotropic (psychiatric) medication
- ☐ Tagamet (cimetidine)
- ☐ Barbiturates

Drug or alcohol abuse

- ☐ Cocaine, PCP, heroin, or marijuana
- ☐ Tranquilizers
- ☐ Diet pills
- ☐ Amphetamines

Vitamin And Mineral Deficiencies

- ☐ Biotin
- ☐ Vitamin B1 (Thiamine)
- ☐ Vitamin B2 (Riboflavin)
- ☐ Vitamin B3 (Niacin)
- ☐ Vitamin B6 (Pyroxidine)
- ☐ Vitamin B12 (Cyancobalamine)
- ☐ Calcium imbalance
- ☐ Vitamin C (ascorbic acid)
- ☐ Low sodium (hyponatremia)
- ☐ Iron deficiency
- ☐ Magnesium or zinc deficiency
- ☐ Pantothenic acid

The Medical Exam

Your medical evaluation will begin with a careful medical history. You will need to be completely honest and frank about all of your symptoms, even those that seem irrelevant or unimportant such as tingling sensations and digestive disturbances. A complete physical and neurological examination should also be part of the procedure. Depending on the findings, an EEG or CAT scan may be required.

The following laboratory tests may be included in the examination:

1. A complete blood count with differential (CBC)

2. SMA 26 (26 blood chemistries and electrolytes)

3. Thyroid tests that include Total T4, the Free T4, and the TSH, which is sometimes known as the BT2 panel. The drug lithium, which is commonly used to treat manic depression, can weaken the thyroid and cause low thyroid, which worsens mood instability. For this reason, anyone with mood instability needs to insist on this test. A simply thyroid screening is not enough.

4. Serum folate level

5. Serum vitamin B-12 level

6. Urinalysis

7. Anti-candida antibody test

If all the above tests are not included in your examination, ask your doctor why. Insist on those tests that are important, especially the thyroid test. You must advocate for yourself to get what you need. Long-term mood instability is too devastating to leave any stone unturned. If your doctor refuses to order particular tests and does not give a satisfactory explanation, insist on having the tests you need. If the doctor still refuses, you may need to find a different doctor.

The Cost

How much can you expect to pay? Medical costs are definitely an issue for most people. If they are for you, discuss your concerns openly with your health care providers. They may be able to steer you to programs that assume some or all the costs of your treatment or medications. Whenever you get the opportunity, speak out for health care that is equally accessible to people with all kinds of symptoms and from all socioeconomic levels.

Choosing Your Health Care Professionals

Selecting Your Primary Care Physician

Shop carefully before engaging a physician to give you a comprehensive examination. The doctor should be sensitive and compassionate to your needs, and willing to listen to and address your concerns. You need to feel comfortable, safe, and affirmed during the examination. Look for a physician who is comfortable telling you the truth.

A person who has a physical disability as well as recurring mood instability says her physician tells her the truth, no matter what, without beating around the bush or trying to make it easier for her. She will not go to a doctor who tries to handle her with kid gloves. She says, "I want it on the line, straight to the point. I feel comfortable talking to my doctor no matter what I have to say."

If you find that your physician is overly pessimistic, however, find someone who has a more positive attitude. As I travel around the country, I meet many people who say they are tired of health care professionals who give them dire projections of the course of the illness and offer no hope. They say it aggravates rather than alleviates their condition. Some people say they leave the doctor's office feeling worse than when they went in. Our health care professionals need to be reminded that mood instability, with proper management and treatment, does get better. Those of us who have depression or manic depression want to feel understood, respected, supported, and validated by our health care professionals.

Creating a Health Care Team

During your complete medical evaluation, you and your physician may determine that other health care professionals are necessary to assist you in making decisions about your treatment and to provide ongoing follow-up. You may find that you also need a psychiatrist, endocrinologist, allergist, gynecologist, urologist, naturopath, and so on. Your health care professionals need to be willing to work together and consult with each other regularly to ensure a well-coordinated approach to your health care. Your own personal preferences and needs must be considered when you choose your team. Most people who get well and stay well rely on a carefully chosen team of health care providers, each of whom is able to fulfill a specific health care need.

A 45-year-old woman who has had mood instability for 15 years and has been stable for the last 8 years says:

> My health care support team consists of a psychiatrist who monitors my medication, a psychologist who counsels me and a family physician who deals with issues of physical health care. My psychiatrist is supportive in both educational and employment areas. He listens to my concerns regarding mood changes and we discuss medication changes. Since I have become well, he listens to my suggestions about medication and respects my self-reports.

A woman whose wellness has allowed her to become a national advocate for people with psychiatric disorders says she considers herself an equal partner with her psychiatrist:

> The doctors should be willing to teach me what they have learned from working with other patients, give a variety of treatment options, and let me make the choices, insisting that I take responsibility for my life and the management of my illness. My doctor values and respects me and gives me hope.

Exploring Medical Alternatives

Competent, qualified health care professionals who practice "alternative" medicine are an integral part of the health care team for many people with mood disorders. More and more professionals trained in Eastern and Western healing arts are able to work cooperatively. Those of us who rely on alternative practitioners for all or part of our care are reaping the benefits of this cooperation.

It's a good idea to make a list of all the members of your health care team to include with your document of treatment preference from chapter 1. Make sure your supporters have a copy of this list. Post your own copy in a convenient place.

Taking Charge

It's best to come armed with information when you visit the members of your health care team. This is especially true when you visit the physician who will do your comprehensive evaluation. Once the examination begins, it is easy to forget information that may be vital to the physician's search for answers.

To get the most accurate diagnosis, make a copy of the information chart on the next page and fill it out before you go for your comprehensive examination. Remember to take it with you.

A doctor told me that some of his patients apologize when they come to see him armed with information and related questions. He says he appreciates the information. It makes his job easier and ensures greater success in getting to the root of problem.

Questions To Ask the Doctor

In addition to bringing your physician information, you can also come with questions. I find it very important to keep a pad of paper handy for several days prior to my doctor's appointment so I can write down questions as I think of them. I have so much on my mind when I go in that I forget to ask for important information. I usually remember after I leave.

Again, don't apologize. A good doctor will appreciate your questions.

Here are some sample questions. They may or may not be questions for you. There is a blank question form for you to zerox at the end of this section. Use it to jot down any specific questions of your own and to record your doctor's answers. These records can be kept in your health care file for future reference.

Sample questions for your doctor:

- Was a complete thyroid screening done? If so, what was the result? If the test was not done, why wasn't this done? Should I be referred to an endocrinologist (a doctor who specializes in the treatment of disorders of the endocrine gland system)?

- Since I have been taking lithium, has my kidney function been assessed at regular intervals? If not, why not?

- What is a neurological exam? How can it be helpful in getting to the root of my depression?

- Who will be available to answer questions and provide support when you are not available?

- What kind of counseling program do you recommend?

- What about alternative, noninvasive treatments?

- Would light therapy be useful?

- Are you willing to work with other health care professionals to determine the most appropriate treatment for me? If not, why not?

- When and how are the best ways to get in touch with you?

- Are you willing to talk and work with other family members or supporters?

Information for the Physician

1. *List all medications, vitamins, and health care preparations you are using.*

Medication   **Dosage**   **When and How Used**

_____

_____

_____

2. *Provide a medical history of yourself and your family. Review the list of possible causes of mood earlier in this chapter. Perhaps something will stand out. You may remember your mother talking about her thyroid disorder, or Uncle Jake talking about his diabetes. Review the list with one or several family members. Look the list over several times in case there is something you have missed.*

Mother's Side of the Family

_____

_____

_____

Father's Side of the Family

_____

_____

_____

3. *Describe changes in:*

   appetite or diet _____

   weight _____

   sleep patterns _____

   sexual interest _____

   ability to concentrate _____

   memory _____

   bowel and urinary habits _____

4. *If you have recently had any of the following symptoms, describe them:*

   headaches _____

   numbness or tingling (where?) _____

   loss of balance _____

   double vision or vision problems _____

   periods of amnesia _____

   mood swings _____

   coordination changes _____

   weakness in arms or legs _____

   fever _____

   nausea or diarrhea _____

   fainting or dizziness _____

   seizures _____

5. *Describe your diet:*

   _____

   _____

   _____

6. *Describe your use of caffeine-containing substances (coffee, tea, chocolate, soft drinks):*

   _____

   _____

   _____

7. *Describe your use of alcohol:*

   _____

   _____

   _____

8. *Describe your smoking habits:*

   _____

   _____

   _____

Question Form

You may find the following format useful. Keep these sheets in your health care file for easy reference.

Question

_____

_____

Response

_____

_____

Question

_____

_____

Response

_____

_____

Question

_____

_____

Response

_____

_____

Action I need to take because of information from my physician

_____

_____

_____

Test Results

Ask your doctor to explain your test results and what they indicate for your overall wellness. This is an important part of assuming responsibility for your own health. The more you know, the better your decisions. Also ask your physician for copies of all test results for your own files, even if they show nothing unusual. You may not understand what they mean (most of us don't), but these copies should be in your possession. This way, the records will be available for other health changes through the years. Check those steps you have taken or need to take and record information below.

☐ *I have had a complete physical examination. The test results showed that I need to address the following issues:*

_____

_____

_____

If the doctor recommends particular medications, diet, exercise programs or other types of treatment, it is your responsibility to thoroughly investigate every aspect of this recommendation. Only then will you be able to determine if the treatment is something you are willing to do and something you can do. Consider the possible side effects and what would stand in the way of implementing of this treatment plan. This will facilitate every aspect of your treatment and help you raise important questions.

Follow-Up Plan

As part of your follow-up plan, keep a record of action that needs to be taken and new information you have learned.

☐ *I am not clear what the results of my examination mean.*

☐ *I need to do some follow-up research.*

☐ *I will make a follow-up appointment with my doctor to ask more questions.*

What information do you need to have?

_____

_____

_____

☐ *I am not satisfied with the results of my examination.*

☐ *I will discuss the results further with my doctor.*

☐ *I will discuss the results with another doctor.*

What are you going to discuss?

_____

_____

_____

Resources

American Association for Retired People. *Healthy Questions: How to Talk to and Select Physicians, Pharmacists, Dentists, & Vision Care Specialists.* Long Beach, CA: American Association for Retired People.
   This handbook helps you evaluate current services and tells you what to look for and questions to ask when choosing new health care professionals. For this free publication, write AARP Fulfillment (EE0589), PO Box 227906, Long Beach, CA 90801-5796.

Billing, N. (1987) *To Be Old and Sad: Understanding Depression in the Elderly.* Lexington, MA: DC Heath.
   This well written book can enhance your understanding of depression in the elderly.

Bondy, P., ed. (1987) *The Merck Manual of Diagnosis and Therapy.*
   An excellent, widely available medical reference that gives a comprehensive overview of a variety of disorders.

The Boston Women's Health Book Collective (1992) *The New Our Bodies, Ourselves: A Book by and for Women.* New York: Touchstone, Simon & Schuster.
   This book, which should be required reading for everyone, includes extensive information about depression, particularly with regard to various life stages. It gives women a better understanding of themselves and men a clearer understanding of women.

Clayman, C. (1989) *Home Medical Encyclopedia.* New York: Random House.
   This two-volume, easy-to-read set contains descriptions of medical and psychiatric illnesses. It's a good home reference.

Copeland, M. (1992) *The Depression Workbook: A Guide for Living With Depression and Manic Depression.* Oakland, CA: New Harbinger Publications.
   Refer to chapter 4, "Taking Responsibility for Your Own Wellness," chapter 5, "Possible Causes of Mood Disorders," and chapter 10, "Finding Appropriate Health Care Professionals."

Glanze, W., ed. (1986) *Mosby's Medical and Nursing Dictionary.* St. Louis: The C.V. Mosby Co.
   This handy reference for "home, school or office" makes all the difficult medical terminology understandable for all of us.

Guinness, A. (1993) *Family Guide to Natural Medicine.* Pleasantville, NY: Reader's Digest Assoc.
   This book is filled with safe, natural alternative remedies.

Extein, I., and M. Gold (1986) *Medical Mimics of Psychiatric Disorders.* Washington, DC: American Psychiatric Press.
   This book will help you to understand those medical problems that have the same—or similar—symptoms as depression or manic depression.

London, Wayne (1991) *Principles of Health.* Brattleboro, VT: London Research.
: *This is an excellent reference that will enhance your understanding of diagnostic test and immune system deficiencies such as hypothyroidism. It contains a wealth of information for anyone concerned with wellness and maintaining mood stability. Self-published. To purchase, write to London Research, 139 Main St., Brattleboro, VT 05301.*

Rosenbaum, M., and M. Susser. (1992) *Solving the Puzzle of Chronic Fatigue Syndrome.* Tacoma, WA: Life Sciences Press.
: *This handbook presents innovative approaches to dealing with a constellation of chronic symptoms including depression.*

Siegel, B. (1986) *Love, Medicine and Miracles.* New York: Harper & Row.
: *Dr. Siegel's healing work is well-known all over the country, and this book, in particular, is a must read for anyone searching for wellness and stability in their life. He successfully addresses the connection between emotional and physiological symptoms.*

——— (1990) *Peace, Love and Healing.* New York: Harper & Row.
: *This book explores the mind-body connection and helps you explore how you can heal yourself.*

Sheehy, G. (1992) *The Silent Passage.* New York: Random House.
: *Sheehy interviews women from diverse backgrounds to uncover myths about menopause. This up-to-date book is a must read for every woman nearing or in menopause.*

Sribnick, R., and W. Sribnick. (1994) *Smart Patient, Good Medicine.* New York: Walker.
: *This guide tells what you have a right to expect from your physician.*

Organizations

Well Mind Association of Greater Washington, Inc.
: 11141 Georgia Ave., Suite 326
Wheaton, MD 20902
(301) 949-8282
This organization provides information on physiological causes of psychiatric disorders and how they can be treated.

4

Taking Medication Safely

A woman who has dealt with chronic mood swings for many years and has finally been well for several years says, "I have learned as much as I can about the medications I take. I am very in tune with my body and this helps me in discussions with my doctor. I have read everything I can find about these medications in books, medical journals, the Physician's Desk Reference, *psychiatric drug books, and newsletters. I also learn what I can from television and videos."*

The decision to use psychiatric drugs to treat your mood disorder is a decision only you can make. Your decision should be based on the best information available from health care professionals who are truly experts in this area and from your own research. Lack of information can lead to misuse of medication or cause harmful interactions between drugs.

This chapter will help direct your research strategy and will explain how to approach drug therapy in a way that offers you optimal benefits and maximum safety.

Choosing the appropriate medication regime takes time and persistence. Your medication must be tailored to you since your response to a particular medication, and the side effects you experience, are physiologically unique. Just because a member of your support group reports excellent success with Prozac, for instance, does not mean that you will find it helpful. I know that lithium causes me to experience severe tremors, yet a friend of mine can take it without getting them.

Seventy-three percent of the individuals who responded to the research questionnaire for my study said they use psychotropic (mood-altering) drugs to help them keep their moods stable. Of that group, 80 percent said the medication gives them at least some relief from symptoms. Some use long-term medication therapy, which they complement with self-help strategies to enhance their medical treatment. Others use medications for the short term to allow time to work on issues, set up systems, learn management techniques, and make lifestyle changes that promote and enhance wellnesss. Some people sense that their moods are too unstable at present to allow them to do this work without the biological support medications can provide.

The most commonly used medications by people in the study were lithium, other mood stabilizing medications, and a wide variety of antidepressants. Some people also take antipsychotic medications and medications that address specific problems such as sleep and anxiety.

In some cases the physician is unable to find any medication or combination of medications that relieves symptoms. In other cases, people who find that psychotropic drugs are effective opt to forego them for the following reasons:

- They fear the long- or short-term side effects

- They feel medications diminsh their quality of life.

- They feel that the medications interfere with normal sexual function, memory, intellectual capacity, coordination, vision, digestion, and so on.

- They feel like a failure if they have to use medications to manage their life

- They have ethical reasons for refusing medications.

- They experience intolerable side effects

Other people chose not to use medication because they are uncomfortable with the idea of using any medication for the rest of their lifes. Some people in my study said lifelong drug therapy makes them feel like they have an incurable illness.

You may have your own reasons for not taking psychotropic medications. What are they?

_____

_____

_____

Given your reasons, is your decision in your best interest? If you are unsure, read on.

Non-Drug Therapies

Psychotropic drugs are not the only therapy available to you. Your health care professional may recommend non-drug therapies such as electroshock treatments or light therapy. See the section on seasonal affective disorder in chapter 5. Find out as much as you can about any recommended therapy before you give your consent. Make several copies of the treatment form that begins on the next page so that you can record the information you obtain. Be sure to add this information to your personal medical files.

Treatment Information

Treatment name:

Other possible names of this treatment:

How does this treatment work?

_____

_____

_____

What do you expect it to do?

_____

_____

_____

How long or how many treatments will it take to achieve that result?

_____

_____

_____

How often will I have this treatment?

Where will I have it?

What are the risks associated with taking this treatment?

_____

_____

_____

What kind of effectiveness track record does this treatment have?

_____

_____

_____

What possible short-term side effects does this treatment have?

_____

_____

_____

What possible long-term side effects does this treatment have?

_____

_____

_____

Is there any way to minimize the chances of experiencing these side effects? If so, what are they?

_____

_____

_____

Are there any dietary of lifestyle suggestions or restrictions when using this treatment?

_____

_____

_____

Why do you recomment this particular treatment?

_____

_____

_____

Have you had other patients that have used it? If so, how have they done?

_____

_____

_____

How is this treatment monitored?

_____

_____

_____

Do you have any printed information on this treatment I can have to study?

_____

_____

_____

Where can I get more information about this treatment?

_____

_____

_____

What tests will I need prior to this treatment?

_____

_____

_____

How often will I need these tests while having this treatment?

_____

_____

_____

What symptoms indicate that the treatment should be changed or stopped?

_____

_____

_____

Making an Informed Choice

Since you are the one who ultimately has to live with the effects of your treatment, don't leave the decision to your doctor. You may need to do your own research so you can intelligently discuss your options with your professional health care team. You may even wish to keep up with the latest scientific research by subscribing to relevant newsletters or journals. People in my study said they found this helpful.

Follow the led of the individual in my study who said:

> I have learned everything I could about the medications I take. This has taken personal long-term research. I read the *Physician's Desk Reference,* and cross-reference that with other sources of information. And I also ask a ton of questions and record the responses and any information acquired. I know that these drugs can cause damage if not monitored carefully. I feel as if I know more than the doctor. It is my body and I always like to know what I am putting in my mouth.

If you don't do your own investigation, you could unwittingly injure yourself. My experience with lithium illustrates this point. When I was taking lithium, I wasn't aware of how important it was for me to maintain body fluids. A brief episode of acute gastrointestinal symptoms caused severe tremors. Fortunately, a quick trip to the emergency room for intravenous replacement fluids alleviated the problem.

Lithium Toxicity.   The shaking I experienced was a sign that lithium had reached toxic levels in my body. Diarrhea and nausea also signal the onset of lithium toxicity. If you experience any of these symptoms, contact your physician immediately.

Because lithium is commonly used to treat manic depression and, less commonly, depression, let me share with you the dynamics that lead to lithium toxicity.

Lithium toxicity is an ever-present danger whenever you lose copious amounts of body fluids, whether through sweating when you are working outdoors on a hot day, or when you're sick with diarrhea or vomiting.

Your body needs a certain amount of sodium to perform normal body functions. When you sweat and lose body fluids, you lose sodium along with the fluid. The body tries to maintain its salt level by adjusting the filtering system in the kidneys so less salt than usual gets lost.

According to an informative report in the newsletter of the Topeka, Kansas, Depressive and Manic Depressive Association, "lithium and sodium are almost identical and your kidneys can't tell the difference between the two. When the kidney's filters hold in salt, they also conserve lithium that would normally pass out of your system. That means the amount of lithium in your body remains high. This can cause symptoms of lithium toxicity including shaking, nausea, and diarrhea."

You can counter this effect by using plenty of salt in your diet when you are working outdoors in the heat. Taking extra salt may make the symptoms disappear quickly, because the salt will cause the filters in the kidneys to release the accumulated lithium. (If you are on a sodium-restricted diet, be sure to consult your physician about the right course of action.)

If you get a flu bug, or diarrhea, contact your doctor for advice on how to manage lithium through your illness. Do NOT stop taking lithium or adjust the dosage without consulting your physician first.

Do make sure you are getting plenty of fluids. It is also essential to get your thyroid tested, on a regular basis, since lithium can sometimes cause hypothyroidism. (For more information on lithium, contact the Lithium Information Center which is listed at the end of the chapter.)

Working With Your Doctor

The more you know about your own body and the idiosyncracies of the medication you are considering, the better off you are. To ensure your safety, a thorough medical examination should precede any new medication regime. Have your health care professionals make sure that you have no health conditions that could be worsened by a particular medication.

A good medical history will help your doctor choose wisely from the available array of drugs. When you are discussing your options, be sure to tell your doctor if any of the following apply to you:

- You are allergic to any medicine.

- You are breast feeding.

- You have seizures, high blood pressure, heart disease, or glaucoma.

- You are taking blood pressure medication, antihistamines, or any other (prescription or nonprescription) medicine.

- You have any other medical problems.

Questions To Ask Your Doctor

When you are considering any new treatment regime, there are two immediate issues to consider: length of treatment and length of time on medication before you will feel better. There is currently much discussion in the mental health field about the pros and cons of long-term use of antidepressant and mood stabilizing medications. The potential for long-term damage is reason enough to seek out a physician who is an expert on psychotropic drugs and has up-to-date information on the most current scientific research.

Be sure to ask how long it will take before you'll notice positive effects from the medication. You may not see any improvement for several days to several weeks. Don't expect to feel better overnight. The improvement is likely to be gradual. In fact, most medications take from two to three weeks to work.

Beginning on the next page is a form for recording pertinent information about particular medications. (Before you record any information on this form, you may want to make several copies of it for later use for other proposed medications or treatments.)

Using Medicine Safely

Learn everything you can about a recommended medication before you decide if it is the right one for you. Find out what systems of the body it affects, the risks of using it, whether there are side effects that can accompany this drug, and if there are food, vitamins, or other drugs you should avoid when taking this drug. Don't be afraid to ask these same questions of your pharmacist.

Medication Information

Generic name: _____

Product name: _____

Product category: _____

Suggested dosage level: _____

How does this medication work?

_____

_____

_____

What do you expect it to do?

_____

_____

_____

How long will it take to achieve that result?

What are the risks associated with taking this medication?

_____

_____

_____

What is the effectiveness record of this medication?

_____

_____

_____

What short-term side effects does this medication have?

_____

_____

_____

What long-term side effects does this medication have?

_____

_____

_____

Is there any way to minimize the chances of experiencing these side effects? If so, what are they?

_____

_____

_____

Are there any dietary or lifestyle suggestions or restrictions when using this medication?

_____

_____

_____

Does this medication cause any adverse reactions when taken with certain other medications? If so, describe them.

_____

_____

_____

Why do you recommend this particular medication?

_____

_____

_____

Have you had other patients that have used it? If so, how have they done?

_____

_____

_____

How is this medication monitored?

_____

_____

_____

What tests will I need prior to taking this medication?

_____

_____

_____

How often will I need tests while on the medication?

_____

_____

_____

What symptoms indicate to you that the dosage should be changed or the medication stopped?

_____

_____

_____

Do you have any printed information on this medication I can have to study? Where can I get more information about this medication?

_____

_____

_____

If you are already taking medication for depression or manic depression, make sure you follow the guidelines below. Check off those steps that have been or need to be taken.

1. You are under the supervision of a physician who is an expert in the use of psychotropic medications. (Your physician has the responsibility to fully inform you of all risks and benefits of any medication prescribed, whether you ask or not.)

   ☐ *I am under the supervision of a physician who has the appropriate expertise.*

   ☐ *I need to find such a physician.*

2. You know the potential side effects of any medication prescribed for you and take personal responsibility to know what goes into your body and what the known side effects are.

3. You have the regular blood tests required for the medication you are taking.

   ☐ *I have been given the regular tests required for the medication I am taking.*

   ☐ *I need to check with my doctor and make sure I am having the required tests for the medication I am taking.*

4. You do *not* change the amount of medication you are taking or stop taking the medication without consulting your physician. (Systems for medication changes and discontinuation vary with each medication and must be monitored carefully to avoid potentially serious reactions. If you are having severe side effects and cannot reach your physician, contact another physician who your doctor has previously recommended as a backup, and ask how to deal with the situation.)

   ☐ *I understand that it is dangerous for me to adjust medication dosages in any way. If I feel a change is necessary, I will be in touch with my physician.*

5. You are completely honest with your physician if you have forgotten to take the medication a few times, or didn't renew the prescription on time. This will allow your physician to accurately assess the effectiveness of the medication.

6. You give your supporters copies of this information and choose one person you trust who can help you find out what you need to know about medication when you are not well enough to do it yourself.

   ☐ *I have designated _____ to help me when I cannot do it myself.*

Making Your Pharmacist Part of Your Safety Team

Consider your pharmacist an active member of your health care team and choose someone who takes a personal interest in you. Also make sure that the pharmacy has a good reputation and a computerized record-keeping system.

I know from personal experience that this is very important. There was a time when I was taking Tegretol, a medicine to control severe mood instability. The medicine helped stabilize me and I was doing well. When symptoms started to recur, my doctor tested the level of the drug in my blood and found that it was below the therapeutic level. He assumed that my body was not absorbing the drug, so he increased the dosage.

At the same time, I ran out of the old prescription and had it refilled. I immediately began having symptoms that indicated I was taking too much Tegretol. When I investigated, I found that the old prescription had been recalled because that batch was not at the correct strength. Unfortunately, my pharmacy—which was part of a large drugstore chain—hadn't taken the trouble to notify me. It took me four months to recover from the effects of changing the strength of the medication and taking too strong a dose. Since then, I've used a small but reputable pharmacy where the pharmacist knows me well.

A good pharmacist will set up a system on the computer that will keep track of how many pills you have left in an old prescription when you change medications. If you ask, the pharmacist could require you to return leftovers before giving you the new prescription. This can eliminate a person's ability to hoard pills for a suicide attempt during a period of severe depression. Consider asking your pharmacist to set up this safeguard for you if you have ever been suicidal or thought of hoarding pills. Check the steps below that you have taken or need to be taken.

- ☐ *My pharmacist takes a personal interest in me, and the pharmacy itself is reputable and uses computerized record-keeping systems.*

- ☐ *I need to find a pharmacy that meets all of the above conditions.*

- ☐ *I have asked my pharmacist to assist me in preventing suicide by monitoring my purchase of medications.*

Taking Responsibility for Your Treatment Regime

Taking medication can become so routine that it is hard to remember whether or not you have taken your daily dose. One way to make sure you do is to take an empty egg carton, mark each egg container with a day of the week, and fill that container with the medicine you need for that day. A quick glance at the carton will tell you whether or not you've taken that day's medicine. Other people prefer setting out their medicine for the day in cups—one for morning medicine, one for afternoon medicine, and so on. Pharmacies also sell small containers that can be used.

Some people find that making a simple checkmark on a daily chart does the trick for them. Others make a daily note in a log designed to provide an accurate long-term record of medication use and symptoms experienced.

If you need to take your medication at a certain time each day, a watch with a timer or a small inexpensive timer that you can purchase at your pharmacy can be a helpful reminder.

Don't be hard on yourself if you forget to take your medication. It is not a personal failure. We all forget. Establish a system for yourself that will most easily resolve the problem. When you realize you have missed several doses of medication, check with your physician to see if you should take the missed doses or continue with the regular single dose.

Guidelines for Taking Medications

Here are some additional safeguards. They were developed by Mary Moller, MSN, RN, CS, of The Center for Patient and Family Mental Health Education in Nine Mile Falls, Washington.

1. Take all medications exactly as prescribed.

2. If the medication may make you drowsy or less alert, curtail activity accordingly.

3. Do not share your medication with others. You never know how your medication could affect another person.

4. Keep all medications in a cool, dry place. Bathroom moisture tends to destroy the effectiveness of medication.

5. Keep all medications out of reach of children and pets.

6. Be sure you have enough medications before vacations and holidays.

7. If you are pregnant or planning on becoming pregnant, tell your physician. Many medications can have a harmful effect on a pregnancy, especially during the first three months.

8. If you are planning to use an over-the-counter medication such as a cold medicine, ask the pharmacist if it can be safely taken with your prescription drugs.

9. Keep all medication in the original bottle. Never mix two medications in one bottle.

10. Remember to tell all your doctors and dentists that you are on medication.

Managing Side Effects

Unfortunately, some psychiatric medications that are very effective can cause unwanted side effects. Many of them are manageable. But if you find that you have checked any of the dangerous side effects listed below, report them immediately to your doctor. *Don't wait!*

- ☐ blurred vision
- ☐ rash or hives
- ☐ nervousness, irritability, shakiness
- ☐ wanting to sleep all the time
- ☐ confusion
- ☐ fainting, seizures, or hallucinations
- ☐ nausea and vomiting
- ☐ slurred speech
- ☐ lack of coordination, stumbling
- ☐ jerking of arms and legs
- ☐ seizures or fainting

- ☐ rapid or irregular heartbeat
- ☐ sore throat or fever
- ☐ insomnia
- ☐ restlessness, incoordination
- ☐ giddiness
- ☐ numbness in hands or feet
- ☐ mental confusion
- ☐ stomach pains
- ☐ swelling of hands or feet
- ☐ ringing in ears
- ☐ large increase in urination

☐ complete stopping of urination   ☐ infection

☐ changes in sex drive, impotence   ☐ changes in menstrual cycle

Even if the side effects you experience aren't on this list, do keep your physician advised of all symptoms that appear after you start taking any medication. Don't assume the symptom is a medication side effect and fail to report it. A serious condition could be needlessly overlooked.

Some common side effects of psychotropic drugs include constipation, dizziness, dry mouth, dry skin, headaches, impotance, irritable bowel syndrome, loss of libido, nausea, tardive dyskinesia and dystonia, thought deficits, tremors, water retention, and weight gain. These side effects can often be managed.

You may find that the side effects you experience are most severe when you begin the medication. After your body adjusts, they may diminish or disappear. I've noticed that I tire easily during the first several weeks I begin taking a new medication. I deal with it by adjusting my schedule so I have less to do and can get more rest.

There are other safe, simple, and effective ways to deal with such side effects. For instance, one man reported that he takes his tricyclic antidepressants with three or four crackers and a full glass of water one or two hours before his bedtime. This helps him avoid stomach upset.

Another says she manages the side effects with exercise, good diet, and a homeopathic medicine for nausea. She accepts her side effects but watches to make sure they don't get out of hand. When they do, she takes it as a warning of an impending episode.

In general, anything that contributes to your overall sense of well-being tends to lessen the incidence and severity of medication side effects. This includes a high-fiber, low-fat diet, plenty of liquids (check with your doctor to find out how much liquid you need with the medication you are taking), daily exercise, and the regular use of stress-reduction techniques. You may find, as many people do, that when life begins to feel "out of control," side effects tend to get worse. See chapter 5, "Developing a Lifestyle That Enhances Wellness," for ideas on how to adjust your lifestyle to enhance your sense of well-being.

Here are ways to minimize or eliminate specific side effects:

Constipation. Many psychotropic medications cause dryness, which increases the likelihood of constipation. This can be prevented by eating high-fiber foods such as whole grains, fruits and vegetables and by getting daily exercise. Using a dietary fiber additive that contains psyllium husks and drinking a quart to a gallon of liquid daily helps elimination. Nonprescription stool softeners may also be helpful.

Diminished sex drive and impotence. When you tell health care professionals about diminished sex drive and impotence, they may minimize the importance of this medication side effect. This is not fair. Clearly people who take medications for psychiatric symptoms deserve full sexual expression just like everyone else. Some people decide to switch medications or discontinue their use because of this side effect. Your health care professional should take it seriously.

Dry mouth. According to the National Institute of Dental Research, dry mouth is a side effect of more than 400 commonly used medications, including those prescribed for depression. This occurs because you are not producing as much saliva as you need. Saliva is an important plaque fighter and tooth hardener, and its absence can lead to gum disease and tooth decay. The National Institute of Dental Research suggests asking your dentist about an artificial saliva to moisten your mouth.

Some people in the study said they eat hard candies to eliminate dry mouth. However, this also causes dental problems. There are many sugarless candies on the market which can be used as a substitute.

Again, adequate fluid intake is essential to successfully manage this side effect. Small amounts of water or juice taken frequently help.

Dry skin. The use of liberal amounts of creams, ointments, and oils helps to alleviate dry skin. There are many unscented products that are acceptable to everyone. Use as little soap as possible and rinse it off quickly. Adequate fluid intake and a healthy diet also help.

Headache and dizziness. Headaches and dizziness may be caused by blood pressure changes. Get up and down slowly. Avoid extreme temperature changes. Consult your doctor about this problem.

Insomnia. Adjusting the time of day when you take medications may help to reduce sleep problems. Some medications help you to sleep, so they can be taken an hour or two before bedtime. Those that keep you awake should be taken in the morning. See chapter 5, "Developing a Lifestyle That Enhances Wellness," for more information on how to get to sleep.

Irritable bowel symptoms (chronic diarrhea alternating with episodes of constipation, and often accompanied by cramps and gas). Symptoms of irritable bowel syndrome are reported by many people who take psychiatric medications or who have mood instability. It is not clear whether the symptoms are caused by the medication, the stress of the instability, or something else.

A study volunteer said, "This can be very disruptive. I've gone to a gastroenterologist and he did a colon examination, found nothing, and prescribed Immodium, which is now available over-the-counter. It works pretty well to stop the spasms and is easier to carry around and quicker acting than Kaopectate. Immodium is actually a narcotic, but it normally doesn't cross the blood-brain barrier, so you can't get high from it."

Dietary fiber additives that contain psyllium husks and an adequate intake of fluid help but do not generally cure this condition. My gastroenterologist says that it takes two weeks to determine how effective it is to use a fiber additive daily. She also recommends Immodium for those times when diarrhea is inconvenient.

A high-fiber, low-fat diet—accompanied by stress reduction techniques, exercise, and adequate rest—may also help to control symptoms.

Nausea. If you experience nausea, taking medication with food or milk may help.

Tardive dyskinesia and dystonia. Antipsychotic drugs such as Haldol, Loxitane, Mellaril, Moban, Navane, Prolixin, Thorazine, Tindal, Trilafon, Stelazine are sometimes prescribed to relieve symptoms of major depression and manic depression. Cumulative exposure to these medications can cause severe side effects, including tardive dyskinesia and tardive dystonia.

Tardive dyskinesia causes uncontrollable movement, varying in degree from occasional minor twitches to severe involuntary movement. The most commonly affected area is the face, where there may be abnormal movements of the tongue, jaw, and muscles around the mouth and eyes. Involuntary movement of the arms, legs, and torso may also be involved. Occasionally a person will experience an irregular breathing rate, speech irregularities, and weight loss.

Tardive dystonia is characterized by muscle spasms that result in involuntary, painful, sustained twisting and distortion of body parts.

These side effects can continue even after you have stopped taking the medication. The movements can be permanent. There is no treatment for tardive dyskinesia or tardive dystonia.

The risk of getting these disorders is about 30 percent for people who have taken the medication for a total of five years (it is estimated that 400,000 to one million people are affected). Occasionally people who have used these medications for a short time develop symptoms. The risk increases as you get older.

Before you begin taking such medication, you should clearly understand the benefits and risks involved. The more you know about the benefits and risks of antipsychotic medications, the more you will be able to make appropriate choices about your treatment. You have a right to know this information, and the prescribing health care professional has a responsibility to help you understand the risks. If you are not well enough to understand the benefits and risks, have a trusted support person assist you in making this decision.

If you take or are considering taking neuroleptic medications, be alert to any signs of tardive dyskinesia.

- Watch for any unusual movement or twitches (supporters are often the first to notice such movements).

- Notify your doctor as soon as you notice any unusual movement.

- Have a tardive dyskinesia checkup every three months. (These checkups must be done by your physician, and take from five to ten minutes.)

It is important to remember that tardive dyskinesia can be masked by the sedating effect of the medication. When the medication is discontinued, the symptoms may increase.

To reduce symptoms of tardive dyskinesia and tardive dystonia, take the following steps:

- Ask your physician about using high doses of certain benign agents such as Vitamin E, choline, or lecithin.

- Use relaxation techniques and stress management daily. (Stress worsens symptoms.)

- Soak in a hot bath or whirlpool.

- Use moist application of heat, or use ice to help reduce acute symptoms and pain.

- Exercise to improve posture and strengthen muscles.

Tremor. Mild to severe tremor affects many people who take psychotropic medications. Adequate rest and strict attention to fluid intake may alleviate this problem somewhat. Relaxation exercises also help.

Soaking in a warm bath sometimes reduces tremors. The effect is enhanced by use of a whirlpool. There are inexpensive whirlpool units available that fit in the bathtub.

Thought deficits. Some people experience thought and memory problems when taking certain psychiatric medication (these are also a symptom of depression). A person in the study said, "One frustrating problem I have is difficulty coming up with a word I want to use—it feels like it gets 'stuck' inside my head." His doctor attributed the problem to the anticholinergic— or drying—properties of his medication. I remember not being able to remember a question long enough to give an answer.

It helps to stay calm when these problems arise. The problem worsens if you get anxious or agitated, but it is minimized if you have a relaxed attitude. It also helps if the people you associate with are understanding and nonjudgmental.

If you are anxious or agitated, do the relaxation exercises in chapter 16, "Responding to Symptoms of Depression," and chapter 18, "Responding to Symptoms of Mania."

Water retention. If you are troubled by water retention, tell your doctor. Your doctor may want you to limit your salt intake.

Weight gain. Weight gain is a common side effect of many medications. If you know a particular medication might cause weight gain, make needed dietary adjustments when you begin using it rather than waiting until after you have gained the weight. It's easier to keep from gaining weight than to lose weight. Weight gain can be minimized by focusing on a diet high in complex carbohydrates (vegetables and grains) and low in simple sugars and saturated fats. See chapter 5, "Developing a Lifestyle That Enhances Wellness," for diet information and the resource list below and at the end of chapter 5 for more information on weight control and dietary issues.

Resources

American Automobile Association. *RX for Safe Driving*. Heathrow, FLA: American Automobile Association.

> *This free booklet describes how drugs affect your ability to drive. To obtain a copy, send a self-addressed, stamped envelope to RX For Safe Driving, Mail Stop 600, 1000 AAA Drive, Heathrow, FL 32746-5063.*

Barnhart, E. (1993) *Physicians Desk Reference*. Oradell, NJ: Medical Economics Co.

> *This book is updated annually and contains technical information on medications. The book isn't all that accessible to the average reader, but it will give you the information you need to ask your health care professionals the right questions.*

Gorman, J. (1991) *The Essential Guide to Psychotropic Medications*. New York: St. Martin's Press.

> *Check out medication recommendations in this up-to-date reference.*

Griffith, H. (1993) *Complete Guide to Prescription and Non-Prescription Drugs*. New York: Body Press/Perigee.

> *This comprehensive reference provides complete information about prescription and nonprescription medications and explains the differences between brand-name medications and generics, and describes the standards for safe medication use.*

John Hopkins University (1993) *John Hopkins Handbook of Drugs*. Baltimore: John Hopkins University Press.

> *Gives information about medications and their side effects to physicians, pharmacists, and the Food and Drug Administration.*

Mondimore, F. (1990) *Depression: The Mood Disease.* Baltimore: Johns Hopkins.
> *A good, medically oriented reference.*

Schein, J., and P. Hansten (1993) *The Consumer's Guide to Drug Interactions.* New York: Collier Books.
> *This book provides essential information on the effects of taking several different kinds of medications.*

Wolfe, S., R. Hope, and Public Citizen Health Research Group (1993) *Worst Pills Best Pills II.* NY: Pantheon.
> *Lists 364 commonly prescribed medications including 119 which should not be used by some people and 113 that should be used only in a very limited way.*

Yudofsky, S., R. Hales, and T. Ferguson (1991) *What You Need To Know About Psychiatric Drugs.* New York: Grove Weidenfeld.
> *This book contains easy-to-understand information about all psychiatric medications, including tranquilizers, sedatives, sleeping pills, anti-anxiety medications, mood stabilizers, antidepressants, and antipsychotics.*

Diet and Medication

Rosenthal, N. (1993) *Winter Blues.* New York: Guilford Press.
> *There is a section in the appendix of this book that gives helpful dietary advice that is useful to people who are taking psychotropic medications.*

Fanning, P. (1990). *Lifetime Weight Control.* Oakland, CA: New Harbinger Publications.
> *A different and very useful approach to weight loss.*

Hoffman, R. (1988) *The Diet-Type Weight-Loss Program.* New York: Simon & Schuster.
> *This book helps you determine the diet that will work for you based on your lifestyle and eating habits. I found it to be very useful in developing a weight control program for myself.*

Kirschenbaum, D. (1994) *Weight Loss Through Persistence.* Oakland, CA: New Harbinger Publications.
> *An excellent, long-term weight loss program based on up-to-date scientific findings.*

Turner, K. (1987) *The Self-Healing Cookbook.* Grass Valley, CA: Earthtones Press.
> *This delightful cookbook shows you how to easily change your style of cooking to one that enhances your wellness. It includes a section on foods that actually help you lose weight.*

Organizations

For more information on Tardive Dyskinesia, contact:

Tardive Dykinesia/Tardive Dystonia National Association
4244 University Way Northeast
PO Box 45732
Seattle, WA 98145-0732

National Institute of Mental Health

Neuroscience Center at Saint Elizabeth's

WAW Building, Room 201

2700 Martin Luther King Jr. Ave. Southeast

Washington, DC 20032

For more information on lithium contact:

Lithium Information Center

Department of Psychiatry, University of Wisconsin

Center for Health Services

600 Highland Ave.

Madison, WI 53792

(608) 263-6171

This center is a storehouse of information on lithium.

PART II

Lifestyle

5

Developing a Lifestyle That Enhances Wellness

It's the hardest thing for me—keeping my life in control and doing for myself the things that I know are best for me.

Paying attention to key areas of your lifestyle—including your daily dose of light, exercise and sleep—can make all the difference in your moods. This chapter will highlight five such areas and explain how to make the necessary adjustments so that each makes a positive contribution to your overall sense of well-being.

Light

Of all the factors, light may be the most critical. In fact, many people, especially those who live in northern climates, fear the onset of winter because they get more and more depressed as the days shorten. Do you experience any of these symptoms as the daylight diminishes and winter approaches?

☐ Drop in energy level

☐ Decrease in productivity

☐ Difficulty getting motivated

☐ Decrease in creativity

☐ Difficulty concentrating and focusing

☐ Impatience with self and others

☐ Difficulty getting out of bed in the morning

☐   Craving for sweets and junk food

☐   Diminished sex drive

If so, the culprit may be Seasonal Affective Disorder, commonly known as SAD. This medically recognized condition is a form of wintertime depression that can be so severe that it incapacitates people.

The incidence of SAD is higher in northern climates than in the South. For instance, an estimated 10 percent of the people who live in New Hampshire suffer from SAD, compared to only 1 percent of those who live in Florida. At the 45-50 degrees latitude mark, SAD affects an estimated 10.2 percent of the people, compared to 1.4 percent in the deep South, where the latitude is 20-25 degrees.

Given these statistics, you might assume that relocating to a sunnier climate would be a good treatment for people who live in the north. This is not feasible for most people.

Fortunately, there is another way to treat SAD. Researchers have found that consistent daily exposure to bright light reduces or eliminates the disorder in up to 80 percent of cases. The intensity of light reaching the eyes is the key to treating SAD. This is why most treatment programs call for supplemental lighting with a light box for about two hours a day. The light emanating from the box can be up to 2,500 lux. (Lux refers to a unit of illumination.) This is far brighter than the 100 lux you'd find in a room with a single light, or the 300 to 500 lux in ordinary indoor lighting.

It is not clear why bright light works in this way, but it may have something to do with the production of the hormone melatonin, which lightens skin pigmentation, among other things. Melatonin is made in the pineal gland and the photoreceptors of the retina, and its production is inhibited by sunlight.

Some researchers believe that people who suffer from SAD are either too sensitive to dim light and manufacture too much of the hormone, or are oversensitive to the amount of melatonin that is usually produced.

Dopamine, a chemical that carries signals between nerves and brain cells, may also play a role in SAD. Depletion of another neurotransmitter, serotonin, may be responsible for the carbohydrate cravings that are a symptom of SAD.

If you think you may have SAD, contact a physician who specializes in treating this disorder. This is especially important if you are considering light therapy and are currently taking photosensitizing medications, or have a condition, like lupus, that causes you to have sun sensitive skin. A health care professional can:

• Confirm the diagnosis

• Make sure that light therapy is appropriate

• Rule out other medical conditions that need treatment

• Work with you to develop a treatment strategy

• Assist you in monitoring the symptoms

• Provide additional ideas and alternative or supplemental treatments

• Give you encouragement and support

The Light Box

Light boxes can often make a dramatic difference in as little as two to four days. "There is a big difference when using this lighting," one of my study volunteers reported. "I feel like some biochemical change has taken place."

Certain companies that sell light boxes now offer them on a short-term rental basis so you can try one out to see if it works for you. Make sure you test the box for at least two weeks before you judge whether or not it is effective. Once you buy a box, be sure to replace the light bulbs regularly so that you are getting the right intensity of light. Some people make their own light boxes, but this is not recommended because it is tricky to wire them, expensive to purchase the components, and difficult to make sure that the box provides sufficient light.

There are several kinds of light boxes. The one I have is a wooden box in a plastic cover fitted with four flourescent bulbs, backed with reflective material. Other models are set on a frame and tilt over a workspace. On average, the boxes cost $350 to $500. While this may sound expensive, consider it an investment in your productivity and quality of life. Many people have spent a lot more than that on treatments that were ineffective. Some insurance companies are even willing to cover the cost of the light box, if your physician prescribes one for you.

To use the light box, sit—with your eyes open—three feet in front of it. You don't have to stare directly at the lights. You can use it instead to illuminate a work surface, or as a source of room illumination. I use my light box to light my office. My plants love the light and respond to it by putting out extensive, lush growth.

The time of day you use the light box is not all that critical, although some people find that a session of light therapy just before bed keeps them awake. This is one reason why some people prefer to get their light exposure in the morning. Others find that early evening fits into their schedule better. What *is* important is to set aside a time that's convenient for you so that you get your light exposure every day. If you skip even a day, your symptoms could return.

I find it best to get up around 5:30 a.m. for my treatment, and to sit at a desk illuminated by my light box. If I miss a session when I'm on the road, I do notice a drop in my mood and overall sense of well-being. If I miss several days, my symptoms worsen dramatically. I am thinking about buying a light visor for when I travel, but for now, I make an extra effort to get outdoors on these days. (Light visors are worn like hats, and direct light into the eyes. They were developed for people whose schedules don't permit them to sit for two hours in front of a stationary light box.)

People who use the light box on a daily basis often taper off light box use as spring approaches, and stop entirely during the summer except when there are stretches of rainy or cloudy days. Others who have an extreme need for light continue therapy through the summer.

Light therapy is well-tolerated by most people. However, if you experience any of the mild side effects, such as headaches, eyestrain, irritability, overactivity, fatigue, dryness of eyes, nasal passages, and sinuses, and sunburn-type skin reactions, decrease your exposure time, use a sunblock, and consult with a health care professional. Even if you don't experience any side effects, it is a good idea to get regular eye checkups.

Once you have begun light therapy, use the Self-Assessment Mood Scale for SAD that begins on the next page to see how it is working. Share this information with your health care professionals.

Self-Assessment Mood Scale
for Seasonal Affective Disorder

Compared to how you feel **when you are in an even or normal mood state,** how would you rate yourself on the following items **during the past week?**

    0 = Not at all
    1 = Just a little
    2 = More than just a little
    3 = Quite a bit, moderately
    4 = Markedly or severely

I have been feeling . . .	Before starting treatment	After 1 week of treatment	After 2 weeks of treatment	After 3 weeks of treatment	After 4 weeks of treatment
down and depressed					
less interested in doing things					
less interested in sex					
less interested in eating					
that I've lost some weight					
that I can't fall asleep at night					
that I wake up too early					
heavy in my limbs or aches in back, muscles, or head, more tired than usual					
guilty or like a failure					
wishing for death or suicidal					
tense, irritable, or worried					
sure I'm ill or have a disease					
that my speech and thought are slow					
that morning is worse than evening					
that evening is worse than morning					
unreal or in a dream state					
suspicious of people/paranoid					
preoccupied/obsesssed that I must check things a lot					
physical symptoms when worried					

Standard depression score   _____   _____   _____   _____   _____

Self-Assessment Mood Scale
for Seasonal Affective Disorder

Compared to how you feel **when you are in an even or normal mood state,** how would you rate yourself on the following items **during the past week?**

    0 = Not at all
    1 = Just a little
    2 = More than just a little
    3 = Quite a bit, moderately
    4 = Markedly or severely

Supplemental Symptoms Chart

I have been feeling . . .	*Before starting treatment*	*After 1 week of treatment*	*After 2 weeks of treatment*	*After 3 weeks of treatment*	*After 4 weeks of treatment*
like socializing less					
that I have gained weight					
that I *want* to eat more than usual					
that I *have* eaten more than usual					
that I crave sweets and starches					
that I sleep more than usual					
that my mood slumps in the afternoons or evenings					

Supplemental depression score _____ _____ _____ _____ _____

Total depression scores _____ _____ _____ _____ _____
(add standard to supplementary scores)

This scale was adapted from the Structured Interview guide for the Hamilton Depression Rating Scale by J. B. W. Williams, M. J. Link, N. E. Rosenthal, and M. Terman. Norman E. Rosenthal holds the copyright on it and it is printed here with his permission.

Get Natural Light, Too

Although few people with SAD find that spending time outdoors can completely meet their need for light, it is helpful to make the effort to spend more time under natural light. Consider the fact that people today are outdoors much less than those who lived 100 years ago. Back then, people walked or traveled by open carriage. Even going to the bathroom involved a trek outdoors—to the outhouse. Today, it is not unusual to get into your car before the sun comes up to make your morning commute to work, where you sit in artificially lit offices without windows, and then travel home just as it is getting dark.

"I get outside for at least 15 minutes first thing in the morning and again in the late afternoon," said one of the women in my study. "It makes me feel better."

When you are outside, gaze at the sky without looking directly at the sun. On snowy days, the amount of light you get is enhanced by its reflection off the snow, but reduced by dark objects such as buildings and trees.

One women who has effectively treated herself for SAD says, "I try to stay outside more than one hour a day or sit near a window when I'm inside."

Incidentally, tanning booths, which only shed light on the skin, do not provide the right kind of light.

It is also helpful to keep your living space well lit at all times. Windows should be uncovered during the daylight hours to let sunlight in. If you work inside, work as close to a window as possible.

Summer Depression

Some people report SAD-like symptoms in the summer. People with summer depressions tend to be more agitated, while those of us who have winter depressions are more sedated. Early research indicates that summer depressions may be a result of temperature sensitivity. Some people have reduced symptoms of summer depression by spending time in an air-conditioned space. While no clear information is available on this subject, it will not hurt to see if spending part of your day in an air-conditioned space helps to relieve symptoms. It will probably take several exposures to reduced temperature before you notice any effect. Adjust the length of exposure to see if that makes a difference.

☐   *I notice that I am more depressed in the summer months. I will spend time in an air-conditioned room to see if it helps reduce symptoms.*

How did you feel before you spent time in an air-conditioned room?

_____

_____

_____

How did you feel after spending time in an air-conditioned room?

_____

_____

_____

What do you plan to do as a result of your findings?

_____

_____

_____

☐ *I will discuss these symptoms and their possible relationship to temperature with my health care professionals for additional suggestions.*

Exercise

One key strategy used by people who have gotten well and stayed well is regular exercise, which is the cheapest and most available antidepressant. It is also very effective.

According to Dr. Edmund Bourne, author of *The Anxiety & Phobia Workbook*, exercise does the following:

- Increases feelings of well-being

- Reduces dependence on alcohol and drugs

- Reduces insomnia

- Improves concentration and memory

- Alleviates symptoms of depression

- Gives greater control over feelings of anxiety

- Increases self-esteem

A woman who has had episodes of depression for 15 years, and who now has her depression under control, says:

I feel physically and emotionally better when I keep up with my exercise routine.

Another who has been well for 10 years says:

I walk about two miles twice a week and bicycle for a mile once a week. It gets my mind off my problems and burns unused energy.

Exercising daily for at least 20 minutes each day is essential to maintaining wellness. Dr. Wayne London, author of *Principles of Health*, recommends that you get three to five 30-to-45-minute sessions of aerobic exercise each week. More exercise than that won't be helpful, because it can make you "sluggish, irritable and depressed," he says.

If you have not exercised regularly, however, consult your physician before you begin any exercise program. Then start with just a few minutes and gradually work your way up. If you start too fast, the resulting aches and pains may discourage you from continuing. A warm bath after you exercise can help reduce those aches and pains.

Sticking to Your Exercise Schedule

Most people find it difficult to exercise in winter and in bad weather. One way to solve that is to buy exercise equipment such as an exercise bicycle or rowing machine, which can be used indoors. These can often be purchased inexpensively, secondhand.

During the onset of depression, it may also be difficult to motivate yourself to exercise. If you address the symptoms early (as discussed in chapters 15 and 16), this won't be a problem.

Some people cite lack of time or lack of enjoyment as a reason to skip exercise. If this is you, try looking at your exercise time as play time. I find that it helps me to stick to my program if I reward myself—my kids call it bribing—at regular intervals. I may put aside a dollar each time I exercise, and use it for clothing or an audiocassette or some other treat. If I keep it up for a week, I may treat myself to a healthy lunch out with a special friend.

Once exercising becomes part of your routine, you won't need to reward yourself because you will find that getting the exercise is ample reward.

What strategy will you use to stick to your exercise plan?:

_____

_____

_____

Scheduling exercise at the same time each day provides structure and helps to ensure continuation of an exercise program.

How many times a day will you exercise? How many days a week? For how long each day?

_____

_____

_____

Combine exercise with other strategies you use to maintain your stability. For instance:

- When exercising indoors, do it in front of a light box.
- Practice reinforcing positive thoughts at the same time.
- Connect with family members and supporters by asking them to join you on a walk.
- Practice peer counseling while walking.

How can you combine exercise with other strategies you use to maintain your stability?

_____

_____

_____

Choosing the Best Form of Exercise

Any kind of exercise—walking, swimming, skating, skiing, dancing—even gardening and raking—is acceptable. You can do the same kind of exercise every day or vary it according to the weather, how you feel, or what you need to get done. Yesterday I spent part of my exercise time shoveling snow and breaking up ice on my driveway. This makes exercise more interesting. You don't have to join an expensive health club (although it is a wonderful treat if you can afford it). The exercise does not have to be strenuous. Even a stroll helps.

What kinds of exercise do you enjoy?

_____

_____

_____

In fact, walking is ideal. Dr. London considers walking the easiest, most convenient, and best exercise. It doesn't require any special equipment except a good pair of walking shoes, which you should have anyway, it doesn't cost anything, and it is very unlikely that you will incur the type of overuse injuries that occur with other types of exercise. People who experience mania find that a walk can help reduce anxiety or the early warning signs of mania.

Diet

As many people who experience depression and manic depression know, diet plays a significant role in mood instability. To feel well, our diet must include:

- At least five servings daily of vegetables

- At least six servings of grains each day

A diet high in complex carbohydrates (vegetables and grains) raises serotonin levels and promotes emotional stability. Low levels of this brain neurotransmitter make you feel out of sorts and depressed. (Some antidepressant medications such as Prozac, Zoloft, and Paxil, also increase serotonin levels.)

Keep It Natural

Nutritionists are learning more and more about the short- and long-term effects of a diet high in refined, processed, and artificial chemical-laden foods. To avoid undetected allergies and improve your general health, it is in your best interest to restrict your diet to fresh, natural food grown without chemicals.

The following substances have been found to increase mood instability. Limit or exclude them from your diet.

- Refined sugar (watch for hidden sugar in many prepared foods)

- Foods that are high in saturated fats

- High-calorie, high-fat, low-food-value junk food

- Alcohol

- Caffeine

A woman who has successfully addressed dietary issues says:

When I found that soda, lots of coffee, sugars, and dairy products were creating mood swings (even though my body had this craving for them), I said it just wasn't worth the constant ups and downs. Once I switched, I noticed a difference right off! A healthy diet keeps me balanced. I changed my diet to a refined one, and my mind changed too!

Through a careful dietary analysis you can identify and eliminate from your diet those foods that are particularly bad for you. For instance, I have found that dairy products upset my digestive system. My mother found them to be very calming and soothing.

What foods increase your mood instability?

_____

_____

_____

Many people have used various amino acid and vitamin regimens to improve their general health and stability. Develop such a program in consultation with knowledgeable health care professionals, such as nutritionists and naturopathic physicians. Also read *The Way Up From Down* by Dr. Priscilla Slagle (in her recommended amino acid formulation, taurene can be substituted for tryptophane, which is no longer available) and *The Amino Acid Revolution* by Dr. Robert Erdmann.

☐ *I am going to explore the use of supplemental vitamin and amino acids to improve my stability. I will consult with the following health care professionals in developing such a plan:*

_____

_____

_____

A good diet, which I know promotes my stability, has often been difficult for me to maintain. When I am very busy, trying to meet a deadline, or preparing for a trip, I tend to put my good eating habits on the back burner. I don't take the time to go grocery shopping or to prepare good food for myself. When I am traveling, I find it very difficult, and in some cases impossible, to find well-prepared, reasonably priced healthy food. I end up dealing with my hunger by snacking on junk foods. I always pay with a general feeling of malaise and acute gastrointestinal symptoms.

To combat this, I need to do the following:

• Make regular shopping trips a high priority so that I will have healthy foods on hand.

• Take the time to cook good foods for myself.

- Keep a supply of easy-to-fix, healthy foods on hand for when I am busy. (I have gotten better at this. When I cook, I freeze the leftovers in meal-size containers and then stick them in the microwave as needed.)

- Identify several local restaurants where I can enjoy a healthy meal.

- Pack a supply of healthy snacks in my carry-on luggage when I am traveling. (I can replenish the supply at a health food store at my destination.)

- Let hosts know of my food needs and ask them to locate restaurants in the area that would meet my dietary needs.

What problems do you have sticking with a healthy diet?

_____

_____

_____

How could you solve these problems?

_____

_____

_____

If you are temporarily house-bound or your schedule is hectic, ask a supporter to pick up groceries for you when they pick up their own. You can return the favor when you are able. If getting out is difficult for you, contact a home health aid service in your area for grocery delivery service. In some areas, nutritious meals can be delivered to your home.

Sleep

A good night's sleep is absolutely essential to stability.

- Lack of sleep worsens mania and sometimes worsens depression. (If you have a history of manic episodes and lose a night of sleep, contact your physician right away. This can be disastrous.)

- Too much sleep worsens depression.

- You need to go to bed at the same time every night and get up at the same time every morning.

- Even when you don't get to sleep at the regular time, you will still feel much better when you get up at the usual hour.

- Shift work, including third shift and swing shift, is particularly bad for people with mood disorders.

The following healthy habits will help ensure a good night's sleep:

- Avoid caffeine, a stimulant. I find that if I have any caffeine during the day, I have a hard time falling asleep and do not sleep well when I finally doze off. Coffee and tea are not the only culprits. There is enough caffeine in chocolate, some soft drinks, and some painkillers to interfere with sleep. Read the labels.

- Avoid the use of nicotine. It is also a stimulant. If you cannot give up your smoking habit right now, avoid smoking two to three hours before bedtime.

- Avoid the use of alcohol. While it may help you fall asleep, it will disturb your sleep later and may cause you to awaken early.

- Eat on a regular schedule and avoid a heavy meal prior to going to bed. Avoid rigid weight loss plans that will cause you to wake up hungry during the night. Distribute your calorie intake throughout the day.

- Be sure you have adequate calcium intake. A calcium supplement often helps people sleep.

- Exercise daily.

- Avoid exercise and other strenuous or invigorating activity before going to bed.

- Have a daily routine so your body knows when it is time to go to sleep.

- Avoid sleeping late or taking long naps during the day.

- Have a pre-bedtime ritual such as washing up, getting into night clothes, and reading a chapter from a book that tells your body it's time to go to bed.

- Consider sex for relaxation.

- Keep your bedroom temperature between 65 and 70 degrees Fahrenheit.

- Make sure your sleeping space is not too noisy or too light. Reserve your bed and bedroom for sleeping and sex only.

What health habits do you need to improve to ensure proper sleep?

_____

_____

_____

Those people who participated in my study said they have discovered a number of techniques to help them get to sleep and stay asleep all night. Here is what they recommend:

- Use progressive relaxation exercises (those in which you tense and relax muscles) to put yourself to sleep. I do this often. I repeat the exercise if I wake up during the night. I keep a relaxation tape in a tape player beside my bed so I can use it when I'm having a hard time getting to sleep.

- Play soothing music on a tape that shuts off automatically.

- Focus your attention on your breathing and repeat the word "in" and "out" silently as you breathe.

- Use your imaging skills to put yourself to sleep. Visualization exercises like painting a landscape in your mind, imaging numbers embellished with various decorations and then mentally erasing a number and going on to the next, or seeing yourself lying on a sandy beach on a warm spring day with gulls flying overhead can also help you get to sleep.

- Read a nonstimulating book or watch a calm television program before going to bed.

- Write in your journal about anything and everything until you feel too tired to write anymore. I keep a journal by my bed. If I wake up during the night and can't get back to sleep because I have too much on my mind, I write it all down and then go back to sleep.

- Eat a turkey sandwich and a glass of milk to raise your serotonin level and make you drowsy.

- Try safe, natural preparations from the health food store. Get recommendations from a naturopathic physician or nutritionist.

- Take tricyclic antidepressants about an hour before bedtime to maximize the drowsiness effect. However, this is not smart if you plan to have sex, because the medication can make you so drowsy that you're really quite out of it.

- If you are not sleeping, don't worry about it. That just makes it worse. Just relax and focus on pleasant thoughts.

What strategies have you successfully used to ensure a good night's sleep?

_____

_____

_____

Only use medications for temporary relief of sleep problems. There is no medication that can cure insomnia. The underlying cause must be addressed. If you are having persistent sleep problems, see your physician or contact a sleep disorders clinic.

Living Space

While living space is commonly overlooked as a contributor to mood instability, how you feel about living space does affect your long-term mood stability. Does yours offer you privacy, safety, easy access to services, and a sense of community? Each of these factors is important.

As one study volunteer said:

A living space should not be hard to maintain, and to avoid stress, it should be affordable. A place close to support systems is important. Also, from experience,

I found that a place with lots of light and master-controlled heating really helps. It should be spacious, clean-looking, and if something malfunctions, you should be able to just call the landlord or a service person.

Another participant said:

I know my living space affects my level of wellness. Where I lived before—a run-down complex—depressed me. Now I live in a nice part of town, in public housing, but it is neat and modern. I feel much better.

I used to live in a dark, cold cabin in the middle of nowhere. While I was very sick I still had to maintain a cabin with no drinking water, no indoor plumbing, no insulation, no light, and a wood stove that ate nine cords of wood a year. It needed to be heated until the end of June. I had to stack those nine cords and couldn't leave the cabin for more than four hours at a time. The snow was always so deep and took forever to melt due to its location. I couldn't figure out why I wasn't getting any better. I finally moved. The move was hard and expensive but worth it.

The following factors need to be explored when considering appropriate living space.

Do you look forward to going home? If not, why not?

_____

_____

_____

What do you need to change about your home to make it a place you would look forward to going to?

_____

_____

_____

Safety. I have lived in several places where I did not feel safe. One place was so remote that no one could have helped me if I had needed help. Another was on a busy street where there were frequent altercations in the middle of the night. Both of these places had minimal locks, which made me feel even more vulnerable. I now live in a condominium in a nice neighborhood where friendly people are close by. I have good locks, back-up locking systems, and—for extra protection, security, and enjoyment—I have a big dog.

Is your home a safe, comfortable haven from the rest of the world? If not, why not?

_____

_____

_____

What do you need to change about your home to make it a safe, comfortable haven?

_____

_____

_____

Privacy. A man in the study who shares a space with several other people but has his own room says:

> I feel the need to have my own quiet area away from others so I can have uninterrupted time to myself. I have a bedroom where I can close the door, read, and relax. I need a space where I can control the environment, including the radio, TV, phone, and where I can exercise, rest, and read. This provides me with a "safe, comfortable retreat." This space is very important to my wellness, which partially depends on my ability to reduce stress. With my job and my responsibilities to my family, I truly enjoy the quiet time I can have. This is how I recharge my batteries.

If you live with others, do you have a space in your home that is just your private space you can decorate to suit yourself, where you can keep your things and they will not be disturbed, and where you can spend time by yourself, involved in your own activities? If not, why not?

_____

_____

_____

What would you need to do to have such a private space for yourself in your home?

_____

_____

_____

Cleanliness. As I reviewed the study responses, participants emphasized over and over again the importance of a living space that is easy to keep clean. For people like me who are pack rats, this is difficult. If you can give up your need to keep everything, your home feels much more comfortable. Lots of "stuff" around increases stress.

Is your living space easy to clean and keep clean? If not, why not?

_____

_____

_____

What do you need to change about your living space to make it easy to clean and keep clean?

_____

_____

_____

Easy access. People who work hard to keep their moods stabilized find that easy access to services is essential. I like to live near town or on the bus route so I don't have to call on others for transportation when I don't feel comfortable driving or when I am adjusting to a new medication.

Several study participants said constant transportation hassles and lack of access to necessary services made their lives more difficult and stressful.

Is your living space easily accessible to transportation and services? If not, why not?

_____

_____

_____

What would you have to do to make your home more easily accessible to services?

_____

_____

_____

Should you live alone? I enjoy living alone. After years of living with others and parenting, I now find my own space is very important to me, my new sense of self and my wellness. However, it is essential that I build into my schedule daily contact with others.

Do you prefer to live alone? If so, why?

_____

_____

_____

If you prefer to live alone, and you now live with others, what can you do to change the situation?

_____

_____

_____

A woman in the study who has controlled her long-term disabling depressions prefers company. She says:

> I have lived in a variety of arrangements over the years. The worst possible arrangement for me is to live alone in a place where I don't know any of my neighbors. For me, isolation leads to devastation. In periods of disabling depression, I have gone to live with my mother, who will provide around-the-clock support if need be. Living with someone who knows you well and knows how to treat you is the best. I now reside in a cooperative living arrangement in a membership community. This works well for me. I have the privacy of my room; but whenever I need some companionship, I can always go to the lounge.

Do you prefer to live with others? If so, why?

_____

_____

_____

If you prefer to live with others, and you now live alone, what can you do to change the situation?

_____

_____

_____

If your living space is not appropriate to your needs or is contributing to feelings of depression, consider finding a place to live that better suits your needs.

☐ *I need to move because of the following reasons:*

_____

_____

_____

What steps can you take to make that happen?

_____

_____

_____

An enthusiastic study participant said, "After moving I went from bounds to LEAPS! I never felt better in my LIFE. A good environment is crucial." I agree.

Resources

American Association of Retired Persons. *Eating for Your Health: A Guide to Food for Healthy Diets* (D12164), Long Beach, CA: American Association of Retired Persons
This brochure describes new labeling systems and gives good information on shopping for special diets. For a free copy, write to AARP Fulfillment (EE0589), PO Box 22796, Long Beach, CA 90801-5796.

Appleton, N. (1985) *Lick the Sugar Habit.* Santa Monica, CA: Choice Publishing.
A good book full of information on how you can get bad food habits under control.

Bourne, E. (1990) *The Anxiety & Phobia Workbook.* Oakland, CA: New Harbinger Publications.
Excellent diet and exercise chapters in addition to being the best book available on dealing with anxiety and phobias.

Catalano, E. (1990) *Getting to Sleep.* Oakland, CA, New Harbinger Publications.
A complete guide to dealing with sleep problems. There is a listing of sleep disorder centers in the appendix.

Copeland, M. (1992) *The Depression Workbook: A Guide for Living With Depression and Manic Depression.* Oakland, CA: New Harbinger Publications.
The chapter "Exercise: Do It" (pp. 251-258) contains charts to help you identify the kinds of exercise you want to do, rate your level of fitness, and keep track of your progress. "Diet" (pp. 241-250) explores why your diet affects the way you feel, weight control issues, the effects of sugar and caffeine on mood, and provides you with a format for understanding how specific foods affect you. "Light, Electromagnetic Radiation, and the Biological Clock" (pp. 259-268) helps increase your understanding of the relationship between these environmental factors and your moods, and how these effects can be minimized.

Erdmann, R. (1987) *The Amino Revolution.* New York: Fireside, Simon & Schuster.
This easy-to-read book contains a chapter on using amino acid therapy to relieve depression.

Food and Drug Administration and the American Heart Association. *How to Read the New Food Label.*
This free brochure is available from the Consumer Information Center, Department 522A, Pueblo, CO 81009.

London, W. (1993) *Principles of Health.* Brattleboro, VT: London Research.
Dr. London shares his observations and thoughts on a wellness lifestyle. This book must be ordered. Write to London Research, 6 Tyler St., Brattleboro, VT 05301. It is an excellent complementary resource for exploring wellness issues.

Rosenthal, N. (1993) *Winter Blues.* New York: Guilford Press.
Dr. Rosenthal's book provides an in-depth discussion of Seasonal Affective Disorder. It must be read by anyone who notices that their mood cycles correspond to the seasons. It includes an extensive list of physicians and facilities where you can get expert treatment assistance.

Slagle, P. (1988) *The Way Up From Down.* New York: St. Martin's Press.
Dr. Slagle describes an amino acid and vitamin protocol that has worked very well for many people.

Turner, K. (1987) *The Self-Healing Cookbook.* Grass Valley, CA: Earthtones Press.
This delightful cookbook focuses on changing your style of cooking to enhance your wellness. The

author addresses the food-mood connection. I highly recommended it. It is the most dog-eared cookbook on my shelf. Wonderful recipes.

Organizations:

National Organization for SAD
PO Box 451
Vienna, VA 22180

Society for Light Treatment and Biological Rhythms
PO Box 478
Wilsonville, OR 79070
(503) 694-2404

National Institute of Mental Health
Building 10, Room 4S-230
9000 Rockville Pike
Rockville, MD 20892
(301) 496-2141

The following companies manufacture light boxes:

The SunBox Company
1132 Taft St.
Rockville, MD 20850
(310)762-1786

Medic-Light, Inc.
Yacht Club Drive
Lake Hopatcong, NJ 07849
1-800-544-4825

Apollor Light Systems, Inc.
352 West 1060 South
Orem, UT 84058

For more information on a light visor, contact:

Bio-Brite
7315 Wisconsin Ave., Suite 900E,
Bethesda, MD 20814
1-800-621-5483

For information on sleep, write:

American Sleep Disorders Association
604 Second St. SW
Rochester, MN 55902

6

Fine-Tuning Your Lifestyle

Since I realized that every aspect of my existence affects my stability, the changes in my life are amazing.

In talking with people all over the country about mood instability, and looking back on my own experience, I have found that there is little discussion about how life's small pleasures can help maintain stability. By "small pleasures" I mean things like surrounding yourself with pleasing colors, taking a nice long bath, listening to soothing music, cuddling with a pet, or actually scheduling time just to have fun.

These things may seem trivial, but they are effective. People who have gotten well and stay well have taken a closer look at their lives and have done some fine-tuning of the details. This chapter will offer you some suggestions about how to do that for yourself.

Make Time for Pleasurable Pursuits

Your life will feel more fulfilling if you take time during the day to involve yourself in activities that are so absorbing you lose yourself in them. These tend to be those pastimes that you know you do well and where performance is not measured.

A woman who has successfully stabilized her moods says:

When I feel good I am very active. I work out at the gym, bike, jog, walk, go to movies, spend time with my nieces, bake, write, and read. To make myself happy, I buy myself a new piece of clothing, let myself be lazy, and indulge in reading. I like biographies and autobiographies, both fiction and nonfiction.

When I looked at these issues myself, I realized there were activities I had stopped doing long ago, such as playing the piano and sewing, that really make me feel good. I was so busy raising children and developing a career that these pleasures were forgotten. They are now part of my wellness tool chest. If I am feeling sad, stressed, or noticing early warning signs of depression or mania, I spend some time in pursuits I enjoy. I feel better and my life feels enriched when I include some of these activities each day. Other activities I enjoy include:

- quilting
- sewing
- playing the piano
- drumming
- baking bread
- writing
- painting a picture
- refinishing furniture
- reading a good book

Some activities named by research respondants that you might want to try include gardening, working with wood or clay, visiting an art gallery or museum, playing with a child or with pets, cooking, or watching a video.

Spend some time thinking about activities you enjoy. You may want to discuss this with a friend or family members who can help you recall things you enjoyed doing in the past.

What activities totally absorb you and make you feel better?

_____

_____

_____

To convince yourself that it really helps to involve yourself in an absorbing activity, note how you feel before you begin this activity.

_____

_____

_____

Then note how you feel after you involve yourself in it.

_____

_____

_____

Take a Fun Break

Scheduling time for fun is a top notch way to lift your mood and balance your life. A fun break is especially important when things are getting hectic. A 60-year-old friend of mine plays with a "Game Boy" when she needs a break. I take a long walk in the woods with my dog, invite a friend out for lunch, spend the evening watching a funny video like *The Gods Must Be Crazy* or *The General*, and play paper dolls with my granddaughters or go roller-skating with them.

Describe a possible fun break.

_____

_____

_____

To convince yourself that it really helps to take a fun break, note how you feel before you take a fun break.

_____

_____

_____

Then note how you feel afterward.

_____

_____

_____

Get Plenty of Laughs

Researchers have found that a hearty laugh is one of the least expensive treatments for pent-up anxiety, fear, and frustration. Laughing improves respiration because as you laugh, your lungs keep filling with fresh air and expelling the stale air. Laughter also increases your heart rate temporarily, in proportion to the duration of your laughter. This is actually good for you, because after you stop laughing, your heart rate drops below what it was before something struck you as funny. If that's not enough, a hearty belly laugh almost always results in total body relaxation.

People in my study found, without exception, that laughter makes them feel better. As two individuals said about laughter:

> If I am feeling slightly manic, a laugh releases the energy. If I am feeling sad, it gives me a lift.

> Laughter neutralizes things and makes me feel better. It greatly enhances my mood.

Even though it is sometimes difficult to find something to laugh about when mood instability is a problem, the people in my study countered this by reading comic strips and joke books, and watching comedy films and comedians.

I make it a point to watch several British comedies on television each week, and I get several good laughs out of them. The comic strips "Calvin and Hobbes," "For Better or Worse," and "Doonesbury" tickle my laughter palate.

What makes you laugh?

_____

_____

_____

Next time you laugh, note how you feel before you laugh.

_____

_____

_____

Note how you feel after you laugh.

_____

_____

_____

Pets

Many, many people in my study spoke of how much they gained from having a pet in their life. A woman who has a cat and a dog said:

> They have taught me a great deal about human intelligence and sensitivity to moods.

Another respondent said:

> I have two dogs that always improve my moods. I recommend having a pet, if possible.

The owner of a female terrier said her dog is a wonderful companion, is entertaining and affectionate:

> I am single and I cannot imagine getting along without her.

Reported one man:

> I have two dogs I thoroughly enjoy. They are always there to give and receive affection. I find it comforting to hold them, talk with them, and play with them.

> I never thought a dog would make such a difference in my life. Several years ago I "dog sat" for my daughter's dog while she was traveling. By the time she came home, I knew I had to have a dog. With an animal there is always something to smile about. I never feel too grumpy. It has also taken care of my problem of sticking to my exercise routine. And I rest easier because I

assume that most people will not bother a dog or the accompanying human being. Dogs are always there for you, even when you are in a bad mood and feel like the rest of the world is against you.

People who have pets cited many advantages. Are any of these statements true for you?

☐ Petting an animal is relaxing.

☐ Pets are not critical, threatening, or judgmental.

☐ Pets keep me focused on the positive aspects of life.

☐ They reduce stress.

☐ My pet keeps me smiling.

☐ My pet improves my state of mind so that when I return to more pressing concerns I can put them in better perspective and cope more appropriately.

☐ Pets are fun.

☐ Pets love me unconditionally.

☐ Pets don't care what mood I'm in.

☐ Pets don't try to change me.

☐ Pets release tension.

☐ Pets convince me that I am lovable.

☐ Pets give my life purpose and meaning.

☐ Pets encourage me to play and laugh.

☐ Pets force me to get my exercise.

In what other ways is your pet helpful?

_____

_____

_____

In addition to all of the above, pets may even help boost your immunity to illnesses and cause a drop in blood pressure.

No matter how good pets are for most people, however, having a pet is a personal choice. Don't force yourself or anyone else to get a pet if that idea is not a comfortable one. You will also discover that some pets are better suited to you than others.

Dogs and cats are the most popular pets, but rabbits, birds and fish are also popular. One woman in my study said she found it very relaxing to watch the movement of fish. Others love guinea pigs, which will cuddle on your lap all evening and squeak when you open the refrigerator door.

When you are choosing a pet, think carefully about issues of cost and lifestyle. What will your intended pet require in the way of your time? How much will it cost to feed the pet and keep it healthy? Can you make that commitment?

If you have a pet, how does your pet enhance your wellness?

_____

_____

_____

If you don't have a pet, why do you think you would like to have one?

_____

_____

_____

Animal shelters are an inexpensive source of pets, especially dogs and cats. When you get a pet from such a shelter, the animal is usually in good condition, has been carefully checked for medical problems, and has received the necessary shots. The shelter will provide you with information on the animal's care.

The other issue you have to consider when you are renting is that in many rental housing units pets are not allowed, even though a well managed and maintained pet is no more dirty or offensive than your average run-of-the-mill human being. Sometimes a landlord will make an exception if you have been a good tenant, or will allow a smaller pet such as a guinea pig or a bird.

Soothing the Senses

Music. Music can be very relaxing, especially when it follows a rhythm of 60 to 70 beats per minute, according to researchers. But what is relaxing to one person may be irritating to you. If you prefer classical to New Age music, or New Age to classical, stick with your preference, to get the most benefits out of it.

People in my study have said the following about how music affects them:

Music makes me feel like I am in another world, floating away from the things around me. It lets me be me. I can do what I feel to the music, act like a teenager or whatever.

I love opera. Leo Deliebes' *Lakme* is my favorite piece. It brings me peace. I also listen to Native American flute music, tapes with birds singing and loons calling. My latest tape purchase was called *Migration* and all you hear are the sounds of migrating birds.

I love the symphony—I love music. I participate in the chorus. I borrow records and tapes from the library. I take courses in music and music appreciation. Music keeps me going.

What kind of music makes you feel better?

_____

_____

_____

Go through your record collection and make a note of those pieces that make you feel more relaxed and peaceful. You may want to combine these selections on one tape, which you can play when you are feeling down or harried.

Color. Many people find that color—whether its the decor, their clothing, or personal possessions—have quite an affect on their moods. I know that I find a very light shade of pink, almost a white with just a little red coloring added to it, very soothing. I painted all the walls this color in an apartment I rented. It felt great. Others have reported a similar experience with a light shade of pink. However, some people reported that other colors had a better effect on their mood.

Choice of color is very personal. Statements from many participants of my research validate this fact. One woman said: "I can't wear red when I feel really down. I wear vibrant colors (red in particular) to brighten my attitude. I love purple, it makes me feel good." Another woman said: "I tried a yellow room once but it didn't lift my mood like it was supposed to. I find blue or green to be soothing." Another said: "I like bright colors. If I couldn't have bright colors around me, I would probably be depressed."

What colors make you feel best when you wear them?

_____

_____

_____

When you are buying yourself new clothes, focus on these colors. When you are having a day when you feel down, wear clothing in these colors. It will help perk you up. Every time you look in the mirror it will give you a lift.

Notice the color of the walls and decor and in those rooms in which you feel best. What color are they?

_____

_____

_____

When decorating your own space, use these colors. If you are living in a space where the colors make you feel down, yet you can't afford to redecorate, try some inexpensive alternatives. A can of paint for a wall or two, or a coverlet from a rummage sale can make a big difference. If your workspace is being redecorated, make your color preferences known. Let your employer know the colors that make you feel best.

Water.   The last time someone told you to take a long, hot bath when you were depressed or agitated, you may have regarded the advice as a simplistic solution to a major problem. And in many cases it is just that. But many people use water such as a shower, bath, whirlpool, hot tub or pool as a soothing part of their daily routine. Hygiene isn't the only reason; it genuinely makes them feel better. Try taking time out during the day if things get hectic or if you are feeling discouraged, to give your body the benefit of the calming properties of water. A man in the study considers water to be "a great harmonizer and balance adjuster."

I had not really considered the therapeutic effects of water on my mood until several years ago. Before that, a morning or evening shower was just one more hurried part of my daily routine. Then, on my birthday, a cold snowy day in January, I was trying to think of something nice I could do for myself. I decided a swim in a heated pool would be just the thing. I called a local motel with an indoor pool and they said that while they usually only open their pool to motel guests or those who have a monthly membership, since it was my birthday, they would make an exception. For six dollars, I spent a delicious afternoon going between the pool and whirlpool, lazily watching the snow fall on the glass roof. I felt so good afterward that I purchased a membership and gave myself this treat several times a week. I relaxed and got my exercise at the same time.

Many community-based recreational centers, motels, and Y's allow easy, inexpensive access to water facilities. In my community, the local mental health center has reserved time at a motel so people who feel self-conscious about being identified with the center can go swimming when the facility is open to the public. If this is something you think you would enjoy, explore the possibilities in your community and see if an opportunity exists or if you can fit a membership into your budget.

You don't have to go to a pool or have a membership to enjoy the benefits of water. Your own bath tub or shower can suffice. Inexpensive whirlpool units give you a sense of luxury and relaxation in your own tub. One woman in the study said: "A hot bubble bath is relaxing and relieves tension. I will sometimes play good music and light candles in the bathroom while enjoying a bubble bath." A man said that he has a rubber duck which he enjoys in his bath. It gives the bath a sense of levity.

Do you already use water to relax and make yourself feel better? If not, how can you explore using water?

_____

_____

_____

Most people find warm water most relaxing. However, others find cooler temperatures work best for them.

To get a sense of how water affects you, complete the following before and after your next "water experience":

What did you do? For how long?

_____

_____

_____

How did you feel before you did it?

_____

_____

_____

How did you feel afterward?

_____

_____

_____

Resources

Padus, E. (1986) *The Complete Guide to Your Emotions and Your Health*. Emmaus, PA: Rodale Press. *This book, a composite of writings and information from many sources, is absolutely full of useful ideas for fine-tuning your life and your lifestyle.*

7

Creating a Career That Works

*It has taken a long time to get to this place—where I really feel like the work
I am doing is the work I am supposed to be doing.*

Depression or manic depression doesn't have to limit your choice of careers. People who suffer from mood disorders have worked as teachers, psychologists, counselors, caseworkers, accountants, dietitians, doctors, nurses, health care professionals, social workers, custodians, surveyors, tool and die makers, electricians, plumbers, etc. The list goes on. You don't even have to work at a career if your finances permit. You can live a full, active, and rewarding life by getting involved with advocacy, or by volunteering, raising a family, caring for elderly parents or relatives with disabilities, or pursuing a particular interest with a passion.

If you do choose to work, however, you'll be better off choosing work that allows you to fully express your talents, and that works within your limitations. The truth is, you *can* find fulfilling work that meets your needs. Finding the right job is a process of discovery. In this chapter, you'll look at the tools that can help.

Before you read further, let's face reality. If you struggle with mood disorders, you may want to reconsider your notions about what it means to be successful. I have. So has Tim Field, an energetic advocate in the mental health field. Here is Tim's perspective on career success:

> Because of the class structure in the United States, it is nearly essential for everyone to be on a "career path" if they wish to be perceived as "one of us" and not as some kind of a failure or "weirdo." This is really most unfortunate. Having a "successful career" or "good job" is the crux of self-esteem for most people. My experience has induced me to simply reject the career path model with its heavy baggage of failure and guilt.
>
> I accept responsibility at work if I feel I am up to it and want to, but I

don't allow myself to get into a position where a large project or an entire department is dependent on me. It has worked better for me to find other sources of reward than career advancement, which by nature requires accepting more and more responsibilities, only to have them taken away when I get depressed. This means a different approach to life goals, but I think it's only prudent. Why beat your head against the wall trying to advance to the "top" at some silly job only to be batted down and humiliated every time you get depressed? There are more important things than a good job, and I focus on these as sources for positive strokes for my self-esteem.

The effects of depression have led me to abandon the upwardly mobile "career path" model and to direct my efforts and sources of self-esteem elsewhere. Perhaps this would have happened anyway. What matters most is finding something that *works*, that is rewarding regardless of my opinion of options I no longer have.

My Path

Before episodes of mania and depression overtook my life, I had several careers. My first was as a homemaker, raising five children and caring for a large home. As the children needed less of my time, I went back to college to complete the final two years toward my bachelor's degree in special education. For a number of years I was a special education teacher and directed a small private school for students with special needs. In the early 1980s I decided a career change was in order. I wanted to focus my energies on a deep, personal passion—environmental issues. I went back to school for a Master of Science in Resource Management and Administration. While in graduate school and for several years thereafter, I worked as a development director in the very stressful position of raising money for several national environmental organizations.

When I was in my mid-forties, the recurring depression and mania that I had successfully controlled with lithium overpowered me and for a time took control of my life. I reluctantly gave up my career because I was no longer able to keep up with the performance requirements. I was supported through social security and other entitlement programs.

My psychiatrist referred me to vocational rehabilitation services to find work that I could manage in spite of recurring episodes. My ongoing relationship with vocational rehabilitation has eased me into a new career, well suited to my interests, talents, and abilities, where I am my own boss, free to do whatever is necessary to keep myself stable. This new career as a mental health educator has given me accomplishment, satisfaction, and security.

When I first went to vocational rehabilitation I had no idea what I wanted to do or how I wanted to proceed. Mental health education was not my original career goal. Through a long process that included a structured evaluation of my education, experience, interests, and talents, along with long-term vocational counseling, I discovered that I was interested in finding out how people with a disorder like mine manage their lives and then sharing that information with others.

My first vocational goal was to be a researcher and technical writer. I decided to develop the skills necessary for such a career by studying people who have depression or mania and depression, compiling the collected data, and writing a technical book on the results of my study. I met these goals with ongoing support and assistance from vocational rehabilitation and the financial assistance of the social security program called Plan to Achieve Self-Sufficiency (PASS). The PASS gave me the funds to purchase a computer, develop research materials, and gather data.

As a result of interest in my research, I gave several presentations that were very successful. When I found that people with depression or manic depression expressed interest in a workbook based on my finding, I set up a new goal for myself—to become a public speaker and author. I got another PASS to help me meet these new goals. My career has taken me to new levels of personal and financial achievement, satisfaction, and independence.

My story is not unusual. Many people with depression, manic depression, and other psychiatric disabilities use the skills they have learned in dealing with these disorders to develop careers in mental health education, support, counseling, advocacy, and administration. Our life experience makes us especially effective in these roles. David Hilton, Director of the Office of Consumer Affairs, uses strengths he has learned in dealing with years of manic depression to effectively establish appropriate programs in New Hampshire for others with psychiatric disabilities.

How To Discover Your "Right" Job

Before you can recognize the "right" job, you must carefully define what you want and what you need. Discovery often occurs as a result of asking the right questions, examining your present situation, and sorting out what works and what doesn't. Scheduling, pressure level, privacy, and the employer's flexibility are all issues to consider.

Here are some questions to get you started:

Is your current work or career satisfactory? Does your work enhance your wellness? What do you like about your work?

_____

_____

_____

What would you most like to change? Would you like to pursue a different career, one that matches your special needs, interests, and abilities?

_____

_____

_____

If you think your work life could stand some improvement, consider the issues that follow.

Scheduling

While most people with depression or manic depression are able to work and do a good job, they often find that their peak performance times do not coincide with those of other workers or with the times an employer would prefer they work. Their performance improved when work was task-related rather than time-related. For instance, rather than work an eight-hour day from 9 a.m. to 5 p.m. each day, they did better when they had an assignment or project to complete within broader time-lines. This is difficult in many work settings. However, other people said they work better and prefer a structured schedule.

☐ *I work best when time schedules are flexible.*

☐ *I perform at my optimum when my schedule is structured.*

People with depression and manic depression should avoid changing shifts—for example, working from 7 a.m. to 3 p.m. for two weeks, 3 p.m. to 11 p.m. for two weeks, and 11 p.m. to 7 a.m. for two weeks. They also don't do well with the 11 p.m. to 7 a.m. shift, perhaps because of insufficient light through the eyes (see chapter 5 on "Developing a Lifestyle That Enhances Wellness").

Pressure Level

People with depression and manic depression do not perform well in pressured work environments. Before I resigned from my job because of severe mood instability and several hospitalizations, I was under a lot of pressure. The organization was operating, as it had been for a long time, with income that was barely meeting its expenses. Employees were in fear of being laid off. The success of key programs was dependent on limited accessible funds. I was a fund-raiser. Intense pressure was my daily companion. It was very hard for me to leave my work behind and enjoy other parts of my life. I burned out very quickly.

☐ *I need a low-pressure position or career because:*

_____

_____

_____

Private Space

Having private space, where you can shut the door, be quiet and alone, is important to many of the people in my study. They did not want a job in which they were isolated, but they did want private space available to them on an as-needed basis.

A woman who has been a guidance counselor for over 20 years says she has never taken off more than six weeks during the school year. She makes her job manageable by having her own office with a door she can close to shut out the world.

I live alone and have my office at home. It gives me quiet time to work. When I want people around, I find a friend to go for a walk or I go into town to do errands. People are as close as my phone. My workshops and presentations also give me needed contact with others. My office is separated from the rest of the house; I can close the door and put my work behind me when I need space from it.

☐   *I need accessibility to private space in my work place.*

Understanding Employers

Some people share their mental health history with their employer. Others, hoping that an episode of depression or mania will not become an issue, have chosen not to divulge that information. In either event, understanding employers may be difficult to find, but they are definitely an asset.

Tim Field shares his recent work experience:

For the last few years I have been completely up-front about my problems with depression, side-effects of medication, etc., when talking with my employer. I may not always volunteer everything, but I feel that I have nothing to hide (because there is nothing to be ashamed of). Everybody has problems, and if I have to be Mr. Clean to work for them, it's not the kind of place where I want to work anyway.

In terms of how I handle downtime from the job, I have made an agreement with the owner of the company that if I'm not up to it, I can be absent. I can take vacation or sick leave until they are used up, and then go on leave without pay. This approach requires being frank and up-front about your situation and having an employer who values the big picture.

If you are being hired for your abilities and accommodations for possible episodes of mood instability are not necessary, then you don't have to tell your employer in advance. However, if you are in a situation in which accommodations would be necessary, then the employer should be notified. By making a careful job choice, accommodations may not be necessary. For instance, if you were being hired to run a machine on a regular basis, and you knew that you were not going to be available to do that work for three months of the year, your employer would need to be told up-front.

The Americans with Disabilities Act (ADA) guarantees equal opportunity to people with disabilities in the areas of employment, state and local government services, and public accommodations and telecommunications. If you feel major depression or manic depression is in any way affecting your work situation or your ability to be employed, contact:

National Rehabilitation Information Center
ABLEDATA Database of Assistive Technology
8455 Colesville Road, Suite 935
Silver Spring, MD 20910-3319
1-800-227-0216 or (301) 589-3563

They have a resource guide which contains information on a variety of ADA materials including guides, manuals, publications, training programs, and technical assistance programs.

Those employers who are willing to take the risk and hire a person with a history of mood instability often find that the employee is able to make up for the "downtime" by increasing productivity after the rough period is past.

☐ *I choose to tell my employer or prospective employer about my depression or manic depression*
☐ *before I am hired*　　　　☐ *after I am hired, for the following reasons:*

_____

_____

_____

☐ *I will not share information with my employer about my depression or manic depression because:*

_____

_____

_____

Creativity

People who experience mood instability are the brightest and most creative people in our society. Therefore they need creative jobs that take advantage of their superior abilities. They do not do well in repetitious, controlled work circumstances.

☐ *Creativity in my career is very important to me. By creativity, I specifically mean:*

_____

_____

_____

Creative Job Development

You may despair about ever finding a job that will meet your needs, particularly if you confine your search to jobs that are currently available. But you don't need to limit yourself in that way. Many people today are discovering the joys of creating their own jobs. I did. Self-employment is often the best way to meet your needs for flexible scheduling, low stress, private space, and creativity.

I developed, over several years, a successful career as a mental health educator, lecturing, presenting workshops, and developing educational resources. When I need a break, I can take one. If I feel like working late into the night, that's all right too. I schedule my work to meet my personal needs. My new career, directed by me, makes good use of my abilities and creativity.

A woman in the study developed a career raising exotic birds after her job as a chef ended due to mania. She feels her work with birds plays an important role in her wellness—their care keeps her going. Initiative was the key! She developed the new career on her own. She reports that a vocational rehabilitation program was somewhat helpful. She said she had a hard time convincing them that she needed to work on her own. She says, "I think they would have been more helpful if I wanted a traditional career, but are supporting my endeavors." She said it's important to let vocational counselors know what you really want and that you want their support in reaching your goal. Think about possibilities of creating your own job. Answer the questions below.

What is your current dream of a new career?

_____

_____

_____

What are the interests, talents, and abilities you want to use in your career?

_____

_____

_____

In what ways will this career meet your requirements for scheduling, low stress, understanding employers, and creativity?

_____

_____

_____

Which criteria will be difficult to meet?

_____

_____

_____

Using your creative problem-solving abilities, describe how you can effectively deal with the criteria that are more difficult to meet:

_____

_____

_____

What is the first step you need to take to begin the process of creative job development?

_____

_____

_____

List intermediate goals such as education, training, or equipment purchases necessary to your career choice.

_____

_____

_____

Traditional Versus Self-Employment

If you have never been self-employed, but are considering that option, do as much research as you can so you can have a solid plan in place. There are now many books available for people who are making the transition. You'll want to familiarize yourself with the potential pitfalls, make a careful estimate of the money and other resources you'll need to stay afloat, and create a business plan. You will also want to take full advantage of the many free sources of help available to you. Several of them are listed at the end of this section.

Training for Career Success

Whether you choose to work for an employer or to build your own business, you may find it helpful to consider vocational rehabilitation, the PASS Plan, or private education. Your local library can also be a wonderful source of information and it's probably the place you should start.

Libraries. Libraries are an excellent source of information to use in the job development process. They are a great way to find educational facilities and programs, career ideas, organizations, corporations, how-to references, etc.

    ☐ *I am going to the library to look up information on:*

_____

_____

_____

Vocational rehabilitation. The federal government, in cooperation with state governments, has set up a nationwide system of vocational rehabilitation services. Vocational rehabilitation services provide various kinds of vocational assistance and support to people with disabilities. If you have lost your job because of depression or manic depression, or because of the mood instability, your job is not appropriate to your special needs. Contact your local or state office of vocational rehabilitation. To receive services, you may need to present medical documents or a statement from your physician to verify your condition.

Don't wait until you know exactly what you want to do. If careers are an issue for you, establish your connection with vocational rehabilitation services right away. They have a wide variety of resources available to guide and assist in all phases of your career development and can help you develop a step-by-step approach to achieving your goals. Check with your Office of Vocational Rehabilitation and Employment and Training Services for information on other programs with services that may be useful.

Which vocational rehabilitation services have you contacted? What assistance did they provide?

_____

_____

_____

☐ *I am going to contact vocational rehabilitation services and ask them to help me with the following:*

_____

_____

_____

PASS. PASS is the acronym for the Plan to Achieve Self-Sufficiency, a social security program. If you have a work history and you receive Social Security Disability Insurance, you may be eligible for funds that would allow you to meet vocational goals that will enable you to resume employment or start your own business. PASS will pay for almost anything that will help you reach your work goal, as long as the total does not exceed the amount of your current benefit. This includes:

- Supplies to start a business
- Tuition, fees, books, and supplies needed for school or training
- Supported-employment services
- Attendant or child care expenses
- Equipment and tools to do the job
- Transportation to and from work
- Uniforms, special clothing, and safety equipment

You can get assistance to set up PASS from a vocational rehabilitation counselor, an employer, or the social security office. For more information, call your social security office and request SSA Publication No. 05-11017, August 1991.

The plan, submitted in writing to the Social Security Administration office for approval, includes:

1. A work goal—a job that you are interested in doing and that you will be able to do at the end of your plan.

2. The length of time it will take to reach your goal. If you need special training that takes two years, for instance, the length of time would be two years.

3. The things you will need to reach your goal—education, equipment, supplies, services, and so on.

4. The cost of the things you need to reach your goal.

5. A determination of how much money you will need to set aside each month to meet your goal.

6. A plan to keep track of the money, such as a separate bank account or record-keeping system.

☐ *I am going to find out more about Social Security PASS Plans.*

☐ *A Social Security PASS plan sounds as if it would work for me. I am going to develop and submit a PASS plan with help and support from:*

_____

_____

_____

Formal education and training.   To meet your career goal, you may also need additional training or education. Doing so can actually enhance your sense of well-being. In fact, a study by the Center for Psychiatric Rehabilitation at Boston University on supported education for people with psychiatric disorders showed that students who attend regularly, complete their course of study, and go on to maintain employment had lower rates of hospitalization and higher levels of self-esteem.

While traditional educational programs may be well suited to your needs, you may find it useful to explore enrolling in an alternative program designed for students with special needs. Community colleges and adult education programs offer a wide variety of education and training options. Vocational rehabilitation and employment and training services will have information on these programs.

I got my Master's degree in Resource Management and Administration in a program that met my scheduling needs for evening and weekend classes. I was also able to get credit for documented life experience. Since my Master's in a counseling psychology program was self-directed, I developed a comprehensive plan for studies, papers, projects, and presentations to meet program requirements. I worked on my own with support and advice from faculty advisers. Each semester, I attended one all-day seminar.

Many schools have an Office of Disability Support Services (ODSS). Let that office know you have a psychiatric disability. You may need documentation, such as a medical report of your disability, to present to the ODSS so that it can provide you with special accommodations. Just remember that your treatment history is confidential and you do not need to disclose it unless you so choose.

Returning to post-secondary education can be exciting and challenging. Take responsibility for your own wellness and develop a program to manage your symptoms. A good support network, both personal and professional, will increase your chances of a successful educational experience. These other guidelines can also help:

- Take a reduced number of classes the first several semesters until you get acclimated to the new environment and lifestyle.

- Become familiar with the resources on your campus. There may be a learning center or its equivalent that will assist you in sharpening your study skills and that provides tutoring services. Some counseling centers provide support groups for students returning to campus after an absence.

- Before you return to school, contact the college's financial aid officer for information on financial awards available, such as Pell Grants. When all other resources have been used, you may be eligible for financial assistance from the Department of Vocational Rehabilitation. This assistance could help you finance your education.

- If disability prevents repayment of student loans, contact the lender immediately and request a medical deferment. Note that granting deferment of your payments is not automatic. You must continue to make payments until you are notified that the deferment has been processed and approved. If you do not, you may be in default. Once your loan is in default, it can be difficult to change that status.

- If you have to leave school, be sure to withdraw officially so that you do not fail your classes by default. In some cases you may be able to have the designation "Incomplete" recorded, thereby earning the right to complete the requirements later.

Resources To Help You Secure a Better Job

You may find the following programs useful if you'd like to upgrade your skills, and intend to work for an employer. Sometimes, the best way to equip yourself to run your own business is to learn what you need to learn while someone else pays you.

Employment and training services. States are federally mandated to provide individuals with free employment and training services such as aptitude testing, job screening, job referrals and placements, and vocational counseling. These offices have comprehensive listings of area employment opportunities.

☐   *I am going to contact Employment and Training Services regarding the following services:*

_____

_____

_____

Job Partnership Training.   Job Partnership Training (JPT) is another federally mandated program. In some states it is administered by Employment and Training Services, and in others by private agencies. JPT provides on-the-job placement services, job training and education, and some expenses such as for equipment and licensing fees needed to get into the job force. JPT is dependent on a yearly funding cycle.

☐   *I am going to contact the Job Partnership Training program in my area to request the following assistance:*

_____

_____

_____

Resources for the Self-Employed

These organizations will help give you a great start if you intend to build your own business:

SCORE.   SCORE is an acronym for Service Corps of Retired Executives. This is a program of volunteer retired executives who give free assistance to people who are starting businesses. Depending on their experience, they will help develop business plans, set up bookkeeping systems, fill out loan applications, develop marketing plans and strategies, etc.

☐   *I am going to contact SCORE and request the following assistance:*

_____

_____

_____

Small Business Administration.   The Small Business Administration guarantees business loans to people in the labor force. Check the phone book for a branch office near you.

Small Business Development Centers.   Each state has federal- and state-funded Small Business Centers which provide in-depth counseling assistance at no cost to people starting new businesses or expanding existing ones. Services include a comprehensive resource referral library, and workshops on a variety of business-related topics. Phone 1-800-SBDC for more information.

Office of Economic Development. Many larger towns and regions have offices of economic development that provide a range of services to businesses. Check the phone book to find such offices in your area.

Women's Support Networks. Gender-related issues often are obstacles to women who want to start their own business or develop a career. Through Women's Support Networks, women can get information on business assistance programs specifically for women. The State Governor's Hotline should have information on these programs.

References

Bolles, R. (1983) *What Color Is Your Parachute?* Berkeley, CA: Ten Speed Press.
> *This is an excellent reference you can use on your own to help you find the career most appropriate to your needs and talents.*

Maze, M., and D. Mayall (1991) *The Enhanced Guide for Occupational Exploration.* Indianapolis: JIST Works.
> *This is a major career reference tool for job seekers. It contains 2,500 of the most important jobs based on information from the United States Department of Labor and other sources. It is available in the reference section of your local library. For more information phone (317) 264-3720*

Self-Employment Learning Project (1992) *Directory of Micro-Enterprise Programs.* Queenstown, MD: ASPEN Institute.
> *This very valuable resource is available from ASPEN Institute, PO Box 2222, Queenstown, MD, 21658.*

Unger, K. *Tips for Students.* Washington, DC: Health Resource Center.
> *Your successful return to educational or training programs can be helped by this guide originally prepared at Boston University. To obtain a copy, write or call the Heath Resource Center: A program of the American Council on Education, One Dupont Circle, NW, Suite 800, Washington, DC 20036-1193, (202) 939-9320.*

U.S. Department of Labor. Bureau of Labor Statistics. *Occupational Outlook Handbook* (1992-1993) Indianapolis: JIST Works, Inc.
> *This is also a major career reference tool for job seekers. It is available in the reference section of your local library. For more information phone (317) 264-3720.*

Whitmyer, C., S. Rasberry, and M. Phillips. (1989) *Running a One-Person Business.* Berkeley, CA: Ten Speed Press.
> *This book covers everything from time management to emotional support systems.*

PART III

Life Issues

8

Minimizing Negative Influences From the Past

I knew there were some things in my life—some current and some from a long time ago—that were making things much worse.

Many people with mood disorders can point to a precipitating event or series of events that preceded the onset of their depression or mania. Others can trace it back to guilt or misperceptions that originated in childhood. If the feelings around these events are left unaddressed, the past events can negatively influence you in the present.

Although you cannot keep traumatic events from happening, you can learn to respond to them, handle them in a self-affirming way, and work through any residual feelings around them. This will allow you to have more control over your moods and your life.

There may also be current circumstances in your life that you need to address so you can get on with your healing. Sometimes major changes are necessary to allow you to resolve the past and take charge of your own journey to wellness. This chapter will help you assess the factors that may be influencing your depression or manic depression and to develop an action plan that will help you minimize their impact.

As you consider your issues, determine if they are major influences or minor ones. I define major issues as those you think about daily and which have a major affect on your moods, thought patterns, and lifestyle. Minor issues are ones you think about occasionally; they have a minimal affect on your moods and your life. Some issues may have been major issues at one time in your life, but are not so now due to the passage of time, life changes, and personal growth work.

When you complete this assessment, you'll know which issues need immediate attention and action, and which require long-term work. The chapters that follow will provide you with the tools and resources you need to do that.

Common Issues

The issues discussed in this chapter are common ones for people who suffer from mood instability. The problem may have occurred in early childhood; or it may be more recent. It may involve a relationship with an intimate other, society at large, or the environment. Please read those topics that pertain to you. Since you may find it useful to reflect upon and describe each pertinent issue in more detail, I've left space for you to do so.

If this process is hard for you, brings up frightening memories (or flashbacks), or makes you feel uncomfortable in any way, don't do the writing exercises. You may want to go through this chapter slowly, over a period of time, and when you are supported by a counselor or someone else who makes you feel safe.

Sexual abuse. Many people with mood disorders report a history of childhood sexual abuse. They feel that this abuse has either caused or aggravated their depression or manic depression. Some have even been diagnosed with Post Traumatic Stress Disorder. See chapter 9 on "Resolving Trauma."

Although experts have known for a long time about the prevalence of sexual abuse, it is only recently that they have come to understand how disastrous its effect is on the psyche of those who have experienced it. Because of ignorance about the issues, those who reported such abuse were often not believed, and, if they were believed, they were told to "forgive and forget." Having to bear this trauma alone often results in poor self-esteem and a wide variety of ongoing symptoms, including mood instability. Fortunately, those who have worked at overcoming the effects of such abuse have regained their sense of security, well-being, and self-worth.

I was sexually abused and terrorized by an older cousin for several years. I told my aunt (my cousin's mother, who was responsible for our care at the time) about the ongoing incidents. She discounted what I had to say and said I must have been leading him on—a response that was demeaning and invalidating. The abuse ceased at that time. Long-term therapy to address this issue has helped to relieve the resulting flashbacks and low self-esteem relating to these incidents.

☐   *I have experienced sexual abuse.*

☐   *I feel this abuse has a major effect on my life and depressive or manic depressive episodes.*

☐   *I feel this abuse has little or no effect on my life and depressive or manic depressive episodes.*

Describe the sexual abuse if this feels like a safe thing for you to do at this time.

_____

_____

_____

Physical abuse. Many people with mood disorders have been physically abused by a relative, peer, or stranger. Some feel the abuse bears little relationship to their mood disorder, while others consider it a major factor. The severity of the abuse and the number of times it occurred seem to be significant. For instance, a woman in my study reports that she was severely beaten by a gang of peers at the age of 16. She feels that there is a strong connection between the beating and her recurring episodes of mania and depression.

☐ *I experienced physical abuse.*

☐ *I feel this abuse has a major effect on my life and depressive or manic depressive episodes.*

☐ *I feel this abuse has little or no effect on my life and depressive or manic depressive episodes.*

Describe the physical abuse if this feels like a safe thing for you to do at this time.

_____

_____

_____

Emotional abuse. Long-term emotional abuse takes a heavy toll on its victims. Those who have been called names and verbally invalidated by authority figures report that the resultant feelings of low self-esteen either cause ongoing depressive episodes or worsen such episodes. For instance, one person who has had recurring episodes of deep depression feels there is a strong connection between these episodes and the emotional abuse he experienced as a child. His parents were constantly reminding him of his shortcomings, he says, and telling him that he would "never amount to anything." It takes real work to counteract the negative self-image and replace the thoughts with more positive ones that boost self-esteem.

☐ *I experienced emotional abuse.*

☐ *I feel this abuse has a major effect on my life and depressive or manic depressive episodes.*

☐ *I feel this abuse has little or no effect on my life and depressive or manic depressive episodes.*

Describe the emotional abuse if this feels like a safe thing for you to do at this time.

_____

_____

_____

Neglect. Those whose parents were absent or who did not consistently meet their child's basic needs for affection, protection, food, clothing, and warmth must also work hard to overcome the long-term effects. Prolonged childhood neglect is devastating. Current research indicates that children who have a history of neglect have a much harder time overcoming its effects than children who have experienced occasional abuse.

A study volunteer whose mother was hospitalized for long periods of time during her childhood, and who had no mother substitute, said she did not become aware of the connection between the neglect and her depression until the issue came up in counseling.

☐ *I experienced childhood neglect.*

☐ *I feel this has a major effect on my life and depressive or manic depressive episodes.*

☐   *I feel this has little or no effect on my life and depressive or manic depressive episodes.*

Describe the neglect if this feels like a safe thing for you to do at this time.

_____

_____

_____

Inability to follow your own path.   A man in my initial research project said that as far back as he could remember, people in his family assumed he would become a medical doctor. As he grew up, he accepted the idea. When he began medical school, he had his first severe episode of mania. His extreme depression became less frequent when he realized that his real gift was teaching. He pursued that career.

☐   *I have been unable to follow my own path and pursue the career goals or vocation of my choice.*

☐   *I feel this has a major effect on my life and depressive or manic depressive episodes.*

☐   *I feel this has little or no effect on my life and depressive or manic depressive episodes.*

Describe your inability to follow the path of your choice if this feels like a safe thing for you to do at this time.

_____

_____

_____

Illness.   People with chronic medical illness such as diabetes, multiple sclerosis, tuberculosis, or Parkinson's disease find that there condition make it difficult to keep depression or manic depression under control.

A woman in the study said that struggling to keep her diabetes stabilized has been hard work that consumes her time and energy. This aggravation has increased the intensity of her depressive episodes and made them more difficult to treat.

☐   *I have a chronic or acute disease.*

☐   *I feel this has a major effect on my life and depressive or manic depressive episodes.*

☐   *I feel this has little or no effect on my life and depressive or manic depressive episodes.*

Describe your chronic or acute disease if this feels like a safe thing for you to do at this time.

_____

_____

_____

Physical handicaps. A 41-year-old woman who has experienced episodes of major depression since the age of 14 feels that her physical handicaps—which include a shunt for hydrocephalus caused by a prebirth injury, head injuries caused by a severe beating, poor vision, and constant leg and back pains—have contributed to her depressive episodes.

☐ *I am physically handicapped.*

☐ *I feel this has a major effect on my life and depressive or manic depressive episodes.*

☐ *I feel this has little or no effect on my life and depressive or manic depressive episodes.*

Describe your physical handicap if this feels like a safe thing for you to do at this time.

_____

_____

_____

Poverty. Those who don't have adequate resources for housing, food, clothing, health care, and other necessities often have no resources left to treat the depression or manic depression that may be a determining factor in their ongoing impoverishment. This can be a vicious circle.

☐ *I currently live in poverty.*

☐ *I have experienced poverty in the past.*

☐ *I feel this has a major effect on my life and depressive or manic depressive episodes.*

☐ *I feel this has little or no effect on my life and depressive or manic depressive episodes.*

Describe your situation with regard to poverty if this feels like a safe thing for you to do at this time.

_____

_____

_____

Stigma. Whether stigma is a response to mental illness or to something else about you which others see as "not OK," it often contributes to depression and mood instability. As Terry McDonough writes in "Alienation," which was published in the *Western New York Mental Health World,* "Part of being mentally ill is worse than the disease itself; the way people respond to you. People have a tendency to walk on egg shells around you.... Many people leave us out of the picture.... People who don't know I'm mentally ill treat me 'normally'. If I choose to confide my condition, I'm suddenly excluded from activities in which I once participated. I'm alienated."

☐ *I currently experience stigma.*

☐ *I have experienced stigma in the past.*

☐ *I feel this has a major effect on my life and depressive or manic depressive episodes.*

☐   *I feel this has little or no effect on my life and depressive or manic depressive episodes.*

Describe your situation with regard to stigma if this feels like a safe thing for you to do at this time.

_____

_____

_____

Poor social skills.   A woman in her forties who had experienced major depression for many years said she realized, after long-term work with an empathetic counselor, that her tendency to be a "chatterbox" overwhelmed others. They had been reluctant to point this out to her because of her depressive episodes and instead withdrew from her.

☐   *I feel that I have poor social skills.*

☐   *I feel this has a major effect on my life and depressive or manic depressive episodes.*

☐   *I feel this has little or no effect on my life and depressive or manic depressive episodes.*

Describe your problem with social skills if this feels like a safe thing for you to do at this time.

_____

_____

_____

Loneliness.   People who experience ongoing depressive and manic depressive episodes often report that they find themselves without a circle of close friends due to the unpredictable nature of the disorder. For instance, a woman who was highly respected for her service to the community, and who had many close friends, found herself very much alone after a severe manic episode that included bizarre behavior and numerous inappropriate confrontations.

☐   *I am lonely.*

☐   *I feel this has a major effect on my life and depressive or manic depressive episodes.*

☐   *I feel this has little or no effect on my life and depressive or manic depressive episodes.*

Describe your situation with regard to loneliness if this feels like a safe thing for you to do at this time.

_____

_____

_____

Work stress. A woman in my study was employed for many years by a major corporation, where she enjoyed her work. She had always assumed that she would work there until she retired. Several years ago, however, in response to a slugglish economy, the demand for the product produced by her company decreased sharply and many employees were laid off. She was not sure when it would be her turn. In addition, she was expected to work overtime and take on additional responsibilities to make up for employees who had lost positions. She had been dealing with depression for a long time. With this increased pressure and lack of security, her depression worsened.

☐ *I am currently under extensive work-related stress.*

☐ *I feel this has a major effect on my life and depressive or manic depressive episodes.*

☐ *I feel this has little or no effect on my life and depressive or manic depressive episodes.*

Describe your situation with regard to work-related stress if this feels like a safe thing for you to do at this time.

_____

_____

_____

Do you feel there is any way you could reduce your work-related stress at this time? If so, how? If not, why not?

_____

_____

_____

Marital problems. A woman who had been married for three years felt that several factors in her marriage were increasing her persistent, deep depression. She wanted to pursue the career she had enjoyed before their marriage, but her husband wouldn't allow her to work outside the home. He did not want her to spend time with family and friends. He also got very jealous when she spoke to another man. Most of their time together was spent arguing over these issues. She felt that she no longer loved her husband and often found herself wishing she had never married him.

☐ *I have marital problems.*

☐ *I feel this has a major effect on my life and depressive or manic depressive episodes.*

☐ *I feel this has little or no effect on my life and depressive or manic depressive episodes.*

Describe your marital problems or your problems in a close relationship if this feels like a safe thing for you to do at this time.

_____

_____

_____

Spouse or family abuse. Those who are being abused by a spouse or other family member find that they cannot make any progress toward wellness while the abuse continues. It is only when the abuse ends, either because they have left the abusive situation or the abuser stops, that they can work toward long-term stability.

☐ *I am being abused by my spouse or a family member.*

☐ *I have been abused by a spouse or family member.*

☐ *I feel this has a major effect on my life and depressive or manic depressive episodes.*

☐ *I feel this has little or no effect on my life and depressive or manic depressive episodes.*

Describe the spouse or family abuse if this feels like a safe thing for you to do at this time.

_____

_____

_____

Divorce. A man in the study said that when he married he believed it would be for the "rest of my life." When the marriage ended, he felt his life was over. That was the beginning of his recurring episodes of deep depression.

☐ *I am divorced.*

☐ *I feel this has a major effect on my life and depressive or manic depressive episodes.*

☐ *I feel this has little or no effect on my life and depressive or manic depressive episodes.*

Describe your situation with regard to divorce if this feels like a safe thing for you to do at this time.

_____

_____

_____

Loss of important people. Another man reported that his wife of 30 years died suddenly and unexpectedly. That event precipitated his first severe mania, although he had always dealt with less intrusive ups and downs. Now he has to be vigilant about his treatment protocol in order to maintain his stability.

☐ *I have lost important people in my life.*

☐ *I feel this has a major effect on my life and depressive or manic depressive episodes.*

☐ *I feel this has little or no effect on my life and depressive or manic depressive episodes.*

Describe your loss of an important person or people if this feels like a safe thing for you to do at this time.

_____

_____

_____

Witness to violence or crime. People who have witnessed violence, particularly violence against a loved one—such as a child witnessing the beating of a parent—suffer intense, long-lasting effects. For instance, a man in the study who saw his mother severely and repeatedly beaten by his alcoholic father had manic depressive episodes for many years. He found it very difficult to overcome the resulting anxiety and panic that aggravated his depressive symptoms.

☐ *I witnessed violence or criminal activity.*

☐ *I feel this has a major effect on my life and depressive or manic depressive episodes.*

☐ *I feel this has little or no effect on my life and depressive or manic depressive episodes.*

Describe the violence or crime you witnessed if this feels like a safe thing for you to do at this time.

_____

_____

_____

Crime victim. The traumatic effect crime has on its victims cannot be overstated. A world once considered comfortable and safe suddenly becomes a terrifying, hostile place. Those who have been the victim of criminal activity such as robbery, mugging, rape, assault, attempted murder, and so on, observed that the mood instability often begins, or gets worse, following the crime. A woman who had manic depressive episodes for 20 years reported a sharp increase in the intensity of her episodes after a brutal rape.

☐ *I am a crime victim.*

☐ *I feel this has a major effect on my life and depressive or manic depressive episodes.*

☐ *I feel this has little or no effect on my life and depressive or manic depressive episodes.*

Describe the crime if this feels like a safe thing for you to do at this time.

_____

_____

_____

War. The Vietnam War brought society to a new level of awareness of the damaging effect of wartime activity on the psyches of those who were involved. One individual who had been in war-related actions for four years felt that the nightmares and flashbacks that resulted from his combat experience made it more difficult to deal with the depression he has experienced since high school.

☐ *I experienced war-related action.*

☐ *I feel this has a major effect on my life and depressive or manic depressive episodes.*

☐ *I feel this has little or no effect on my life and depressive or manic depressive episodes.*

Describe the war activities you were involved in if this feels like a safe thing for you to do at this time.

_____

_____

_____

Natural disasters. Hurricanes, floods, earthquakes, fires, mud slides, and other disasters that disrupt daily life, interfere with supportive social relationships, and increase feelings of insecurity take an additional toll on people who already have to work hard to stay on an even keel. At a recent conference held in Iowa after the disastrous summer floods of 1993, a conference participant shared how difficult it was to keep his moods stabilized when he realized he couldn't raise any crops for a season.

☐ *I am a survivor of a natural disaster.*

☐ *I feel this has a major effect on my life and depressive or manic depressive episodes.*

☐ *I feel this has little or no effect on my life and depressive or manic depressive episodes.*

Describe your situation with regard to natural disasters if this feels like a safe thing for you to do at this time.

_____

_____

_____

Can you name any other issue that may be affecting your depression or manic depression? Describe this issue if this feels like a safe thing for you to do at this time.

_____

_____

_____

Taking Action

Immediate action needed. Life situations that present a serious threat to your safety, such as ongoing physical abuse, demand immediate action. Make a list of those situations and specify what you are going to do to alleviate the situation and protect yourself. For each situation, answer each of the following questions.

Which situations require immediate action?

_____

_____

_____

What action are you going to take?

_____

_____

_____

When and how are you going to take this action?

_____

_____

_____

Who is going to support you in taking this action?

_____

_____

_____

Long-term intensive work. Review the list again. Do any of the situations affecting your depressive and manic depressive episodes need long-term intensive work? Which problems are ones that you know you can't resolve overnight, but will need work over the long run for you to regain your stability and wellness?

Which issues do you feel are not appropriate to address at this time but will need attention in the future?

_____

_____

_____

Addictions

Substance abuse. It is well documented that people who are addicted to alcohol or illegal drugs cannot overcome recurrent episodes of depression and manic depression until they have dealt with addiction issues. Many people reported that they originally began using alcohol or street drugs in their quest to find relief from ongoing depression or manic depression.

Tim Hamilton, a founding member of Dual Recovery Anonymous, which works to promote mental health and improve services for and attitudes toward people with mental illness, knows well the battle with chemical dependence and manic depression. It was this experience that prompted him to write *The Dual Disorders Recovery Book: A Twelve Step Program for Those of Us With Addiction and an Emotional or Psychiatric Illness.*

He was frustrated for a long time about not being able to get help. From ages 19 to 24, he saw fifteen different health care professsionals. As he explains:

> I felt like a total failure in all areas of my life and I had failures to prove it. One of the biggest was I couldn't stay off drugs. I may have been the only drug user whose daily goal was not to use. The best I did was move from shooting drugs to taking prescription drugs or drinking daily. That was my biggest accomplishment.
>
> Nobody picked up on the fact that there were distinct mood cycles. Summer was traditionally a time when I experienced a lot of depression. The closer we moved toward fall and winter, the more hyper and manic I got.
>
> Recovery started with my day in court with the judge. It wasn't in the doctor's office, but in the judge's chamber, as a result of multiple alcohol-related driving charges that had piled up. The court sent me to a chemical dependency evaluation counselor before sentencing. She asked the assessment questions. My answers gave me a clear picture. There is an illness and there is something I can do about it. That gave me a clarity that I hadn't gotten from anybody. Validation and empowerment took on real meaning at that point.

Tim then called a doctor whom he trusted and went for treatment. He was in the psychiatric unit of a hospital for ten days, where he went through withdrawal and all the evaluations. Unfortunately, they diagnosed him with either chemical dependency or mental illness, not both. What should have happened, in his opinion, was that they should have said, "We have a young man who is chemically dependent and bipolar and who will need to be followed very closely in the next two years of abstinence because of his mood cycles." Tim's hospitalization was followed by inpatient hospital treatment for six weeks, plus six months at a halfway house where he was actively involved in 12-step programs.

Eventually, Tim began working professionally in the field of chemical dependency. Nobody noticed his mood swings right away. When he was manic, he was very productive, lecturing and writing. His depression was characterized by atypical symptoms like headaches, disturbed sleep, fluctuating weight, poor memory, and concentration problems. Finally he got appropriate medical help. It took numerous medication trials to stabilize his moods. He has since gone on to do advocacy work.

☐ *I have abused alcohol or drugs in the past.*

☐ *I currently abuse alcohol or drugs.*

☐ *I feel substance abuse has a major effect on my life and depressive or manic depressive episodes.*

☐ *I feel substance abuse has little or no effect on my life and depressive or manic depressive episodes.*

Describe your situation with regard to substance abuse if this feels like a safe thing for you to do at this time.

_____

_____

_____

☐ *I going to work on giving up my addiction to alcohol and drugs.*

If you have decided to overcome your addiction, be aware that the detoxification process can cause severe medical symptoms. That's why you need to go through this process at a detoxification center. It is dangerous to detoxify without medical attention and other qualified support. In fact, the process can be so painful that you will resort to using the addictive substance to ease the symptoms. Have a complete physical examination before treatment begins, to address any medical conditions that might affect your progress.

After you have gone through the detoxification process, a specialized rehabilitation program will help prevent relapse. You can get information on detoxification and rehabilitation programs from the following sources:

- Your doctor
- Hospitals
- Phone book
- Library

- Other health care professionals
- Mental health and social service agencies
- Members of twelve-step programs
- Drug/alcohol rehabilitation agencies

☐ *I am going to enter a detoxification program to deal with my addiction.*

List as many people as you can that you can safely ask for guidance, assistance, and support in this process.

_____

_____

_____

If you don't feel anyone will support you in this way, don't let that stop you. As you begin the treatment process, you will meet new supporters.

If you have a long-standing addiction to alcohol or drugs, you may need several courses of treatment. Don't get discouraged. Your life is worth it.

Other addictions. There are many addictions that can impede the progress of people who are seeking to alleviate depression and manic depression. For instance, a woman in the study said she had a food addiction that has caused her to be 100 pounds overweight. This addiction has lowered her self-esteem and made her feel sluggish and depressed. Coming to terms with addictions and overcoming them often give a huge boost to your overall sense of well-being. In order to address addictions, most people need professional help and ongoing support.

☐ *I am addicted to* _____ .

☐ *I have been addicted to* _____ *in the past.*

☐ *I feel this has a major effect on my life and depressive or manic depressive episodes.*

☐ *I feel this has little or no effect on my life and depressive or manic depressive episodes.*

Describe your addictions if this feels like a safe thing for you to do at this time.

_____

_____

_____

☐ *I going to work on giving up my addiction to* _____ .

List as many people as you can that you can safely turn to for guidance, assistance, and support in this process.

_____

_____

_____

You will also need specialized support and assistance in letting go of your addiction. You can get this help from organizations such as those listed here:

- Gamblers Anonymous

- Debtor's Anonymous

- Overeaters Anonymous

- Sex Addicts Anonymous

- Sex and Love Addicts Anonymous

You can learn of still other organizations and resources in your area through any one of the following:

- Your doctor
- Hospitals
- Phone book
- Library
- Newspaper

- Other health care professionals
- Mental health and social service agencies
- Members of twelve step programs
- Drug and alcohol rehabilitation agencies

Also refer to the Resources section below.

Resources

Birkedahl, N. (1990) *The Habit Control Workbook.* Oakland, CA: New Harbinger Publications, Inc.

Hamilton, T. (1993) *The Dual Disorders Recovery Book: A Twelve Step Program for Those of Us With Addiction and an Emotional or Psychiatric Illness.* Center City, MN: Hazelden.

Hamilton T., and P. Samples (1994) *The Twelve Steps and Dual Disorders.* Center City, MN: Hazelden.

Jampolsky, L. (1991) *Healing the Addictive Mind.* Berkeley, CA: Celestial Arts.
This book gives helpful solutions to addiction issues. I found it to be a valuable aid when I worked on giving up some of my addictions.

Matsakis, A. (1992) *I Can't Get Over It: A Handbook for Trauma Survivors.* Oakland, CA: New Harbinger Publications.
This book offers good information and resources that can help you deal with addictions.

Sandbek, T. (1986) *The Deadly Diet: Recovering From Anorexia and Bulimia.* Oakland, CA: New Harbinger Publications.
This book offers help for those suffereing from serious food disorders.

Steketee, G., and K. White (1990) *When Once Is Not Enough: Help for Obsessive Compulsives.* Oakland, CA: New Harbinger Publications.
This easy-to-read, helpful manual provides techniques and strategies to relieve obsessions and compulsive activity.

9

Resolving Trauma

*I always felt something was wrong with me, like I was somehow "tainted." I
didn't know where these feelings came from and I couldn't make them go away.*

A history of abuse, victimization, or other traumatic experience is common among people with
mood disorders. In my study, three-fourths of the people who have gotten well and stayed well
reported that they experienced physical, sexual, or emotional abuse, ongoing neglect, seeing a
violent act against a loved one, being a crime victim themselves, or loss through a natural disaster.

As I explained in the last chapter, trauma can trigger episodes of depression or manic
depression or exacerbate a mood disorder that already exists. If you suspect that trauma is at
least partly responsible for yours, you can at least take some comfort in knowing you are not
alone. This is what some people had to say about the link between their mood disorder and their
past history:

A 32-year-old woman said:

I've just begun to explore and experience the pain of physical abuse as it relates
to the moods of manic depression. Members of my family were verbally abusive
to one another.

A 42-year-old man said:

My father used to punish us—I have three brothers—by beating us over our
heads. I think "we left" during this trauma.

A woman in her fifties said:

Trauma has worsened my mood disorder. I have difficulty learning how to experience stress in critical times in a way that is necessary for stability.

A 33-year-old woman, whose mood instability began when she was 22, feels that her brother's death from drug abuse and her experiencing a violent rape caused her condition to deteriorate.

A 50-year-old woman, who has had ongoing major depression, experienced a rape as a teenager, marital rape, the loss of several loved ones, and emotional abuse by a parent who told her over and over that she was no good, fat, and ugly.

The Recovery Process

No matter what the source of the trauma, the path to wellness is essentially the same. There are several key tasks to accomplish along the way. This chapter will explain what they are, outline the process of healing, and acquaint you with the resources that can help.

Trauma is so damaging to your sense of well-being because it can rob you of the following:

- Your sense of connection to others

- Your sense of self

- Your sense of control over your world, and of feeling safe

You often feel isolated, invalidated, and powerless to influence the events in your life. To recover the confidence that all is right in your world, your recovery process must help you reestablish your connection with other people, validate your experience, and regain the personal power that was lost. You must also learn how to keep yourself safe.

The process of reducing the effects of the trauma and integrating such events in a positive way into your life takes time and persistence. Don't expect miracles overnight. Sometimes you will make a lot of progress. At other times, you will need to take a break from this work and focus on other parts of your life. Everyone's path to healing is different.

The following steps to recovery can be worked on simultaneously or separately. You are in charge of your recovery process. It needs to feel right to you.

Task 1: Recognition

Few people recognize the impact of a trauma or deal with it directly, especially when the trauma is fresh. There are several reasons for this. One is that health care workers, family members, and "uneducated" supporters tend to ignore the effects of trauma. They may tell the person who has been traumatized that the experience was their fault or to "forgive and forget and just get on with your life." This only makes the injured party feel invalidated and inappropriate for experiencing some *very* appropriate reactions.

An invalidating response often leads the individual who has been traumatized to assume that they deserved what happened and are at fault in some way—whether through a basic character flaw or actions that invited the horrifying event to occur. This colors the individual's self-image and becomes the basis for their relationship to the world. People who come to perceive themselves as victims are often victimized again and again.

Another reason why trauma goes unrecognized is personal choice. Human beings, by nature, seek to avoid pain. Most people who have been traumatized would prefer to deny what happened or avoid feeling the pain, rather than confront it directly. For others, the experience is *so* overwhelming or horrifying that the psyche defends against it by blocking it out and chooses instead to integrate the experience over a long period of time, rather than all at once. "Forgetting" can also happen when the trauma occurs so early in childhood that the faculty for memory is not fully developed.

Unfortunately, denial, dissociation, and repression of feelings tend to perpetuate experiences of victimization. Even those traumatic events that cannot be consciously recalled exert an influence on the way you think, feel, and perceive yourself and your world. For some people, the inner tension created by an unresolved trauma finally erupts into symptoms so severe that the individual requires hospitalization in a psychiatric ward. This is why it is so necessary to consider your personal history and see if you have emotionally resolved each painful episode in your life. If you are unsure of whether this exploration will yield anything, consider whether you exhibit any of the symptoms below. The presence of such symptoms *may* indicate that a past, painful event is currently interfering with your life—a question you will want to explore with a qualified counselor.

Symptoms. Do you experience any of the symptoms on this list? (Notice the overlap between these symptoms and those experienced by people with depression or manic depression.)

☐ mood instability	☐ depression
☐ nightmares	☐ insomnia or sleep disturbances
☐ flashbacks—recurring intrusive thoughts, feelings, and images	☐ revictimization (abuse continues to occur)
☐ feeling always on the alert; hyperarousal	☐ feeling powerless to create change in your life
☐ feeling unsafe in your body	☐ anxiety and panic attacks
☐ feeling like your emotions, thought processes, and life are out of control	☐ dissociation (the feeling that you are not in your body, or are disassociated from yourself and your life experiences)
☐ lack of self-confidence	☐ inability to experience pleasure
☐ unexplainable grief reactions	☐ hopelessness
☐ poor concentration	☐ difficulty making decisions
☐ alcohol and substance abuse	☐ food or other addictions
☐ the impulse to engage in self-destructive acts	☐ a vague feeling that something unidentifiable is wrongs

- [ ] contemplating suicide
- [ ] suicidal thoughts
- [ ] desire to hurt or mutilate yourself
- [ ] lack of confidence in the future
- [ ] uncontrolled fear
- [ ] feeling that nothing makes sense

- [ ] unexplainable outbursts of temper
- [ ] sexual problems
- [ ] inability to trust appropriate people
- [ ] poor self-esteem
- [ ] chronic muscle tension
- [ ] unexplainable physical discomfort (headaches, stomachaches, dizziness, and so on)

Are there additional symptoms that you feel may indicate your depression or manic depression are related to experiences related to abuse or trauma? If your answer is yes, what are they?

_____

_____

_____

Two medically recognized trauma disorders. Post Traumatic Stress Disorder (PTSD) was recognized in 1980 in response to symptoms exhibited by veterans of the Viet Nam War. It soon became apparent, however, that these symptoms were not limited to Vietnam vets or soldiers who had seen combat. Because the recognition of this condition is still so new, many people who have PTSD go unrecognized and do not receive needed help and support. According to current estimates, this condition may affect up to 8 percent of the population.

Significantly, not everyone who suffers from PTSD can remember the specific traumatic event or series of events that caused it. Others may not recognize that there is anything unusual or damaging about the emotional abuse or ongoing neglect they suffer. This lack of awareness prevents people from seeking treatment. For more information on specific causes of PTSD, refer to chapter 8 on "Minimizing Negative Influences From the Past."

In rare instances, people who experience extreme and ongoing abuse since early childhood develop a condition called Multiple Personality Disorder (MPD). Individuals with this disorder form other personalities as a way to "spread out" the pain of the abuse when it becomes too overwhelming for the central personality to bear alone. This is done for survival, and serves an important role temporarily, in that it may prevent these individuals from committing suicide, or from engaging in other extremely dangerous and maladaptive behaviors.

In the past, people with MPD were often misdiagnosed, and spent many years in and out of psychiatric treatment programs. Today, much more is know about the condition. Therapists tend to be more informed and many are now able to diagnose this disorder correctly.

Here are some indicators of Multiple Personality Disorder:

- You lose periods of time that you cannot account for.

- You find clothing in your closet that you do not remember buying.

- You are greeted by people you do not know but who seem to know you.

- You hear voices.

- You find yourself in places without knowing how you got there.

If you suspect you might have MPD, go to a qualified therapist who is an expert at dealing with this condition. With the correct treatment, the chances that you will recover are good. The process will not be easy, however. The longer abuse goes untreated, the greater the repression and the more ingrained the symptoms. In general, symptoms tend to be most intense and acute when the abuse occurs in children who are too young to accurately assess what is happening, when a trusted adult is the perpetrator, when the abuse continues over a long period of time, and when physical violence, coercion, and deception are involved. These circumstances are often involved in Multiple Personality Disorders.

Task 2: Early Intervention, When Possible

Severe reactions to trauma, such as Post Traumatic Stress Disorder and Multiple Personality Disorder, can often be prevented if appropriate treatment is provided shortly after the trauma occurs. The person who has suffered through the experience requires understanding, respect, and support, and needs to be given the opportunity to express all of the feelings related to the trauma. If such steps are taken, the negative effects of the experience have a better chance of diminishing with time.

Such foresight is not unusual today. When a trauma such as a suicide or shooting occurs in a school, for instance, special counselors are brought in to deal with student reactions. Similarly, crime victims may receive intensive counseling and support. When support is not forthcoming, possibly because others do not know the abuse is occurring, or the trauma happened in the past, symptoms may persist and become overwhelming.

Task 3: Establish Safety

People who have been abused or traumatized find that they tend to re-create in their lives the circumstances that allow for the continuation of abuse or trauma-related injuries. They often continue to live in chaotic and violent relationships, with people who physically or emotionally abuse them. They also tend to spend time or live in places that are not safe, such as bars or dangerous sections of town. If you follow this pattern, the best way to break the cycle is to connect with people who respect and care for you.

For several years, I lived with a husband who threatened me and my family, was emotionally abusive, and on occasional physically attacked me. My low self-esteem—the result of childhood issues—led me to believe I deserved this treatment. Through a good counseling program and self-help trauma-related recovery work, I realized that I needed to leave that situation and find space with safe people.

☐ *I spend time with people who treat me well and respect me.*

☐ *The people I spend time with are sometimes hostile and abusive and do not contribute to my sense of safety and well-being.*

☐ *I need to spend time with people who are respectful, caring, and supportive.*

Who will you spend time with?

_____

_____

_____

Who will you avoid?

_____

_____

_____

The actual space where you live may not be safe. It may be in a section of town where there is a high crime rate. It may not have a good lock, strong doors, or other barriers, allowing easy access to anyone who wants to enter. The space may be too isolated for easy access to help and protective services.

I lived for a time in a quaint, rustic log house in the country. It seemed idyllic. However, the fact that it was far from other people and police services made me an easy mark for anyone who wanted to hurt me. The locks were flimsy. There were no alternative routes to use when I left the house. I could never relax there, especially at night when the surrounding forest seemed dark and foreboding.

I now live in a condominium with good locks and strong doors, not easily accessible to people who don't live here. I have neighbors on both sides who will assist me in difficult circumstances. I have a wonderful dog who lets me know when anyone is around. The condo is close to town and easily accessible to police.

☐ *I live in a safe space.*

Why do you feel safe in this space?

_____

_____

_____

☐ *I do not live in a safe place.*

Why don't you feel safe in this space?

_____

_____

_____

☐ *I need to find space to live where I am safe.*

What action are you going to take to find yourself a safe space to live?

_____

_____

_____

Task 4: Rebuilding Support and Trust

Sometimes when you have been traumatized or abused you lose your trust of others and isolate yourself. You may have plenty of acquaintances but feel close to no one. Reconnecting with trustworthy people who validate your experience, affirm you, and offer support is an essential step in the healing process. Support groups, health care professionals (including a counselor), and trusted family and friends who respect your healing process will help you reconnect with positive people.

Health care professionals and supporters who assist you in the healing process:

- Validate your experience, listen to what you are reporting, and believe you
- Give appropriate advise, encouragement, care, and support that is always under your control
- Assist you in reclaiming your power
- Help you redefine yourself as a separate person in charge of yourself and your life
- Reduce your sense of loneliness and isolation
- Recognize your experiences, strengths, and abilities
- Direct you to resources

In my own case, I didn't share information about my abuse history because, when I was a child, I told adults that were supposed to be protecting me from the abuse. The adults told me that *it must have been my fault* and *to forgive and forget*. As a result, I felt that there must be something wrong with me. I didn't recognize the truth: that something was very wrong with the abusers. I withdrew and avoided contact with others. Even as an adult I felt distanced from others, unliked, and unlovable.

I have learned, as many others have, to reconnect with people through counseling, peer counseling, support groups, and involvement in activities with people I enjoy.

Ways To Rebuild Trust

Counseling. Many people who are healing from the effects of trauma choose to work with a trusted counselor who will support and guide them through the process. The counselor is an ally who shares useful knowledge, resources, techniques, and possible solutions.

Counseling is most effective when you feel that you and your counselor are equals, and that you are in charge of your healing process. The counselor is there simply to assist you in that process and to present choices, without making decisions for you. The old dynamic, where the counselor plays the role of benevolent parent, is not effective in healing trauma because the parent/child dynamic serves as a constant reminder of how it felt to have your power taken from you by another person. Direct intervention by the counselor is only permissible if you are a clear and indisputable danger to yourself or others. Even then, you, the client, need to be given as much choice as possible.

There are many counselors who are trained to work with people recovering from trauma. Get referrals from your physician, mental health center, crisis center, or help line. See chapter 10 on "Making the Most of Counseling" for more information on finding a counselor.

Support groups. Special groups are available in many areas, often free of charge, for people who have been abused or traumatized. Support groups give you the opportunity to share what has happened to you, and to feel accepted and validated. They can help you develop close, positive relationships and a feeling of safety. You will also find that you are not alone, that others have had similar experiences and feel the way you do. Just as significantly, you will see for yourself that others with symptoms like yours have gotten better.

While the size of these groups vary, five to seven people seems to work best. Most meet weekly, but may choose to meet more often when the group is first starting. Members are often required to come from a background that includes abuse or trauma, agree to confidentiality, and also abide by the other rules of the group. Group members may work together to develop individual safety plans and create strategies.

The discussion at support group meetings tends to focus on such issues as the flashbacks—what they are and where they come from, the difference between flashbacks and hallucinations, delusions, being considered "crazy"—and the use of self-mutilation and other defense mechanisms to get rid of the pain of flashbacks. Group members may review safety plans, learn relaxation and stress reduction exercises, write to perpetrators, and discuss activities that will help them to understand their own power.

To locate support groups in your area, ask your counselor, call the crisis center or help line in your area, or check the local newspaper. The group should provide a comfortable, safe place in which you can share your experience and receive validation and affirmation. If you do not feel comfortable in a group after several sessions, find another group that's more comfortable.

For a more detailed discussion of this topic, see chapter 2 on "Creating a Support Network."

Peer counseling. Peer counseling lets you share and integrate memories, thoughts, and feelings in a safe setting, supported by a person you trust. Many people prefer peer counseling because it's free, it gives them a sense of control, and they get to give something back to the other person. For more on peer counseling, see chapter 11 on "Peer Counseling."

Activities. A good way to reconnect with people is to take part in activities of mutual interest. I like to hike and cross-country ski. I often ask friends to join me on these excursions. When people are engaged in an enjoyable activity together, it helps them to feel safe and comfortable.

Task 5: Remembering and Sharing

Sharing abuse memories takes away their power and helps you to reevaluate experiences, which in turn reduces symptoms and other aftereffects. Before you share, make sure you are in a safe place where validation is assured. You need to be able to say whatever you think and feel, even if you don't know whether or not it's real. You need to be able to repeat the same thing over and over, to say it any way you want, and to express any emotion you feel as you share. This process can stir up very strong emotions. It might be helpful to undertake it early in the day, so that you can either call your counselor or go back later to deal with any feelings that have become too overwhelming to handle on your own. No one else should put any pressure on this process. Share only when you are ready and only what you want to share.

Set parameters around the process of uncovering and sorting out painful memories. Don't let them take control and overwhelm your life. Instead, set aside a block of time with a counselor or trusted peer to work on these issues. Complete the session with an activity that brings you back to the present, like talking about what you are planning to wear to work the next day, what you are planning to have for supper, or your impression of a current event. Also set limits on the time you spend to remediate the aftereffects. Then focus your attention on the present, taking care of your responsibilities and doing things you enjoy.

A woman working on the aftereffects of trauma said:

> I deal as best I can by not allowing myself to dwell on that which caused the trauma. I work on the pain for a time and then refuse to continue without a "time-off" period.

Thoughts, feelings, and flashbacks sometimes intrude and become obsessive, triggered by some factor in the environment of which you may or may not be aware. When this becomes overwhelming, it helps to talk to a supportive person, to write about what's happening, or to express the feelings by drawing, painting, or working with clay. Whatever you choose to do, continue until you feel complete. Write until it is all out of you, at least for now. Paint until you don't feel like painting anymore. Talk until there is nothing more to say. Don't worry about style, technique, etc. Whatever comes out is acceptable. You are in charge of this process. It is up to you to decide what you are going to do and how you are going to do it.

Take good care of yourself in every way while you are doing this work, as you should at all times. Eat right. Exercise. Keep your living space attractive. Do activities you enjoy. Spend time with people you really like. Honor yourself and your experience.

At some point, you may think you have dealt with every trauma-related issue that ever affected you. Then you read an article in the paper, hear a name, feel a breeze blow across your face in a particular way and all the feelings are back. This happens. You cannot predict when it is going to happen. Be gentle with yourself. Use techniques you have used throughout the healing process to help you feel better.

Task 6: Changing Negative Beliefs About Yourself to Positive Ones

People who have experienced abuse and trauma tend to develop negative, inaccurate, and inappropriate beliefs about themselves, and this hampers the recovery process. If this is true for you, you need to build a new view of yourself and of the world. Cognitive therapy, a process of identifying negative beliefs and changing them to positive ones, can facilitate the recovery process. You will find yourself building a whole new self-image based on reality rather than on what was imposed upon you by someone, or something, outside of yourself.

The following negative beliefs are common among people who have been traumatized. Each one can be changed by developing a positive rebuttal statement and repeating the statement over and over to yourself until you feel that you know and believe it. A good resource for learning other ways to reinforce positive thoughts is *Thoughts and Feelings: The Art of Cognitive Stress Intervention.*

Negative Thought	*Nobody ever liked me.*
Positive Thought	*Many people have liked me.*

List the people who have liked you:

_____

_____

_____

Negative Thought	*Nobody likes me.*
Positive Thought	*Some people like me.*

List people who like you:

_____

_____

_____

Negative Thought	*I have never been safe.*
Positive Thought	*I have been safe.*

List times when you have been safe:

_____

_____

_____

Negative Thought	*There have never been any positive people in my life.*
Positive Thought	*There are positive people in my life.*
Negative Thought	*I am a bad person.*
Positive Thought	*The people and things that happened to me were bad. I am not bad.*
Negative Thought	*The bad things that happened to me were my fault.*
Positive Thought	*The bad things that happened to me were not my fault.*

Negative Thought	*I can't take care of myself.*
Positive Thought	*I am a competent, capable adult now. I can take care of myself. No one can do bad things to me. I keep myself safe. I stay away from people who do bad things. I am powerful. I am in control of myself and my life.*
Negative Thought	*I deserve to be treated badly.*
Positive Thought	*I deserve to be treated with dignity and respect at all times.*
Negative Thought	*I do not deserve to be alive.*
Positive Thought	*I have a right to be alive.*
Negative Thought	*I am a bad person.*
Positive Thought	*I am a unique and wonderful person.*
Negative Thought	*People don't like me.*
Positive Thought	*Many people like me.*
Negative Thought	*I want to die*
Positive Thought	*I want to live. I deserve to live.*
Negative Thought	*My body is dirty.*
Positive Thought	*My body is clean and wonderful.*
Negative Thought	*Sex is bad.*
Positive Thought	*Sex is a beautiful thing when shared by people who love and respect each other.*
Negative Thought	*I don't trust myself, my thoughts, or my feelings.*
Positive Thought	*I trust myself, my thoughts, and my feelings.*
Negative Thought	*I can't take care of myself.*
Positive Thought	*I am a self-reliant, independent person.*
Negative Thought	*I am not in charge of my life.*
Positive Thought	*I am in charge of my life.*
Negative Thought	*I can't do anything good for myself.*
Positive Thought	*I can take positive action in my own behalf.*

Negative Thought   *I can't do anything right.*

Positive Thought   *I do many things well. They include:*

_____

_____

_____

Negative Thought   *I have never accomplished anything.*

Positive Thought   *I have accomplished many things in my life. They include:*

_____

_____

_____

Negative Thought   *I never feel close to anyone.*

Positive Thought   *I feel close to some people. They include:*

_____

_____

_____

Write a personal, positive affirmation of yourself that you can repeat over and over. For instance, one that I have used as part of my recovery is this one:

I am an amazing person for having survived. I am responsible for getting myself to this good place where I am in charge of my life and my recovery. I am an amazing person. I have created a safe place for myself in the world.

Your personal affirmation:

_____

_____

_____

Task 7: Self-Nurturance

Change the way you feel about yourself by nurturing yourself. Those who have been traumatized or victimized often have the misperception that they do not have any value and do not deserve anything good in their lives. Consequently, they do not treat themselves well. To contradict this negative thinking, treat yourself very well. Pretend you are your own best friend. Then do for yourself as you would do for this friend.

- **Make your living space very comfortable and pleasant for yourself, even if it means some redecorating.** Think of the kind of space that would nourish you and create it for yourself. If cost is a problem, inexpensive and attractive coverlets, curtains, rugs, and accessories can often be purchased at rummage or yard sales.

- **Avoid the company of people who do not treat you well and have negative attitudes.**

- **Eat well.** Prepare food for yourself that you enjoy and then serve it in style. Odd pieces of very lovely china can be purchased at yard sales and flea markets.

- **Treat yourself regularly to a soothing, warm bath instead of a hurried shower.**

- **Spend some time each day doing something you really enjoy—such as painting, sewing, going to a movie, rapping with a friend, playing basketball.**

- **Wear clothes that you enjoy and that look nice on you.**

☐ *I am going to do the following things to nurture myself:*

_____

_____

_____

See chapter 14 on "Raising Your Self-Esteem" for other ideas on how you can develop a positive self-image.

Task 8: Self-Empowerment

Once you have made the decision that past trauma or abuse is no longer going to control the way you feel about yourself or the quality of your life, empower yourself to take positive action on your own behalf. This is essential to your recovery.

You must take charge of every aspect of your recovery. Do allow others to validate you and your experience, and to offer advice, support, assistance, affection, and care, but realize that only you can heal yourself. This recognition is essential to regaining power over your life. People who insist that you follow their directive—even if they are health care professionals, members of your support team, relatives, or acquaintances—are not supportive and cannot help you in your recovery process. The process is very personal and only you can be in charge.

As an abuse victim, I have regained my power by insisting on my rights whenever appropriate, by becoming an advocate for others who have been abused, and by working on a committee to develop a safe place for abuse victims.

Here are ways to empower yourself (check the ones you are going to pursue):

☐ Take a self-defense course

☐ Volunteer for the local crisis, switchboard, helpline, or hotline

☐ Advocate for abuse victims and survivors

□   Volunteer at a crisis center

□   Study self-help resources on assertiveness, advocacy, and self-empowerment

□   Take an assertiveness training course

List other ways you can empower yourself.

_____

_____

_____

Important Points About Your Recovery Process

Your recovery program needs to have the following characteristics.

- It should be flexible and based on your own needs and feelings. No one can define your recovery process for you. It is yours and needs to proceed as you see fit. There may be times when you work on recovery intensely and other times when you choose not to deal with trauma-related issues.

- It should be directed by you. You need to ask for what you need and want for yourself, persisting until you get it.

- It should be focused on your strengths.

- It should be sensitive to issues related to cultural diversity, religious background, race and gender.

When flashbacks overtake you, experience them, honor them for the role the experiences have played in making you the wonderful person that you are, and then let them go.

Try not to let flashbacks and feelings overwhelm you. This is easier if you recognize that what happened to you is not happening now. That was then. *This is now.* Concentrate on the present as much as possible. Replace these feelings by doing things you enjoy.

List the things you can do to take your attention away from flashbacks and the bad things that have happened to you.

_____

_____

_____

People who have experienced trauma or abuse often have the uncomfortable and unsettling feeling of being in a constant state of hyper-arousal. Use relaxation and stress reduction techniques to reduce these feelings. In some cases, medication can help reduce symptoms that are overwhelming and make it easier to begin the recovery process. If you are considering using medications, review chapter 4 on "Taking Medication Safely."

Resources

Herman, J. (1992) *Trauma and Recovery*. New York: Basic Books.
> *This book contains an in-depth description of the recovery process.*

Matsakis, A. (1992) *I Can't Get Over It: A Handbook for Trauma Survivors*. Oakland, CA: New Harbinger Publications.
> *This handbook for trauma survivors gives a comprehensive view of PTSD, including symptoms and biochemical considerations. It describes an intensive long-term healing program that includes self-help exercises. It has chapters dealing with specific types of trauma such as rape and sexual assault, domestic violence and sexual abuse, natural catastrophes, vehicular accidents, and war.*

McKay, M., M. Davis, and P. Fanning (1981) *Thoughts and Feelings: The Art of Cognitive Stress Intervention*. Oakland, CA: New Harbinger Publications.

Sanford, L. (1990) *Strong at the Broken Places*. New York: Random House.
> *In this fascinating book, Sanford reports the results of her study of 20 people who had been abused as children. It was her intention to discover the source of their strength and success later in life.*

Organizations

The Hope Chest, Inc.
> 70 Dell Ave. #A4
> New London, CT 06320-3342
> (203) 447-2932
> *This organization provides a newsletter and informational articles for adult survivors of childhood trauma.*

Incest Survivors Enlightened and Empowered
> PO Box 82
> Milton, VT 05468-3525
> *This group provides a newsletter, and a resource and referral service for survivors of sexual abuses*

Incest Survivors Anonymous
> PO Box 5613
> Long Beach, CA 90805
> (213) 422-1632

National Child Abuse Hotline, Childhelp USA, 1-800-4-A-CHILD
> National Coalition Against Domestic Violence
> PO Box 15127
> Washington, DC 20010
> (202) 232-6682

National Organization for Victim's Assistance
> 1757 Park Road NW

Washington, DC 20010
(202) 232-6682

Group Project for Holocaust Survivors and Their Children
345 East 80th St.
New York, NY 10021
(212) 737-8524

National Resource Center on Child Sexual Abuse
106 Lincoln St.
Huntsville, AL 35801
(205) 533-KIDS or (800) KIDS-006

Childhelp USA
5225 Wisconsin Ave. NW suite 603
Washington, DC
(202) 537-5193
This group provides information on federal programs and legislation.

Healing Paths
PO Box 599
Coos Bay, OR 97420-0114
This group provides a newsletter.

American Association for Protecting Children
63 Inverness Drive East
Englewood, CO 80112-5117
(800) 227-5242
This organization provides professional publications and information regarding child protective services and child abuse and neglect.

Foundation for America's Sexually Exploited Children
RT 9 Box 327A
Bakersfield, CA 93312
This organization is dedicated to public awareness and prevention of sexual exploitation of children.

10

Making the Most
of Counseling

This journey is difficult. My counselor has been there with me through all the hard times. Her support has been consistent and unwavering.

In my study, 73 percent of the people who have gotten well and stayed well have used counseling as part of their overall treatment strategy. Before the current medical treatments became available, counseling or psychotherapy was often the only hope for people with depression or manic depression. Today, there are many more treatment choices. Counseling is often used as one of several components of a multi-strategy, holistic approach aimed at relieving the symptoms of mood instability and eliminating the causes.

The Benefits of Counseling

Counseling provides an opportunity to share experiences and discuss predicaments. It often reduces symptoms, helps you feel better, deepens your self-understanding, and may even teach you new approaches to life's challenges. Counselors can listen, encourage, and support you, monitor your progress, and provide understanding, feedback, advice, information, and education. People with mood instability often benefit from this kind of professional support.

Counseling doesn't work automatically, however. You have to approach it with care. As a study volunteer said, "Change doesn't just happen by the magic of the counselor or the process—a commitment to the wellness process and a willingness to work are imperative."

This chapter will help you explore the various issues you need to consider to get the most out of your counseling.

Here is what many people had to say about how they use counseling.

A woman who has been successful in stabilizing her moods after years of severe mood swings said:

I work through situation-based tensions. It puts structure in my day and helps me to be more creative in problem solving. At a counseling session, I talk about whatever feelings arise out of situations that I have experienced. The counselor challenges my negative thoughts about myself. She lets me know when she sees changes in my behavior and gives me positive feedback on my progress. The counseling, which I have been in for 15 years, has created a great deal of change in my life. An ideal counselor allows you to unfold your complexities as you are ready and encourages you to look at the good as well as the problem areas.

A man in his fifties who has had recurring deep depressions with alternating mania said:

Counseling helps me to know myself better by giving me some outside feedback. I have a tendency to think negatively when I am feeling down and to get into risky behavior when I am higher, so getting feedback about these things helps me to be more grounded. We discuss any significant changes in mood, medication as prescribed by my physician, and ways I have dealt with these things. Positive thinking is reinforced.

From a man in his forties:

I have a tendency to downplay changes, especially when my mood starts going higher. My counselor challenges my irrational thoughts and helps me to be more grounded in reality. I may not like what he says at times, but I can trust him to be honest and helpful

Said a mother in her thirties:

Counseling is helpful to me because it gives me a chance to share my thoughts and feelings without being judged. My counselor shares my excitement when I share my hopes about changing.

A man in his sixties who experienced deep depressions for 20 years said:

Counseling helps me distinguish between the things I can have an impact on and can change, and those I cannot.

A 40-year-old man who has been stable for five years said:

I expect counseling to be able to change my thinking and get rid of the negative emotions—anger, fear, low self-confidence, and low self-esteem—to learn to accept myself as I am, accept others as they are, practice detachment with other people, and help me set short- and long-term goals that are realistic. My counselor listens to me and provides emotional support.

A 44-year old woman who has not had any episodes of mania or depression for 10 years says a good counselor should reduce pain and stress, help her find freedom from abusive people, and help her resolve the past.

What would you like counseling to do for you?

_____

_____

_____

Counseling Comes in Many Different Forms

Before you consider a specific counselor, you may want to consider whether there is a specific style of counseling that will work best for you. There are almost as many different approaches to counseling as there are people who counsel. Most counselors use a variety of methods, depending on what works best for their client. Use the resources listed at the end of this chapter if you would like to investigate the different styles and kinds of counseling.

Another issue to explore is whether you prefer a counselor who waits for you to draw your own conclusions, or one who readily gives you direction and advice. A study participant who has been in a variety of counseling situations said:

> My bias is that nondirective counseling is the best kind *except in crisis management*. It allows us to discover ourselves rather than the shorter term, superficial fix of becoming what the counselor thinks or ordains we should be. We don't like to be told what to do. That approach is not helpful to healing.

Length of Counseling

The length of time you will need to be in counseling is also something to consider. Some therapists emphasize short-term, solution-focused therapy; others prefer to work with clients over a longer period of time. Treatment length may be an issue for you, particularly if you have financial constraints or your medical insurance policy is less than generous about reimbursement for psychotherapy sessions.

The only truism is that length of treatment varies with each individual. People stay in counseling relationships from six months to "forever." Most people in my study have remained in counseling for several years. I have had two counselors for extended periods of time, the first for eight years. I have been seeing my current counselor for the last four years. Counseling relationships have been a very important part of my overall treatment strategy.

Unfortunately, financial considerations often dictate the length of counseling. Many health plans will not cover sessions. Those that do often limit the number of counseling sessions they will cover, or they place a cap on the amount of money that can be spent in a year (or a lifetime) on mental health-related services. Again, advocacy for appropriate coverage is needed.

Optimally, you can see your counselor on a regular basis for as long as necessary. When intensive counseling is no longer needed, the counselor could be available for occasional sessions.

Choosing a Counselor

Choosing a counselor is a very personal matter. Regardless of the counselor's credentials, experience, and reputation, the only counselor that can work effectively with you is one you respect, whose judgment you value, and with whom you have rapport. Health insurance plans, family members, and friends may try to steer you in one direction or another. Money, no matter whose it is, spent on therapy with a person you do not respect and with whom you do not enjoy a personal rapport is money down the drain. It doesn't help.

Most people expect from counseling a confidante relationship, with a person who is specially trained to listen objectively and provide insight.

Take care to choose your counselors when you are stable, not when you are in the midst of a crisis or having early warning signs of depression or mania. To establish stability, you need to have in place a counselor who knows you and your situation, knows about mood instability, and can give good advice and support when you are in a crisis or trying to maintain stability. Your counselor is your steadfast ally on the road to recovery.

☐   *I am going to estabish a relationship with a counselor when I am feeling stable.*

☐   *I am not going to establish a counseling relationship for the following reasons:*

_____

_____

_____

Counseling Credentials

According to the respondents in my study, the counselors' educational background had little to do with their effectiveness. Clients were just as pleased with those who have associate degrees as those who have their doctorate. Of course, those with advanced degrees will have had more supervised counseling experience, more information, and more experience with a variety of counseling techniques. They may have researched specific areas of interest, or have specialized training in treating depression, trauma, marital conflict, family conflict, and addictions. However, some excellent counselors do not have impressive academic credentials or experience.

Is a counselor's educational background important to you? If so, why? What educational background would you prefer?

_____

_____

_____

Counselors also vary with regard to experience. Some have been counseling for many years and others, such as graduate students or interns, are just beginning their counseling career.

Some have extensive experience in working with depression or manic depression. Others, particularly those who practice in rural communities, work with people with a variety of symptoms and issues. You may be the only person, or one of several people, the counselor sees who experiences mood instability.

Is a counselor's experience important to you or not? Why?

_____

_____

_____

As you search for the right counselor, you may hear anecdotal reports on particular counselors. Consider whether the source is reliable and whether the issues discussed are valid to you. For instance, one person in the study said she wouldn't go to a particular counselor because the counselor was too young. She felt their age difference would limit the effectiveness of the counseling. Of course, this is not an issue for everyone. In another case, the issue was over lack of support and inappropriate advice. How important are such reports to you?

Is your counselor's reputation important to you or not? Why?

_____

_____

_____

Many women said they would prefer working with a female counselor and many men said they would prefer working with a male. They feel that having a counselor of the same sex allows them to be more open about personal issues and that a same-sex counselor would have a deeper level of experience with their issues.

Would you prefer having a counselor of the same sex or not? Why?

_____

_____

_____

Most say they prefer to work with a counselor who is willing to confer with other health care professionals as needed, and to work as part of an overall wellness team. They found that this increases the effectiveness of counseling and enhances the entire healing process.

☐ *I want a counselor who is willing to confer with my other health care professionals and to work as part of my health care team.*

People in the study said the ideal counselor would have the following qualities. Check those that are important to you:

☐ respectful   ☐ warm

☐ nonjudgmental   ☐ gives unconditional positive regard

☐ intelligent   ☐ perceptive

☐ compassionate   ☐ confrontive

☐ considerate   ☐ professional

☐ consistent   ☐ honest

☐ supportive   ☐ listens

☐ advises   ☐ educates

☐ confidential   ☐ interested

☐ caring   ☐ concerned

☐ provides referral to resources

☐ has experience working with people with depression or manic depression

☐ has experienced depression or manic depression

☐ knows a lot about depression or manic depression

☐ has academic training in dealing with depression or manic depression

☐ coordinates with other health care professionals

☐ knows the warning signs of depression and manic depression and knows what to do if these signs appear

What other attributes would you like your counselor to have?

_____

_____

_____

Setting Up the Interview

Interview several therapists before making a commitment. Get recommendations on who to interview from your physician, other people who have depression or manic depression, health care organizations, and friends. Request a free initial interview to help determine if this is the right counselor for you.

Who can you ask to recommend counselors you can interview?

_____

_____

_____

When you have several names of possible therapists, call and ask for an initial interview.

☐ *I am going to ask the following counselors for interviews:*

Therapist   **Interview date**

_____   _____

_____   _____

_____   _____

_____   _____

The right counselor must feel right to *you*. No one else can choose your counselor for you. Some people are compatible for a counseling relationship and others are not.

Here are some issues you may want to address in the initial interview.

☐ Payment. (Deal with payment issues in this first meeting so it does not get in the way of your relationship.)

☐ Counselor's background and experience.

☐ Focus of training.

☐ Accessibility between appointments.

☐ Availability of backup if counselor is not available.

☐ Willingness to confer with family members and supporters.

☐ Attitudes about medication use.

☐ Your goals in counseling. (Your goals in counseling need to be clearly understood by both you and your counselor.)

☐ Your expectations.

☐ Counselor's approach. Is it directive or non-directive?

What other issues would you like to discuss with the counselor in the initial interview?

_____

_____

_____

You may want to make copies of the Prospective Counselor Interview Form on the following page for use at interviews.

The Counseling Session

There is no way to describe a typical counseling session. They vary as much as counselors and people being counseled.

Prospective Counselor Interview Form

Name: _____

Address: _____

Phone: _____

Cost and payment options: _____

If associated with an agency, what is the agency? What services does it provide in addition to counseling?

_____

_____

Areas of specialty: _____

Education: _____

Licenses or accreditations: _____

Experience: _____

Accessibility: _____

Backup availability: _____

Willingness to confer with other health care professionals:

_____

Willingness to confer with family members or other supporters:

_____

Willingness to be part of a health care team:

_____

How did you feel about this counselor? Is this a person you would consider as your counselor? If so, why? If not, why not?

_____

_____

Expect the counseling session to be a safe and supportive place to feel your moods and get assistance in monitoring them as they change. Also expect to receive guidance, reassurance, and encouragement as you express your thoughts and feelings and learn to help yourself.

Sometimes, due to the nature of mood instability, sessions tend to focus on your management and crisis control rather than on exploring the issues that might be causing or exacerbating the disorder. This is often frustrating. Counseling seems more satisfying when management and crisis control are no longer the focus of each session.

Here are a few descriptions of how people in my study use counseling.

From a woman who has not had a severe episode for 15 years:

> I expect the counseling session to be a safe place to allow myself to feel my moods and express my thoughts. I expect guidance when I begin to get off track if I'm not aware of this or not allowing myself to acknowledge it. I expect reassurance and encouragement when I experience more depression, because it is too easy to begin feeling "things will never change." Counseling plays a vital role in helping me maintain my wellness. I realize that I must do the work and be responsible, but the counseling helps me gain more insight and awareness so that I can make better decisions when my mood changes are affecting my thinking and feeling.

Another woman, for whom counseling is an essential part of keeping her moods stabilized, said:

> In counseling, I just talk about what is bothering me. When I don't make myself clear the counselor asks questions. She gives me things to think about. I expect from her reinforcement for my way of thinking and available options that I can't think of.

In counseling for three years, a man remarked:

> I work just as hard as my counselor and fully understand that she does NOT have any magical powers or all the answers—this is a team effort. I discuss any issues of importance to me since previous appointment. We discuss any significant changes in mood, medication as prescribed by my physician, and ways I've dealt with these things. Positive thinking is reinforced.

A woman whose episodes at one time overwhelmed her life said:

> My counselor monitors my health through my charts and speaks with other physicians, and I feel she really cares. Without counseling, I would be lost with a lot of boxed-up old junk! We talk about feelings that arise out of situations that I have experienced. She challenges my negative thoughts about myself. She lets me know when she sees changes in my behavior and gives me positive feedback on my progress.

One woman, who prefers a female counselor, said:

> The session content depends on how I feel and what I want to talk about. I expect her to listen and be interested. If I did not go to counseling, I would still keep all

these things inside of me, and I know I cannot do that anymore. If I did, I would never get well.

A middle-aged woman who is bipolar and has had no episodes for five years said that she feels therapy, in addition to her medication, is responsible for her long-term wellness. About counseling she said:

> I usually have an immediate problem I want to discuss, but sometimes the counselor initiates the talk. I expect it to help me discern if problems I have are real or if my view of things is distorted. Ongoing contact between my therapist and doctor is really helpful.

Many of us find it helpful to keep lists of things to discuss with the counselor to make sure we cover all pertinent issues. A 58-year- old man who is bipolar and who has kept his moods under control for 14 years says the sessions are better when he goes prepared with issues to discusss. He has done work around family communications, career change, and personal feelings. His counseling sessions sometimes involve other family members.

☐ *I am going to take a list of issues I want to discuss with my counselor at each session.*

Some people find it helpful to keep a journal to record the focus of counseling sessions, specific points to remember, and action that was decided upon. It also provides a useful record of progress. For instance, a counselor advised a woman to take afternoon naps so she wouldn't be tired in the evening. The journal was a good place for her to keep track of her naps and how they made her feel.

Some counselors suggest "homework," such as contacting a physician to ask questions about medication side effects. The journal is a good place to keep track of the "assignments" given to facilitate your healing process.

☐ *I am going to keep a journal related to my counseling.*

Your Responsibilities in the Counseling Relationship

Counseling is a two-way relationship. To keep unneccessary tensions from entering into the dynamic with your counselor, there are certain courtesies you must observe. First, expect counseling to be confined to the agreed upon hour. Counselors have schedules that they need to follow. Second, be strict in adherence to payment arrangements. The counselor is dependent on this money for income. Lack of payment can seriously hamper your relationship with your counselor and the effectiveness of the process.

Keeping Yourself Safe

When it comes to safety, your first responsibility is to yourself. Good counseling can help, but bad counseling can harm you. If you don't feel respected by your counselor, if the counseling makes you feel worse about yourself, or if things just don't feel right, you do have the right to end the counseling or find a different counselor.

In one of my first counseling relationships, I worked with a counselor who was using an approach that involved excessive, inappropriate, and critical interpretations of my feelings and actions. This made me feel less adequate and more depressed. Unfortunately, I thought that whatever the counselor said or did was right, so I internalized the negativity. I was not yet able to look at the relationship objectively and understand that it was not helpful. Instead, I thought something was wrong with me.

Because it is difficult to look at your counselor objectively, here is a list of red flags. Counseling *should not* make you:

- Feel judged, blamed, criticized
- Feel like the counselor is better or more knowledgeable than you
- Feel you are being told what to do
- Probe into areas and issues you are not ready to address
- Go faster than is comfortable for you
- Remember things you don't remember
- Feel the counselor is trying to impose his or her own views on you

Some people in the study said that counselors tried to make them think that they knew everything or that they were superior to their clients. Feelings of inadequacy and misperceptions about the way others feel are common for people with depression. Being up front with the counselor and talking it out may help.

Also be on guard if a counselor says any of the following:

- "Just call the center in the morning."
- "You're just feeling sorry for yourself."
- "Why are you so quiet?"
- "I know best."
- "Pull yourself up by the bootstraps."
- "It's all in your head."
- "If you would just try harder, you could do it."
- "Are you trying to hide something from me?"

Protecting Yourself From Sexual Abuse

Also beware of the therapist or counselor who suggests, encourages, attempts, forces, or claims that any type of sexual contact is necessary to the therapeutic process or relationship. If your counselor makes advances, leave the relationship immediately. Do not see the counselor again under any circumstances. Report the person to the state licensing board or other government body responsible for such matters in your area. If you do not know how to file a report in your area, call your state government information line, a legal aid lawyer, or your attorney. A reputable counselor will never suggest or allow any type of sexual or inappropriate contact, or any contact that makes *you* feel uncomfortable.

People who are struggling with difficult life situations can fall prey to unscrupulous practitioners who are not making decisions or taking action in the best interests of their clients. Sexual contact with a trusted therapist is always damaging and devastating.

Also be wary if your therapist tells you to:

- Stop relationships with family members or friends.

- Trust him or her completely.

- Not to discuss your session with anyone else. (Be just as wary if the counselor threatens you in any way or offers to protect you from others.)

Reserve Counseling Time To Work on Issues

Making sure that you have a responsible counselor who follows through on payment and scheduling agreements, and affords you a clear space in which to work most effectively on your particular issues. See chapter 8 on "Minimizing Negative Influences From the Past" if you'd like help exploring which of your life events and concerns you should bring to counseling. You may also want to share your writing exercises from that chapter.

☐   *I am going to share my writings from chapter 8 with my counselor.*

Give your full attention to your issues *during* sessions, but don't allow your issues to take over your life. When you leave the counseling session, leave those concerns behind and get on with the good things in your life. Use the time outside of counseling or peer counseling to manage your life and have a good time. It may be helpful to visualize putting all your issues or troubles into a box and storing the box away after each counseling session. You can bring it out again and reexamine the contents during times reserved for working on such issues.

If setting your concerns aside is as difficult for you as it is for most people, try this visualization:

Get into a comfortable position. Feel yourself settle into your chair, with your back resting on the back of the chair, your feet firmly on the floor. Close your eyes. Take three deep breaths. Now visualize a box. It can be a heavy wooden box or a strong metal box; it can be ornate or plain. Make sure it has a strong lock and you are the keeper of the key. As you review each issue that you discussed in your session, put it in the box. When you have put in all your issues, concerns, cares, difficult memories, close the box and lock it. Now visualize yourself storing the box on a high shelf in a special place. Make a promise to yourself not to take the box down or examine the contents until your next session. Now give yourself credit for a task well done, and slowly bring your attention back to the room.

End your counseling sessions by refocusing attention on the good things that are currently happening in your life. Good questions to ask yourself are: "What am I looking forward to this week?" "What am I going to do to make myself feel good this afternoon?" "What is my favorite way to spend an evening?" "What is my favorite outfit?" "Whom would I most like to meet on the street when I leave here?" "Which two people would I enjoy being in touch with this week?"

I find that it helps me to have a plan for what I am going to do right after a counseling session. Usually I find myself going to the health food store and getting a healthy but delicious treat or stopping at the florist to look at the flowers and choose a special one for myself. Spending time chatting with a friend or shopping for groceries also helps to bring my focus back to the present.

What activities that help you focus your attention back on the present after a counseling session?

_____

_____

_____

If You Are in Counseling Now

Perhaps you are already seeing a counselor. You may want to answer the following questions to assess how the counseling is working for you.

What are you dealing with?

_____

_____

_____

Why is counseling working well for you?

_____

_____

_____

In what way is it not helpful?

_____

_____

_____

What do you need from counseling that you are not getting?

_____

_____

_____

How can you change this situation to make the counseling experience more effective?

_____

_____

_____

Resources

American Psychological Association. "If Sex Enters Into the Psychotherapy Relationship." American Psychological Association.

> *For a copy, write to: Order Department, American Psychological Association, Box 2710, Hyattsville, MD 20784*

Catherall, D. (1992) *Back From the Brink.* New York: Bantam Books.

> *This book provides information on finding the right therapist.*

Copeland, M. (1992) *The Depression Workbook: A Guide for Living With Depression and Manic Depression.* Oakland, CA: New Harbinger Publications.

> *Includes information on kinds of counseling and how to find the right counselor.*

Department of Health and Human Services. (1993) *Depression is a Treatable Illness: A Patient's Guide.*

> *For a copy of this pamphlet, write to the Department of Health and Human Services, Agency for Health Care and Policy Research, 2101 East Jefferson St., Suite 501, Rockville, MD 20852. Ask for publication number AHCPR 93-0553, April 1993.*

DePaulo, J., and Ablow, K. (1989) *How to Cope with Depression.* New York: Fawcett Crest.

> *This book contains descriptions of the various kinds of therapies.*

Fisch, S. *Choosing a Psychotherapist: A Consumers Guide to Mental Health Treatment.* Waterford, MI: Minerva Press.

> *To obtain a copy, write to Minerva Press, 6653 Andersonville Rd, Waterford, MI.*

Greenspan, M. (1983) *A New Approach to Women and Therapy.* New York: McGraw-Hill.

> *Greenspan describes a model for feminist therapy.*

National Coalition for Women's Health. *Women and Psychotherapy, A Consumer Handbook.*

> *To obtain a copy, write to Women's Studies Program, Arizona State University, Tempe, AZ 85287.*

Organizations

Association for Women in Psychology

> Feminist Therapist Roster
> 1200 17th St. NW
> Washington DC 20036
> *This group provides a list of feminist therapists.*

11

Peer Counseling

I peer counsel every Friday afternoon with a good friend. It lifts my depression and feelings of isolation when I'm low, and helps to bring me down when I am high.

Many people have found peer counseling, a structured form of mutual attention and support, valuable because of the opportunity it provides for them to express themselves honestly and openly with a trusted ally.

Janet Foner, who has used a form of peer counseling called reevaluation counseling to help her stay in charge of her life after an extended psychiatric hospitalization in the late 1960s, says that the process "helps people reclaim their own power and encourages people to change society and make it work for them instead of against them. . . . It promotes profound positive changes within oneself, new recognition of inherent capabilities, the ability to think anew about solutions to various problems, and the disappearance of old fears and low self-concepts. It is not, however, a panacea. It is only as effective as the people who use it—that is, it can work if you make it work."

For some people, peer counseling is the key to their wellness program. They find that when used consistently, peer counseling is a free, safe, and effective self-help tool. It can put you in control of your own healing process and help you to confront and express your real feelings. For this reason, peer counseling is very useful in addressing the problems identified in chapter 9, "Resolving Trauma."

Peer counseling is also known as exchange counseling. Reevaluation Counseling Communities, a well known international network, calls the process co-counseling or reevaluation counseling and provides training through classes, workshops, and publications. They do not permit use of these names to describe peer counseling classes unless people using the names are certified to teach it by the Reevaluation Counseling Communities. I have attended classes and workshops sponsored by this network and highly recommend them. Write Reevaluation Counseling Communities, listed at the end of this chapter, for more information and to find the contact person in your area. People who want to learn this process through the classes must be able to listen effectively and counsel as well as receive counseling.

Every human being encounters a wide variety of situations that can be disturbing and, if not addressed, can rob them of their vitality. If past experiences of hurts, trauma, and misinformation are not healed through emotional release, you may experience ongoing episodes of depression, "mania," mood instability, sadness, anxiety, fear, embarrassment, guilt, shame, low self-esteem, and lack of self-confidence.

Peer counseling gives you a forum where you can carefully examine past experiences, hurts, trauma, and misinformation, and where you can express emotions. It is based on the premise that people know what to do to heal themselves and can do just that, given the right tools. Another premise is that you know the solutions to your problems and can re-evaluate your beliefs. A third premise is that all of us are born as intelligent, loving, creative people with enthusiasm for life and its adventures and that our life experiences divert us from this reality. Peer counseling can restore that lost wholeness and inspire you with creative solutions to present-day struggles.

In the version of peer counseling called co-counseling, you look at information in light of present-day reality, express emotion, and correct misinformation. For instance, because of the circumstances of my childhood, I have always felt that people didn't like me, especially those people I am close to. Through the peer counseling process, I discovered where these feelings came from, laughed and cried about it, and began to incorporate into my consciousness the truth, which is: *people do like me, even when we are close.*

Co-Counseling Sessions

In a co-counseling session, two people consent to spend a previously agreed upon amount of time together. They divide the time equally, and take care during the session to pay attention to each other's true nature, as well as each other's issues, needs, and distresses. Sessions usually last two hours but can be shorter or longer. Each person gets equal time in the roles of talker and listener.

Co-counselors have an ongoing agreement to provide complete confidentiality. Judging, criticizing, and giving advice are not allowed.

While most people prefer to do the sessions face to face, sessions can be held over the phone when necessary. Schedule them in a comfortable, quiet atmosphere where there will be no interruptions or distractions, and where you cannot be heard by others. Disconnect the phone, turn off the radio and television, and do whatever else is necessary to eliminate other distractions.

The content of the session is determined by the person who is receiving attention—the talker. If you are the talker, you can use this time any way you choose. It may include eager talk, tears, crying, trembling, perspiration, indignant storming, laughter, reluctant talk, yawning, shaking, singing, wrestling, or punching a pillow. You may want to spend some time planning your life and goals. The only thing that is not OK is hurting the person who is listening to you.

Often you may find it most useful to focus on one issue and keep coming back to it, even if you'd rather avoid it. At other times, you may need to jump around from subject to subject. At the beginning of a session, you may want to focus on one particular issue, but as you proceed, you may find other issues coming up that take precedence.

The person who is listening and paying attention needs to do only that, to be listening attentively in a supportive way. If both partners agree, the person who is paying attention can ask questions (but only those that will help the speaker focus or will encourage emotional expression.) The person who is paying attention must never demand anything of the other person. Full control must remain at all times with the person who is receiving attention.

The expression of emotion around issues is essential to the process. The release of emotion is facilitated if the counselor encourages the person to repeat over and over a statement that contradicts erroneous belief patterns. For instance, in dealing with my low self-confidence, my partner encourages me to repeat "I have the ability to do whatever I need to do." After repeating this several times (or many times) I start to cry or laugh, releasing emotion around the issue. After releasing the emotion, I always feel much better. I have done this repeatedly in peer counseling, working on a wide variety of issues. Some issues take only a session or two to resolve. Others will be ongoing for a long time.

In peer counseling, the expression of emotion is *never* seen as a symptom. Many people feel that supporters view expression of emotion as symptoms of illness rather than as a vital part of the wellness process. We have been treated inappropriately and even hospitalized for expressing emotion. Many people have learned not to express emotion because it is not safe, and this interferes with our wellness process. My mother was first taken to a mental hospital because she spent many days crying. As I look back, I wonder if her life had gotten overwhelming and she needed a good, long crying session. Several study volunteers reported they were warned by other patients in psychiatric facilities to avoid expressing emotion, as it would lengthen their hospital stay or penalties would be incurred against them. It took me a long time to feel safe expressing emotion, even in the peer counseling setting.

A woman in my study who has had many episodes of major depression said:

> When I am depressed I choose to seek out someone who will listen to me without trying to "fix" me or "change" me or "take care of me," someone who will listen to my "crazy" thoughts without telling me "I am wrong," "I'm overreaching," etc. Sometimes just saying my fears out loud dispels them. My friend just held me while I cried last night. I appreciate someone allowing me to cry in their presence.

The person receiving attention can make requests of the assisting person. For example:

"Tell me what you like about me."

"Hold me."

"Pretend you are _____ (*parent, child, peer, employer, friend, etc.*) so I can safely tell that person how I feel or practice telling that person how I feel or what I want."

Some people feel that, because they are having a difficult time in their own life, they can only listen or share for a short time. They need to honor those feelings, and only increase the length of sessions if it feels right to do so.

Occasionally, the counselor will feel that the other person has so much to work on or is having such a hard time that all the session time for that day should go to the talker. This is not a good idea. People who peer counsel have found that sessions without mutual sharing are not effective. Everyone needs time to listen as well as be heard. If a person cannot listen at a session, arrange a time when he or she will be available to listen.

Sometimes people find that three-way or group peer counseling is helpful. The time is divided equally between the participants. When you are receiving attention, you are receiving it from several people instead of one. This can be very validating. It also means you have to listen to all that the other people share.

Many people have never felt heard around their issues, concerns, and feelings. When sharing with a person who is committed to paying close attention, it's amazing what can be accomplished.

I have always had low self-confidence, which contributes to my depression. When I become aware that I'm beginning to feel depressed, it is usually feelings of low self-worth that are intruding. I have several friends with whom I peer counsel regularly. I have addressed this issue repeatedly in peer counseling sessions. After the sessions I feel a great sense of relief. When those thoughts begin to intrude and become obsessive, I arrange another peer counseling session. I feel I have made significant progress through regularly scheduled weekly peer counseling sessions, with additional sessions set up on an as-needed basis. If I obsess in my mind about my lack of self-confidence, feelings of depression deepen.

If you are having symptoms of mania or depression, are in a crisis, or if it just feels like the right thing to do, ask the peer counselors you work with for additional sessions. Have several counselors that you work with so there is always one available when needed. They can be the same people who are on your list of supporters. Refer back to chapter 2 on "Creating a Support Network." Also see "Steps for Peer Counseling" at the end of this chapter.

Focusing Attention on the Present

When feelings of depression or mania are making you feel uncomfortable and keeping you from doing the things you need to do and enjoy doing, it is best to focus counseling sessions on getting things back in order in your life and to focus away from past issues. A study volunteer was deeply depressed because his relationship, housing, and work situations were uncertain and unstable. He needed the opportunity to explore choices and make decisions for himself while feeling safe and supported. Using the session to address and resolve these problems was more helpful than focusing on other issues.

At least once a week, focus your peer counseling session on the present, putting your attention on pleasant things and your current reality. Keep the counseling session contained so that time outside counseling can be used to do things that make you feel good and to take care of responsibilities. The session can be kept contained by the following activities:

1. At the beginning of a session the counselor reinforces the good that is happening in your life by asking you to share several good things that have happened in the last week (or day or month). This provides a starting point for the session.

Three good things I shared with a counselor in a recent session:

- Over 60 people attended a workshop I presented in Alaska.
- I took a fun walk with my daughter and we watched birds and looked for shells.
- I saw four bald eagles today.

2. At the conclusion of the session, the person who is listening brings the other person back to focus on the present by asking the person a benign question. The question can be a nonsense or "wrong answer" question.

Sample concluding questions:

- What are computers for?
- What color do you like the least?
- What do you use couch cushions for?
- Where do you think the car that just went by is going?
- What do people wear hats for?
- Who is the most important person in the world?

At the end of a session (actually, anytime it is appropriate), it is useful to remind yourself to stay in the present by repeating the following affirmation:

☐ *I don't have time to focus on difficult issues. There are many things I would rather do. I decide to focus my attention away from distress and onto pleasant and rewarding things in life.*

Make a list of things you would rather do than focus on difficult issues.

_____

_____

_____

It is often very difficult to focus your attention away from problems and issues when not in a session. Ongoing reminders facilitate the process. Until shifting your focus becomes a positive habit, you may need to remind yourself. Say to yourself:

☐ *I am going to stop thinking about my problems and do* _____ *whenever I find myself thinking about difficult issues.*

Sometimes I have to remind myself almost every moment to stay focused on the present when I am not in a peer counseling session or using counseling, focusing, or writing to deal with my issues. But I feel so much better when I focus on the present.

Don't be critical of yourself if this is hard for you. It is very hard for most people. It will improve with consistent practice.

Intensive Peer Counseling

Occasionally some of us feel the need for longer, more intensive sessions—several hours, a day, or more—with counselors taking turns giving and receiving attention. For example, one young

Peer Counseling Record

Date: _____

Counseled with: _____

Length of session: _____

Issues discussed: _____

_____

_____

Comments: _____

_____

_____

How I felt before the session: _____

_____

_____

How I felt after the session: _____

_____

_____

Important directions explored or taken in the session: _____

_____

_____

Next peer counseling session date: _____

Time: _____

Place: _____

With whom: _____

woman was hospitalized for symptoms that might be described as mania. Some time after her release from the hospital, she was again beginning to feel symptoms of mania—agitation, lack of sleep, and racing thoughts. She set up around-the-clock reevaluation counseling sessions, for four days. The "manic episode" subsided. She is now a highly effective and respected teacher and mother.

A woman who has had recurring episodes of both mania and depression said:

I share time one hour each week with a fellow employee providing mutual support. In addition, we talk whenever we want. This is a valuable time for both of us. She has experienced a major depression and has relatives with mood disorders. It is helpful to have an understanding person to share things with. It gives immediate support if needed—confidential, understanding, and encouraging.

Another study volunteer said:

I use peer counseling daily with peers at a drop-in center. I find it to be very helpful. I get good feedback and have learned to trust my own judgment.

Another woman hospitalized with mania many years ago said:

I have had training in peer counseling. I do it every day. My counseling partner is a friend and it is very helpful to her—especially the fact that we give no advice. It lets me see there are two ways to solve a problem—if you choose this way, this might happen and if you choose that way, that might happen, so you decide which way you want to handle this matter. You have to think for yourself.

Record Keeping

Many of us who use peer counseling as an essential component of our wellness program keep notes on various aspects of each session as a way of keeping track of progress and reminding us of issues to address.

A spiral notebook can be used or the form that follows can be copied and clipped together for an ongoing record of your progress and experience.

Peer counseling workshops and classes are available in many areas. Watch your newspaper, mental health newsletters, or contact the Reevaluation Counseling Communities.

☐ *I am going to get more information on peer counseling by doing the following:*

_____

_____

_____

☐   *I am going to ask the following people to peer counsel with me:*

_____

_____

_____

☐   *I am not going to try peer counseling because:*

_____

_____

_____

Steps for Basic Peer Counseling

Here are Janet Foner's guidelines for basic peer counseling.

- Find someone you feel comfortable with whom you think will be able to pay attention to you well.

- Agree to exchange time listening to each other on a regular basis (weekly, daily, biweekly).

- Agree on the amount of time you'll set aside. (This may vary from week to week but can be five minutes each way on the phone or one hour each way in person, or any other time.)

- Find an environment where you will not be disturbed; take the phone off the hook or have calls held, and find a child care person or a babysitting cooperative if necessary.

- When it is your turn to listen, put aside your own distractions and give your partner your full attention. See if you can become aware of where the person is hurting. This may take you a number of sessions.

- Figure out all possible ways to illuminate that hurt by contradicting it (not arguing with it, but presenting its opposite).

In a recent peer counseling session I was being very hard on myself and recounting many ways I felt I was inadequate. The person who was listening suggested that I repeat over and over again, "I am fine just the way I am," contradicting my thought and feelings. I tried it. At first it felt very uncomfortable and brought up a lot of feelings. Gradually, it felt better and better. It was a very useful exercise for me.

In another session, I was talking about feelings of distress that relate to my inability to accept caring from others. The person who was listening suggested that I repeat, "I know that many people care about me." Again, it felt uncomfortable to repeat this at first, but gradually I came to understand the reality of this contradictory statement.

Here are more of Janet Foner's guidelines:

- If one way doesn't work to help the other person release emotions, try another way.

- Practice sharing your caring for the other person, sharing your confidence that the person can triumph over this hurt. Trust your own thinking and the other person's own best thinking about himself.

- As talker, trust the listener by sharing all that you can about yourself.

- Say what you *really* think, as much as you can.

- Expect the listener to be able to help you.

- Take charge of your own time when you are the one who is sharing. Bring up what will help you most, figure out what will contradict your distress, and share it with the listener.

- Outside of session times, take action to contradict your own distress and decide over and over again not to pay attention to it but act as if it were already gone.

- Whether you are in the role of listener or talker, the more difficult the distress, the lighter you should try to be. The more you cannot take it seriously, the faster the emotional release will come.

- There is no cookbook of techniques to use. The best technique is the one you invent at that moment.

- Celebrate your successes as listener and as talker.

- Start sessions by recounting something new and good that happened in the past week.

- End sessions by doing the same or some other activity or conversation to draw attention away from one's problems into the delightful world around you.

- Build the safety of your relationship with each other by trusting each other more and more, listening with more and more awareness to each other and caring for each other more and more.

Resources

Personal Counselors, Inc. (1982) *Fundamentals of Co-Counseling Manual.* Seattle: Rational Island Publishers.
This practical manual of co-counseling is essential for anyone exploring this very effective technique for alleviating distress.

Organizations

For more information on Reevaluation Counseling contact:

Reevaluation Counseling Communities
Harvey Jackins
719 Second Ave. North
Seattle, WA 98109
(206) 284-0311

12

Focusing on What's Really Bothering You

So simple, yet so important and helpful.

Focusing is a simple, safe, free, noninvasive yet powerful self-help technique that was brought to my attention by friends in England. They report that this method is used successfully to relieve the feelings that can escalate into mania. Based on their strong recommendation, I attended a focusing workshop led by Dr. Neil Friedman, a student of Eugene Gendlin, the founder of this method.

Once I had basic instruction in this technique, I began my own regular practice of focusing. Whenever things felt too busy, confused, or hectic, I found myself a comfortable space and went through the steps of a focusing exercise. It helped! Instead of feeling "so scattered," I got a sense of what was really bothering me. And with that "focus" came a shift in the way I felt. The shift may have been slight or profound. Either way I felt relieved and more stable. Often, the insight included ideas on the next step or steps to take to rectify the situation.

I left sessions calm, relaxed, and with a clear sense of direction. I used focusing when I noticed early warning signs of mania or early warning signs of depression. It worked well in both circumstances. In some cases the feelings evoked were profound. At other times, they were simpler and gentler. I now include "focusing" in my growing repertoire of important techniques that, used regularly, increase my level of stability.

The focusing sequence uses a series of well-defined questions or steps to help people focus on what is really bothering them at the moment and prevent them from being distracted by issues that are not so central. This allows a connection to be made with the feelings generated by the issue. When you connect with your feelings and explore them, you are likely to experience a positive change in your overall sense of well-being. As a result, you'll gain a new level of understanding, which will translate into feeling better—calmer or less depressed.

Some people may find focusing difficult at first. You may not be used to deliberately working with yourself in this way. With daily practice it becomes easier. It is also easier if you have a teacher when you are learning the technique. Information on teachers in your area is available through the Focusing Institute, listed at the end of this chapter.

A problem that many people have with focusing is differentiating between a physical feeling, that is, a queasy stomach or an aching back, and the physical "feeling sense" that occurs with a change in perception or understanding of problems and issues. Again, this becomes easier with practice.

Focusing is something like meditation, but it's not meditation. Meditation is an effective quieting and healing process in which you empty yourself and give yourself a chance to just be. In "focusing" you respond, feel, and gain insight.

Focusing Instructions

The best way to gain a clear understanding of focusing is to try it. Here are two sets of focusing instructions. Use the one that feels right to you or use them as a guide to develop your own set of focusing instructions.

Basic Instruction

Have a person you trust and with whom you feel safe slowly read you the following instructions, giving you time between each step to follow the instructions in your mind and body. If no one is available, record the instructions, again allowing time for action, and play it to yourself.

1. **Make yourself comfortable.** Do whatever is necessary to make yourself comfortable. Lie down or sit on a comfortable chair. Loosen clothing that is restrictive. Take several deep breaths and allow yourself to relax fully.

2. **How are you feeling?** How are you? What's between you and feeling fine? Don't answer; let what comes in your body do the answering. Several issues may come up. Don't go into anything. Greet each concern that comes. Put each aside in your memory, acknowledging but not addressing. Except for these things, are you fine?

3. **Review the list of things that stand between you and feeling fine.** Which one stands out the most, seems the most important, is having the most effect on how you are feeling? Choose that problem to focus on. Don't go into the problem. What do you sense in your body when you think about all aspects of the problem? Feel all of it. Where do you feel it in your body? What does it feel like?

4. **What is the quality of that feeling?** What one word, phrase, or image comes out of that feeling? What quality word, image, memory, music, poetry fits it best? Take several minutes to explore the possibilities and find the one that feels right.

5. **Go back and forth between the word or image and the feeling.** Do they match? If they don't quite fit together, explore further until you come up with the right word or image. When it feels like they match, let your attention go back and forth from the feeling to the word or image several times.

6. **Let yourself feel that for a minute.**

7. **Ask yourself what it is about this problem that makes you feel this way.** Let the answer come to you. If an answer doesn't come easily, ask yourself: "What is the worst of this feeling? What's really so bad about this? What does it need? What should happen?" Don't answer; wait for the feeling to stir and give you an answer. Now ask: "What would it feel like if it was all OK? What is in the way of feeling OK?"

8. **Feel the change in your feelings that comes from having this new information.** Welcome and feel the feelings and information that comes to you. Be glad it spoke. Know that it is only one step in this problem, not the last. Now that you know where it is, you can leave it and come back to it later. Don't analyze it or criticize it.

9. **Ask your body if it wants another round of focusing, or if this is a good stopping place.**

Alternative Instructions

Have a person you trust and with whom you feel safe slowly read you the following instructions, giving you time between each step to follow the instructions in your mind and body. If no one is available, record the instructions, again allowing space for action, and play it to yourself.

1. **Get into a comfortable position, either sitting or lying on the floor.** Take a few deep breaths, relax, and close your eyes.

2. **Ask yourself, "How do I feel inside right now?"** Image a searchlight, searching through your body, finding places that feel good and places where tension exists.

3. **Ask, "What is keeping me from feeling fine right now?"** Let whatever comes up, come up. Image a stack of your problems or feelings with you some distance away from them.

4. **Choose one problem to work on right now.** Pick the one that seems to stand out or demand the most attention.

5. **Focus on what that one thing feels like, how it makes you feel inside your body.**

6. **Find a word, phrase, sound, gesture, or image that fits the feeling while you are feeling it.**

7. **Say the sound, word, phrase, or gesture back to yourself—over and over.** See if it matches the feeling. If it doesn't feel right, try another until you find one that fits.

8. **Keeping your attention on the feelings, ask for words, images, or memories to come from the feeling itself.** Now exhale what you received.

9. **Ask yourself the following questions, taking deep breaths between each question:**

   - What is the crux of the feeling? What is it about? Answer with your body, not your head.

   - What's wrong?

   - What's the worst thing about this feeling?

   - What does this feeling need?

   - What is a good small step in the right direction for this thing?

   - What needs to happen?

   - What would my body feel like if this thing were all cleared up? Allow yourself to feel how that would feel.

   - Ask yourself what is exactly the right question to ask yourself at this time. Now let yourself respond, not with your head, but with your feelings.

10. **Use the next minute to stretch and relax.** Then to open your eyes and come back to the present.

Focusing on Feeling Good

Some of us focus so much on problems and issues that we never get to "feel good." Enhance the positive experiences in your life through focusing. They deserve attention as well.

Try focusing using the following questions:

1. **Do whatever is necessary to make yourself comfortable.** Lie down or sit on a comfortable chair. Loosen clothing that is restrictive. Take several deep breaths and allow yourself to relax fully.

2. **How are you feeling?** How are you? What is making you feel good? Don't answer; let what comes to your body answer for you. Several things may come up. Don't go into anything. Greet each good thing that comes. Put each aside in your memory, acknowledging it but not addressing it. Are all these the things that are making you feel fine?

3. **Review the list of things that make you feel good.** Which one stands out the most, seems the most important, is having the most effect on how you feel? Choose that to focus on. What do you sense in your body when you think about all aspects of this good thing? Feel all of it. Where do you feel it in your body? What does it feel like?

4. **What is it about this whole thing that makes you feel this way?**

5. **What is the best thing about this feeling?**

6. **How did you create this feeling? What did you do to make yourself feel this way?**

7. **What does this feeling need from you in order to stay or be with you more often?** Or what does it need from you to be there when you what it?

8. **What is the next step for you to take?** Can your body let you feel the next step in this progression?

How did you feel before focusing on a positive issue?

_____

_____

_____

What good things came up for you when you were focusing?

_____

_____

_____

Which good thing did you focus on?

_____

_____

_____

Describe the feelings that came with this good thing.

_____

_____

_____

What word or image resonated with these feelings?

_____

_____

_____

Describe changes in feeling that occurred in the session.

_____

_____

_____

If there are any, describe any small steps you are going to take as a result of this session.

_____

_____

_____

How did you feel after the session?

_____

_____

_____

Did the instructions as given work well for you? If not, how would you change them?

_____

_____

_____

Focusing for Early Warning Signs of Mania

I remember a particular day I was getting ready to go on an extended speaking tour. I still had last minute arrangements to make and packing to finish. I needed to make some key decisions about presentations. I noticed that I was feeling uncomfortably scattered and overwhelmed—for me, early warning signs of mania. I knew that I could increase my effectiveness and feel better if I took time out to focus.

I changed into a sweatsuit, which is more comfortable and less restrictive than my usual attire. I sat on the sofa in my living room, a very private and quiet space. I took several deep breaths, and brought myself to a place of deep relaxation. I felt better already. Then I asked myself the following focusing questions. These were my responses:

1. **How are you feeling?**
   I am feeling like I have too much to do, so I have to race around to get it all done. It doesn't feel good. I feel very stressed and uncomfortable.

2. **What's between you and feeling fine?**
   The issues that came into my body were:

   - There's too much to do.

   - I won't make it.

   - I will forget something important.

   - I don't trust myself that I can get all this done.

   - If I only went faster, I could get all this done.

- What if I don't make it?

- What if I am not really good at what I do and they don't like me?

As these issues came up, I just set them aside, remembering them but not thinking further about them.

3. **Except for these things, are you fine?**
   Yes, except for these things, I am fine.

In reviewing the list of things that stand between me and feeling fine, the one that stood out the most was "I don't trust myself that I can get all this done." I chose that problem to focus on. When I thought about the problem my body reverberated with uncomfortable tightness and tension all over, especially in my upper chest. I lay there and felt these uncomfortable feelings.

In exploring the tension I came up with the image of a steam engine hurtling too fast down a railroad track. I went back and forth between the feeling of tension and tightness in my chest and the image of the train going so fast it was out of control. It felt like a good match. I lay there and resonated with the feeling for several minutes.

I asked myself, "What is it about the problem that makes me feel like a train hurtling down a track out of control." The answer that came to me was "lack of confidence in my competency." Understanding that my long-term problem with self-confidence was getting in the way gave me a physical feeling of relief, a sense of aha, it's that old problem coming up again. If it was OK, I would have the ability to go ahead with my tasks and they would all be done well and on time. That would feel great. Warm all over. I am competent. I can do it that way. What I felt was a slight change that took me a bit closer to complete understanding of my level of competence. I understood that negative beliefs about my level of competency are getting in the way of feeling OK.

I allowed myself to feel the change in my feelings that came from having this new felt information. Suddenly I felt better and relieved, and sensed that I had let go of some of those old negative feelings. I know that this issue needs more work, but I welcomed this change and luxuriated in the new way of feeling for a few minutes.

My body told me this was a good place and time to get back to my tasks. I could come back to the issue of negative feelings about my level of competence another time. For now, I could go back to my tasks, feeling renewed and refreshed. I now had a piece of information I didn't have about myself before this session—the fact that my feelings of low self-confidence and lack of competency are creating uncomfortable tension in my body.

As a result of this exercise, I realized that when I start to feel tense, I can remind myself that I am competent and can easily accomplish the necessary tasks.

Focusing for Symptoms of Depression

This is an example of a focusing session done by someone who is well acquainted with the focusing process and is working to reduce his symptoms of depression.

> I awakened this morning as usual, feeling depressed . . . but with some good
> energy around the margins of the depression. I decided to focus to see whether
> I could tease out the various emotions that were feeding the mood "depression."

I sat comfortably in a chair in a calm and clear space, closed my eyes, went inside and asked myself, gently, "How am I from the inside? . . . What am I feeling?"

In response to the question, it was as if there were a ball of twine inside and I could pull apart a few separate threads of it.

The first thread was labeled "sadness and grief." It was a big thread: a big piece of my depression was sadness and grief about the loss of a love.

But that was not the whole story. After I took a breath, there was a second thread to untangle. It was called "anger." A part of me was angry about this loss; I wasn't just sad.

Sitting with the anger felt better. There was more energy in it and I didn't feel so much like a victim when I felt the anger.

But this was not all. The ball of twine returned as a visual image, and another thread appeared. This one came with the label "fear." Part of the depression was fear that I would never love that way again. This fear was an integral part of the depression.

At this point I was no longer depressed. I was sad, angry, and fearful. Having disentangled these feelings from the overall mood ("depressed"), I was able to listen to each, get more from each, and see what thread from the ball of twine I wanted or needed to pursue further. I had some feelings with which to go further rather than just this large, unmanageable mood called depression.

Describe Your Focusing Session

Some people like to keep written records of their focusing sessions in a journal. It allows them to review a sequence of sessions and feel a sense of their accomplishment. It also reinforces the results of the sessions.

You can use the Focusing Session Record on the following pages as a guide to recording your sessions.

Most people feel very calm and peaceful after completing such an exercise.

Additional Suggestions

Some people find it helpful to make a special, quiet, private, comfortable, and convenient place and reserve it for focusing.

If you haven't tried focusing, and you find this technique intriguing, attend a focusing workshop. The references at the end of this chapter are also very helpful.

The focusing process is extremely safe and can be used by anyone. You are completely in charge of your own process and you need only pursue a direction of your choice.

Some people "focus" when they notice early warning signs of mania or depression. Others focus on a regular basis, often daily, at a scheduled time, such as after lunch. Do what works best for you.

Again, try focusing! It's helps!

☐   I am going to try focusing because:

_____

_____

_____

☐   I am not going to try focusing because:

_____

_____

_____

References

Gendlin, E. (1981) *Focusing*. New York: Bantam Books.
This inexpensive book will enhance your understanding of the effectiveness of focusing and help you learn the technique.

Organizations

The Focusing Connection
2625 Alcatraz Avenue #202
Berkeley, CA 94705
This informative newsletter gives ideas that will enhance your focusing practice as well as information on focusing workshops and resources. To receive a copy, write to the newsletter publisher at 2625 Alcatraz Ave. #202, Berkeley, CA 94705.

The Focusing Institute
401 S. Michigan #710
Chicago, Ill 60605
Contact the institute for a list of coordinators and teachers throughout the world and a catalogue of focusing resources.

Focusing Session Record

How did you structure your session? Did you have someone read the instructions to you? (Who?) Or did you record the instructions yourself, or go through them in your mind?

_____

_____

_____

How did you feel before you focused?

_____

_____

_____

What issues came up for you when you were focusing?

_____

_____

_____

Which issue did you focus on? What feelings came up with this issue?

_____

_____

_____

What word or image resonated with these feelings?

_____

_____

_____

What changes in feeling occurred during the session?

_____

_____

_____

If there are any, describe the small steps you are going to take as a result of this session.

_____

_____

_____

How did you feel after the session?

_____

_____

_____

Did the instruction as given work well for you? If not, how would you change them to better meet your needs?

_____

_____

_____

How well did the structure of the session work? Would the session have been more effective if a different person had read the instructions? Or, if you recorded the instruction or went through them in your mind, would you have done something differently? Describe any changes you would make and explain why.

_____

_____

_____

13

Using Your Journal for Release

My journal is my best friend. It has seen me through the worst and the best of times.

People have kept diaries and written accounts of activities, events, and feelings since the beginning of time. But only recently have we become aware of the power of personal writing to ease various kinds of emotional difficulties, including depression and manic depression. The popularity of self-help workbooks also attest to the usefulness of writing for release and resolution.

A woman who works daily to keep extreme moods under control says:

> Journaling is an important tool for me in managing mania and the psychotic thoughts that come with it. It helps to process the thoughts that come so easily in a confused, jumbled way. Journaling can help stop racing thoughts and loose association and psychotic confusion by bringing order to all the stuff in my head. Writing it down and looking at it and organizing it help sort my thoughts out and keeps my mind from cycling more out of control.

The kind of deep inner exploration and evaluation that the journaling process encourages is a valuable asset to the wellness process.

Why People Journal

Many people who have gotten well and stayed well have effectively used journal writing as part of their wellness process. Study volunteers said:

> My journal is always available. It is a completely trusted friend when no one else is around.

It affirms and validates me to keep a chronology of my life.

Journal writing is fun and it feels really good.

My therapist suggested I keep a journal of our work together. It makes the counseling process easier and more effective for me.

I like journaling because I don't need to depend on anyone else to do it and no one else is telling me what to do.

I use my journal to monitor mood changes.

When I write, it helps keep me from internalizing negative thoughts.

It helps me to get my anger and pain out and onto the paper.

Journal writing leaves a trail of my thinking [and gives me] reflections to return to.

When I opened my journal to 1989 and reflected on where I was at that time, I was awed by the progress I have made. My journal has also helped me chart my moods and mood swings during seasonal changes.

My journal has helped me get over my addiction to food. When I feel like munching and know I have had plenty to eat, I write in my journal instead.

After my psychotic episodes I had to learn to write again. My thoughts would not come out correctly. I would have to rewrite my thoughts many times before they stopped being all jumbled. Through regular writing in my journal, this skill has improved greatly.

A 45-year-old woman who was diagnosed with manic depression for 15 years, and who has had two extended hospitalizations that were disruptive to her and her family said:

When I was very ill and first out of the hospital, I used journaling to express my thoughts and feelings because it was very difficult to verbalize them. This also helped me when talking with my psychiatrist. When I received therapy from him, it was a way to share my experience and a way to begin sessions when it was difficult to talk.

I have had an ongoing journal since I was a child. I have written on everything from the back of junk mail to lovely, cloth-bound diaries. Most of my recent writings are on the computer. I print them out and keep them in a folder. My "journals" are stacked on a shelf in my closet. Sometimes I write daily. At other times my journal writing has taken a vacation of several months. When I feel drawn to my journal, I again pick up the pen and begin. At 53, I look back, impressed with all the writing I have done and how my life has changed over the years, and I realize how important this tool is to me.

During a long hospitalization for deep depression, a journal was the only thing I could relate to. I wrote, almost nonstop for days. It is the most valuable writing I have ever done. The process of all that "stuff" pouring out was clearing and cathartic. The hospital staff was encouraging and kept me supplied with notebooks. They respected my process and didn't interrupt my writing to go to meetings or classes. When I had poured out all I needed to, I felt very relieved and much better.

As one person said of her writing:

My journal is a safe place to let go of feelings I can't vent in other ways.

Think about how you view writing down your thoughts and answer the questions that follow.

Describe your experience of journaling.

_____

_____

_____

What role has journaling played in your wellness?

_____

_____

_____

A study volunteer said:

I use journal writing in my wellness process. It allows me to let go of the day's stresses. I begin by writing whatever thought comes first and then I write how I feel—not just about the thought but how I feel about how I feel—and go on from there, writing everything that comes to my head.

☐ *I am going to continue my relationship with my journal.*

☐ *I am going to start journaling.*

For about a month I had very high energy, the kind of feeling that precedes a manic episode, related to reminders and recurring memories of old abuse issues. I would wake every morning at 3 a.m. and be unable to get back to sleep. I kept my journal beside my bed . When I woke up, I wrote and wrote and wrote. Soon I would get tired and go back to sleep. In that time I worked through some very important issues. It was a very healing process.

What You Need To Begin Journaling

Paper. Use whatever paper is available and whatever feels right to you. Choices range from the backs of old envelopes and mail, to simple pads of paper, computer paper, spiral notebooks, to bound journals with fancy covers. Many people like to honor their journaling process by purchasing a specially made journal with an attractive cover. My fantasy is to have a very large journal, perhaps three feet high and two feet wide, which would allow me to write to my heart's content while laying on my belly on the floor.

Writing instrument. Whatever feels right to you is fine—a pencil, magic marker, ball-point pen, fountain pen, crayon, brush, typewriter, or word processor. Again, some people like to honor their journaling process by reserving a special writing implement for journaling such as a ballpoint pen with colored ink or a fountain pen they used in school.

A study volunteer said, "It's the cheapest kind of therapy—all you need is paper and something to write with."

A place to keep your journal. Have a safe, private space to store your journal—like in the bottom of your underwear drawer or on a high shelf. Other people in your household should respect your right to a private journal. Because I live alone, I keep my journal on my night stand for easy accessibility if I awaken in the middle of the night. If the privacy of your journal cannot be assured, you may want a trusted friend to keep your journal for you. If it is stored elsewhere, a three-ring binder might work best. Keep a supply of paper on hand, write when you feel like it, and take the pages to your friend at another time.

Journaling Rules

This is easy. There are no rules. Write anything you want, anything you feel. It doesn't have to make sense. It doesn't have to be real. It doesn't need to be interesting. It's all right to repeat yourself over and over. Whatever is written is for your value only. This is yours.

You don't have to worry about punctuation, grammar, spelling, penmanship, neatness, or staying on the lines. You can scribble all over the page if that makes you feel better. I have done that and it made me feel great—a wonderful way to get rid of tension.

Choosing to share writings is a personal choice. It is strictly confidential. The privacy of the journal should not be violated. You don't have to share your writings with anybody unless you want to. Some people find it helpful and feel comfortable sharing writings with family members, friends, or health care professionals. This is a personal choice. Others require privacy. As one study volunteer said, "I can express any emotion I want while writing without being criticized or judged."

It helps to set aside a specific time every day for journaling, such as early in the morning or before going to sleep at night, but this is not necessary. Spend as little or as much time writing as you want. Some people like to set a timer.

You can write in your journal anytime—daily, several times a day, or weekly. You don't have to commit to keeping a journal for the rest of your life—just when you feel like it.

You can write at any speed you want, fast or slow. You can write as much or as little as you want.

Ways To Get Started

Write your name, address, and phone number inside the front cover if you carry your journal with you. Add a statement something like this: "This contains private information. Please do not read it without my permission. Thank you!"

Some people like to quiet down before starting their writing. You can do this by taking several deep breaths and then focusing on something pleasant for a moment or two, such as a flower, a piece of fruit, your pet, or the view out the window. You might want to take a warm bath or go for a short walk—whatever quiets you down. Then, claim a quiet space to journal. Turn off the phone, and ask others to respect your need for quiet and privacy. Moms and dads may choose to journal when the baby is napping, the children are in school, or after the children have gone to bed.

You may choose a special place in your home that you decorate and reserve for journal writing. Lighting candles may feel good. I sometimes like to write in my journal by candlelight. Writing outside sitting under a big special tree or on the beach in the warm sunshine also feels good. Consider journaling while listening to your favorite music.

Date your entries if you want to. It helps keep things in perspective as you review what you have written over time.

Don't fix your mistakes. Just keep writing. Draw or paste pictures or words in your journal. Doodle.

I choose to keep my journal writings. Most people do. Others discard them. I have a friend who burned all her old journals as a way of celebrating an extended period of wellness. She said she needed to start anew.

Write as quickly or as slowly as you want. Don't think too much about what you are writing, just let the writing flow.

Journaling Goals

If you are thinking about using journaling as one of your wellness strategies, you may want to write some journaling goals to get started, but only do it if you want to. This could be your first journaling session.

Some possible journaling goals:

- To understand why I get depressed
- To enhance my understanding of myself
- To gain an understanding of how I use my moods
- To guide me on a journey to wellness
- To help in achieving life goals
- To write my own personal history
- Just for the fun of it
- To get over a relationship
- To assist in problem solving
- To facilitate the counseling process
- To track cycles and mood changes
- To work on issues that have been getting in the way of stability
- To help understand life issues that affect my moods
- To give myself credit for my progress
- To get to know myself better
- For a deeper understanding of issues
- For a deeper understanding of others
- To grieve a loss
- To develop spontaniety
- To explore different aspects of my personality

- To explore dreams
- To get in touch with feelings
- To improve relationships
- To keep track of life changes and growth
- To safely work through feelings
- To enhance creativity
- To keep a record of counseling or peer counseling sessions or other activities

- To pinpoint and address stressors
- To become more comfortable writing
- To understand why I get manic
- To discover the good things in my life
- To explore creativity
- To reevaluate beliefs and behaviors

Did you find any goal in the list that you want to choose as your personal writing goal?

List your journaling goals, if you want to:

_____

_____

_____

Journaling Exercises

If you have had a hard time starting to journal, some of these exercises may help you. Make your answer as revealing as possible. Write as long or short a response as you'd like.

If my life could be any way that I want, what would it be like? Start your journal using a separate piece of paper, a notebook, or a special book you've purchased.

- What I like about myself:
- What is making me feel good today?
- What made me feel low today?
- What made me feel high today?
- What are the stressors in my life?
- What makes me happy?
- My favorite people are:
- What makes me feel so good when I spend time with:
- The best thing that ever happened to me was:
- The worst thing that ever happened to me was:
- Write a letter to someone you would like to tell off but it wouldn't be wise or who is not available.
- Write a letter to yourself, pretending you are your own best friend.

- List the best things that have happened this day (or month or year) in your life.

- Make a list of all the reasons you want to be alive.

- Write five things you need to do today and how you feel about doing them.

Here are some additional ideas:

- Take an inventory of your life.

- Write your own prayer.

- Write yourself a question and then answer it.

- My ideal place to live would be:

- My ideal place to work would be:

- If I had one day left to live, I would:

- I am proud of myself because:

- Describe yourself.

- Describe someone else.

- Describe a special moment.

- Write a dialogue with another person, event, or thing.

- Dialogue with a part of your body.

- Dialogue with a famous person.

Make lists. Describe things you want to do in your life, why you like yourself, why you like someone else, why you feel stressed, why you want to be alive, fears, reasons to stay with your partner, reasons to have a child, reasons not to have a child, losses, things to do when depressed, things to do when manic, things you would never do again, what makes you laugh, what makes you cry, what makes you happy, what makes you sad, your favorite people.

A woman in the study said she learned about journaling as a self-help tool by attending several workshops. She says journal writing allows her to let go of stress. She begins a journaling session by writing whatever thought comes first and then she writes how she's feeling, not just about that thought but how she feels about how she feels, and she goes on from there writing everything that comes into her head.

Resources

Adams, K. (1990) *Journal to the Self.* New York: Warner Books.

Baldwin, C. (1977) *One to One: Self-Understanding Through Journal Writing.* New York: M. Evans & Co.

Baldwin, Christina (1991) *Life's Companion: Journal Writing as a Spiritual Quest.* New York: Bantam Books.

All three of these books give valuable information on journal writing.

14

Raising Your Self-Esteem

If only I felt good about myself, I know I would feel so much better.

Lack of self-confidence and low self-esteem are rampant in today's society, but this is particularly true for people who suffer from mood disorders. Every individual in my study had something to say about how negative self-perceptions tend to limit them in their daily lives, making it hard for them to attain their goals and maintain mood stability.

Low self-esteem is characteristic of depression. The inability to get anything done, or fulfill any responsibilities while in this state of mind, just makes things worse. And even though mania seems to make people feel very good about themselves, when they sink into depression, the picture changes radically. As you may know, self-esteem that is already low can be further diminished by guilt over actions taken in a manic phase.

Fortunately, there are ways to rebuild self-esteem. It takes time and practice, but you *can* do it. The methods I'll share in this chapter are safe for anyone to use. However, if you've experienced physical, emotional, or sexual abuse, or been severely oppressed or the victim of violent crime, you may find this easier if you get the assistance of a counselor or join a support group. (See chapter 2 on "Creating a Support Network" and chapter 10 on "Making the Most of Counseling" for more information.)

Be patient with yourself during this process. It is often very difficult to rebuild self-esteem after years of invalidation. Those negative thoughts you have about yourself can become very deeply ingrained, especially if they had been reinforced by others in your childhood. I have been working at raising my self-esteem and self-confidence for many years. I find that when I am under a lot of stress, my self-esteem drops. I counter that drop in self-esteem by participating in activities that help me to feel good about myself.

How Poor Self-Image Develops

Sometimes it helps to look back and discover where your poor self-image comes from. Did it come from a very critical teacher? A jealous older sibling? A well-meaning aunt? Ads on television? Peers? Colleagues? You may want to explore the source of your negative self-esteem with a supporter. It helps to be with a trusted ally when working on difficult issues.

Low self-esteem and lack of self-confidence can come from numerous sources. Many people tend to blame their parents. While it is true that parents who were never taught good parenting skills may contribute to the problem, there are many other factors to consider. Educational institutions, the media, the business world, and social and religious institutions also influence the way people feel about themselves. So do our intimate others, peers, colleagues, and the health care professionals we patronize.

The images promoted by television, radio, and print advertising, along with movies and television programs, play a big role. I know that television advertisements helped me define myself as a child and young adult. I thought I was supposed to look like people in the ads and do things the way they did.

The only reliable way to counter this sense that there's something wrong with you, if you don't fit the image, is to develop a strong sense of individual worth that is not dependent on others or society to maintain.

How do you feel about yourself right now?

_____

_____

_____

How self-confident are you?

_____

_____

_____

How would you like to feel about yourself?

_____

_____

_____

A strong sense of worth can help you to remain clear about your "self," even when others are unable to mirror you in a positive way. As a study volunteer said:

So often we tend to give someone else the power to determine how we feel about ourselves. We must not give away our personal power to anyone. We must not let anyone else define who we are. We must, in a very positive way, determine who we are and stick to it.

I've had to put this to the test. I recently received negative feedback from an angry family member. In the past, such input would have devastated me. Now, while I am very sad that this person feels this way, my sense of myself and who I am is so strong that this episode did not affect my self-esteem.

Negative Feedback

Children don't have the ability to screen out the negative, inappropriate messages they receive about themselves. Instead, they tend to believe anything that is said to them by their peers and adults. Unfortunately, this can create problems that continue to affect them when they're adults. My older brother teased and ridiculed me incessantly. He did not give me appropriate input about the kind of person I am. However, since I was only a child, I believed much of what he told me about myself.

Who fed you negative information about yourself?

_____

_____

_____

Were these messages appropriate?

_____

_____

_____

A person in the study said she had a teacher in school who criticized her and the other students *personally*. Instead of focusing on the students' actions, the teacher said things like, "You nasty little girl," "You will never amount to anything," and "You were born bad." These stayed with the girl into adulthood.

How To Short Circuit the Message

No one has the right to do long-term damage to your self-esteem. You may find it useful to give the negative source that fed you erroneous information about yourself a name such as klutz, stupid, jerk, dumbbell, bozo, good-for-nothing, or worthless. Close your eyes for a minute and find a name that most closely fits the source that is so critical of you.

Whose name comes to mind? Does the name really fit?

If it doesn't, keep working on it until you find a name that really fits. It is much easier to get rid of a source that has a name, rather than one that just exists in some general way. It's a way of packaging the information and making it easier to deal with.

Once you have found a name that works, use it to help you let go of negative thoughts and feelings about yourself. When they come up, say to yourself, "Oh, Tom made me feel that way." Then let the thought or feeling go. You may have to repeat this many times to really get rid of those negative thoughts and feelings.

Constant criticism from the important people in your life is particularly damaging to your self-esteem. A woman in the study said her sister was very critical of her. She criticized the way she looked, the way she acted, the way she decorated her house, the way she raised her children, her career choice—every aspect of her being. It was a pattern that developed in childhood. When the woman told her sister how this made her feel, her sister was willing to work with her to correct the situation.

The Importance of Validation

People who have gotten well and stayed well have only those people in their lives who affirm and validate them. If the people, family members, friends, or colleagues you associate with treat you badly, try to correct the situation by explaining how devastating their comments and actions are to you. They may not realize the damage they are causing.

☐   *I am going to tell the following people how they are treating me is making me feel about myself and ask them not to do it.*

_____

_____

_____

If they persist in giving you inappropriate negative feedback, you need to limit or avoid contact with these people as much as possible.

For a time, I went to a doctor who was very critical and abrupt. When I left her office, I felt so bad about myself that it sometimes took me several days to get over it. Although her guidance on health care issues may have been right, it was negated by the terrible way she made me feel about myself. I changed doctors.

A study participant said her father left the family when she was very young. Her on-going efforts to make contact with him were often ignored, which made her feel like she was not worthy. She eventually gave up, choosing instead to spend her time with other family members and friends who appreciate her.

Another woman in my study also addressed this. "I used to think people could control me with their cruelty and manipulations. Only in the past few years have I decided to control my own emotions in a way in which their comments and actions don't defeat me. I immediately rattle off all my good points when others try to make me feel small. I am constantly telling myself that I have unique, good qualities that nobody else has. I use these affirmations at work, when there is tension. I use them when I am sure someone isn't giving me credit for what I do."

Is there anyone in your life right now who is feeding you negative, inappropriate messages about yourself?

_____

_____

_____

How do these messages make you feel?

_____

_____

_____

What are you going to do about it?

_____

_____

_____

☐ *I am going to spend time with the following people who affirm and validate me:*

_____

_____

_____

☐ *I am going to avoid contact with the following people because it is so damaging to my self-esteem:*

_____

_____

_____

When Life Circumstances Color Your Worth

A variety of life circumstances can also contribute to low self-esteem. Years of mood instability that get in the way of meeting life goals have a disastrous affect on self-esteem. The following circumstances were noted as contributing to low self-esteem by people in the study:

- Loss of jobs and career opportunities
- Unstable or failed relationships
- Estrangement from, or poor relationships with, family members

- Inability to be self-supporting
- Inability to complete educational programs and meet educational goals
- Loss of credibility in the community
- Embarrassment, shame, and guilt from manic behavior

What circumstances of your life have lowered your self-esteem and self-confidence?

_____

_____

_____

How valid were these circumstances as determinants of your worth?

_____

_____

_____

The best way to protect yourself from negative input, whether it is situational or inflicted by someone in your life, is to develop a clear picture of yourself and who you are, so you can judge for yourself whether there is any validity in what another person is saying or what the circumstance seems to be telling you about yourself.

I have a positive statement of my own worth that I have internalized to help me deal with difficult situations. It affirms me and has been my savior when I experience the low self-esteem that is an early warning sign of depression. Here it is:

> *I, Mary Ellen, am an amazing, unique, valuable, and wonderful person. Others like me because I am friendly, warm, and compassionate. I like people and have a strong empathy for others. I always do the best I can and am competent and responsible. I am honest and trustworthy. I have a good education, have successfully raised five wonderful children, and have helped many people improve their lives.*

Now write a statement of your own. What are you really like? What kind of a person are you? What wonderful things have you accomplished? Do it as if you were doing it for someone else. No negatives are allowed. You will notice that I have left lots of space. Fill it up.

_____

_____

_____

_____

_____

_____

Make several copies of this statement. Keep them in convenient places, such as your bedside table, pocket, purse, glove compartment. Alternatively, you can tape it to the mirror in the bathroom, or stick it to the refrigerator door.

Read it over and over to yourself until you memorize it. Then, whenever, you start thinking negative thoughts about yourself, repeat it silently if you are with others, or aloud if you are alone. As you feel better about yourself, you may realize that you can update your statement of your own worth to make it even more positive.

Breaking the Cycle of Negative Self-Talk

People with a history of mood instability often develop negative perceptions of themselves. Unfortunately, engaging in negative self-talk can stimulate the onset of depression, creating a vicious circle. The negative thoughts worsen the mood instability, which then causes more negative thoughts. These negative thoughts and the resulting low self-esteem can be positively addressed through an intensive program of cognitive therapy, which emphasizes changing negative thoughts into positive ones.

Tim Field, a mental health activist said:

Dealing with the thought problems is different. I find my thoughts are plenty "disordered" when I am depressed. What happens to me is that negative thoughts and useless worries *intrude* upon my normal thinking. Suddenly a thought such as "You're a bad person" or "Why don't you kill yourself?" or "How are you going to afford to get your car fixed?" will superimpose itself on whatever I was thinking about, like a tape-loop from hell, an evil spirit whispering in my ear.

I keep track of how often this happens as a measure of how depressed I am. On a normal day, the intrusions may occur just four or five times or maybe not at all. If they begin to happen 50 times an hour or more, I find myself quite impaired. As the intrusion escalates, so do the obsessive worries. I worry about everything, and can't stop it.

I think contending with the intrusions and worries are the taxing elements that deplete my usual energy. Normal decisions that I make 100 times a day seem to become vastly complicated and overwhelming and more than I can handle at the moment. One way I deal with this is to make every effort to *put off* decisions or actions that seem too overwhelming. If something can't be put off, I ask someone in my support team for advice and/or help if I don't feel up to it or I'm not sure what to do.

One woman in her sixties said:

Some nights I pull an "all nighter." That means I don't sleep. When I have been awake for 36 plus hours I find I start thinking negatively. So I change my thoughts by inserting something positive. It really works. Or I can go to sleep and wake up talking very positively.

I try to find the good in everything that happens. I don't carry grudges. "I don't know if I can do this" becomes "Yes, I can do this." If I think I can, I will do it. Think that you can do it and you will do it.

A woman who used to tell herself, "I'm no good," now makes a list of her good points instead. When she is taking on too much at one time and feeling self-critical because she doesn't get it all done, she responds by doing a little something for herself each day. The thought *I have no time to do anything I want* is opposed by actually taking time out each day to do something she enjoys—crafts, reading, or watching television.

A 44-year-old woman who has been well for 10 years has taught herself to say, "I am OK, everything is not my fault," and "I don't have to please everyone."

A man who is 58 and has been well for 14 years says he uses the affirmation "I am calm" to avoid "bolting" while standing in line at unemployment.

A woman who has had manic depression and has had no episodes for eight years said:

I work on this daily. I try to be aware of negative thought patterns and "reverse" them by reframing the thoughts around the situation. My therapist and several self-help resource books have assisted me in this process.

A woman said:

I always have difficulty when I am sliding into a depressed phase because I think the bottom may fall out, I will lose control and need to be hospitalized. I worry that it would ruin all the growth I have made professionally. I then tell myself I have not been hospitalized since 1985, and that I have felt this way before and have been able to make it through. I know I can always talk with my therapist and doctor.

A man in the study said:

I tell myself over and over "I am a capable human being," especially when I am starting to feel the depression hit.

A woman who has been well for seven years uses the following affirmations, especially on days when she's feeling low, worn out, or worrying a lot. She uses these while walking or driving in her car:

- I am a good person.
- I am intelligent.
- I enjoy my new life.
- I must continue to go forth.

- I am worth loving.
- I am confident.
- There is hope in faith and strength.

When I find feelings that are difficult to deal with, I stop and say the affirmation in my head, and it becomes easier to let go of that feeling.

Other examples of negative thoughts that study participants have changed to positive ones include:

Negative Thought	Positive Thought
I can't control any of my depressed feelings.	I control my depressed feelings.
I am stupid.	I am smart.
I'm not OK.	I am OK.
I've had it. I'm going to give up.	I'm going to stay the course.
This situation is going to last forever.	This situation will improve.
I can't handle it.	I can handle it.
I am incompetent.	I am competent.
I am a bad person.	I am a good person.
I can't do anything.	I can do anything I want to do.
I am weak and ineffective.	I am a strong and powerful person.
My personality stinks.	I have a fantastic personality.

Use the following space to write down your negative thoughts and their positive counterparts.

Negative Thought	Positive Thought
_____	_____
_____	_____
_____	_____
_____	_____
_____	_____

The following techniques will help you think positive thoughts and increase your self-esteem.

Thought stopping. Every time a negative perception comes up, say to it, in a firm voice (in your mind if you are with others), "Shut up!" "Stop!" "Be quiet!" "Go away!"—whatever works for you. Try wearing a rubber band on your wrist and whenever this negative thought comes up, snap the rubber band.

Affirmations. Write positive statements on a piece of paper. Carry it with you. Repeat the statements over and over to yourself when you are waiting at a street light, waiting for an appointment, or before you go to bed at night. Say your affirmations as many times as you can each day until the thought becomes second nature.

Meditation. Use progressive relaxation techniques to relax. Then repeat the positive thought while you are in this relaxed state.

Visualization. Relax your body using progressive relaxation techniques. Then picture how you would feel if you really experienced your affirmation as true.

Journaling. Use your journal to write about the process of changing negative thoughts to positive ones.

Signs. Post signs around your home that have positive statements that you developed. Read them several times when you see them.

Peer counseling. Get together with a friend you trust and take turns repeating positive thoughts about yourselves over and over. Then take turns describing changes you are working on.

Counseling. Regular meetings with a counselor you trust can help raise your self-esteem and self-confidence. Share with the counselor your lists of negative perceptions and positive affirmations.

Which of these techniques are you going to try?

Many people find that when they are repeating positive thoughts about themselves it seems to bring up some emotion, usually crying. Expressing the emotion helps to reinforce the positive thoughts.

Refer to chapters 10, 11, and 12 on counseling, peer counseling, and focusing for more information on enhancing your self-esteem by changing negative thoughts to positive ones. The resources listed at the end of this chapter can also help you in this process.

Enhancing Your Self-Esteem

Use the following activities to give your self-esteem a boost. Incorporate one or several of the following activities into your daily schedule each day, especially on those days when you are feeling very low or down on yourself.

1. **Do something you enjoy that you know makes you feel better about yourself.** This can include fixing something, cleaning your space, painting a picture, taking a walk, playing a musical instrument, singing, reading a light novel, going to a good movie, and so on. What do you enjoy doing?

2. **Do something that makes you laugh.** Watch a sitcom on television, watch a funny video, read a comedy that you find funny, get together with a friend who has a good sense of humor.

3. **Do something nice for yourself.** Buy yourself a gift or a flower. Light a candle to yourself. Give yourself a massage. Take an afternoon off to read a good book. Allow yourself time to watch a gorgeous sunset.

4. **Do something special for someone else.** Read a child a story, shop for a sick friend, send an "I'm Thinking About You" card to someone special, buy a friend an unexpected gift, or volunteer at the local hospital.

5. **Pretend you are your own best friend.** If you were your own best friend, what would you tell "you" about yourself? Would you recommend that you take good care of yourself, eat right, do something fun, give your body needed nourishment and care? Would you remind yourself, or say to yourself, *"You are a great person, I love you"*?

6. **Make a list of your accomplishments in a day, a week, or a month or in your life.** Don't leave things out. Give yourself credit for whatever you have done. Do not compare yourself to anyone else. Post the list in a prominent place. Then read it every time you start to get down on yourself.

7. **Set up a space to honor yourself.** This could be a bureau top, a wall, the refrigerator door. Then fill the space with pictures of yourself, trophies, and other mementos. Spend a few minutes each day reviewing the contents of the space. Change the items as you feel like it. I use the top of my dresser for this purpose. I have pictures of myself and special people in my life, trinkets I enjoy, gifts, cards and dried flowers.

8. **Have pictures of yourself in prominent view around your living space.** When you walk by each one, tell yourself something good about yourself. I filled a frame with pictures of myself at different ages. I included a special quote from a supportive friend. I have it hanging at the top of the stairs where I have to look at it each time I go up or down the stairs. It constantly reminds me of how special I am.

9. **Look at a child.** Think of all the good things you would like to tell that child about him- or herself. Then tell yourself the same things. Through my life, I have looked back on my childhood and said to myself: "Why didn't you do this that way or that this way?" "Why didn't you keep your room neat like your sister did?" "Why didn't you try harder in school?" I also had the habit of obsessing about things I did that were embarrassing to me—like running into a parked car with my bicycle when waving to an elderly friend on a porch. One day last year when I was walking by a school playground I saw lots of little boys and girls at play. I thought to myself, *you would never judge those children in the harsh way that you judge yourself as a child.* From that time on, I have been much more compassionate with my thoughts about myself as a child. It has translated into better feelings about myself.

10. **Get together with a trusted friend and share the time.** You may decide to divide a block of time in half, ten minutes each. Then take turns telling each other everything that is good about yourselves. Just think, ten minutes of compliments! The first time I tried that exercise, I found it was very easy to give the other person compliments,

but very difficult to receive compliments about me. I have made it a point to get used to sharing compliments and having that make me feel good. This can be done regularly as part of peer counseling.

11. **Ask for what you want and need for yourself.** Advocate for yourself. Don't allow anyone to treat you badly. Don't allow yourself to be a victim! Be your own best friend. You deserve it. If you need to develop this skill, please go back to chapter 1 on "How To Advocate Effectively for Yourself." What do you need for yourself now? Is it a better housing situation, better treatment on the job, help with chores from family members, attention from health care professionals?

12. **Have a celebration.** Celebrate the fact that you got up, made the bed, worked every day this week, wrote a long overdue letter to a family member, or made a difficult phone call. Be creative. Then give yourself a little party. Invite a special supporter, a family member, or a child to join you. Or celebrate by yourself. Have a good time. The celebration can be as long or as short as you want it to be.

These activities will all help raise your self-esteem if you use them consistently.

Resources

Beck, A., B. Rush, B. Shaw, and G. Emery (1979) *The Cognitive Therapy of Depression.* New York: Guilford Press.
   This is a good resource for understanding and using cognitive therapy.

Burns D. (1980) *Feeling Good.* New York: Morrow.
   This is another easy-to-use guide to cognitive therapy.

—— (1989) *The Feeling Good Handbook.* New York: Plume.
   This handbook is an excellent addendum to Burns' first work, and provides a program that an individual can use alone or as part of a therapeutic process.

Copeland, M. E. (1992) *The Depression Workbook: A Guide for Living with Depression and Manic Depression.* Oakland, CA: New Harbinger Publications.
   The chapters "Building Self-Esteem and Self-Confidence" and "New Ways of Thinking" supplement the information in this chapter.

Davis, M., E. Eshelman, and M. McKay (1988) *The Relaxation & Stress Reduction Workbook.* 3rd ed. Oakland, CA: New Harbinger Publications.
   Use this guide to learn the visualization exercises that are recommended in this chapter.

Fanning, P., and M. McKay (1992) *Self-Esteem.* Oakland, CA: New Harbinger Publications.
   This book is highly acclaimed as an excellent self-help resource for developing a positive sense of self.

McKay, M., M. Davis, and P. Fanning. (1981) *Thoughts and Feelings: The Art of Cognitive Stress Intervention.* Oakland, CA: New Harbinger Publications.
   This workbook is an essential resource in any cognitive therapy program.

Audio Tape

Combatting Distorted Thinking. (1987) Oakland, CA: New Harbinger Publications.

Copeland, M.E. (1993) *Living With Depression and Manic Depression.* Oakland, CA: New Harbinger Publications.

Video Tape

Copeland, M.E., and W. Hood (1993) *Coping With Depression.* Oakland, CA: New Harbinger Publications.

PART IV

Addressing Specific Issues

15

Preventing Depression

This has been the biggest challenge of my life—getting rid of these horrid depressions which overwhelm and debilitate me.

Depression is dangerous. If it becomes severe enough, it can lead to suicide. That is why it is essential for you to do everything you can to prevent depression, and to also get competent professional help, when you first feel the onset of depression

If you have experienced depression, you can probably relate to the following descriptions provided by people who responded to my study:

> Depression is like being in the bottom of a deep, dark hole. All the world is bleak and cold. I don't want to do anything. I don't want to move. All the energy has left my body. I feel there is no hope. Nothing will ever change. I am worthless. This is all my fault. My life is over. I just want to die.

> The despair, the pessimism, the hopelessness fill my life. I want to sleep. All I do is cry. I can't pay bills. I can't keep appointments. I can't do chores. I hide out. I take the phone off the hook, read and watch sad stories. My body aches. I am ugly and agitated.

> I want to stay in bed. I don't want to shower, get dressed, or take care of myself. I don't want to talk to friends. Nothing pleases me. Money gives me no pleasure. I want to die all the time.

Medically speaking, a person is considered clinically depressed if they have five of the following nine symptoms. This list comes from the *Diagnostic and Statistical Manual of Mental Disorders (DSM-III-R)*, a publication of the American Psychiatric Association:

1. A depressed mood most of the day, almost every day.

2. Diminished interest or pleasure in almost all activities of the day, nearly every day.

3. Significant weight loss or gain when not dieting, and decreased or increased appetite nearly every day.

4. Insomnia or hypersomnia (excessive sleep) nearly every day.

5. Abnormal restlessness or a drop in physical activity nearly every day.

6. Fatigue or loss of energy nearly every day.

7. Feeling worthlessness or excessive or inappropriate guilt nearly every day.

8. Diminished ability to think, concentrate, or make decisions nearly every day.

9. Recurrent thoughts of death, or recurrent suicidal thoughts without a specific plan, or a suicide attempt, or a specific plan for committing suicide.

Sometimes, depression is the result of another illness. (See chapter 3 on "Eliminating the Physical Causes of Mood Disorders.") If this is the case, treat the illness. But if *no* illness is present, and the individual is not suffering loss but is experiencing depression almost every day and has lost interest in almost all activities every day, then that individual is considered clinically depressed.

Even when there has been a loss, a complete physical examination is a good idea if the depression persists for an extended period of time or interferes with day-to-day responsibilities. The self-help techniques in the last section can also help.

Taking Preventive Action

There is no "up" side to depression. That's why those who have experienced depression or the depressive phase of manic depression are usually willing to put preventive measures in place to prevent depression. The first step is to realize that wellness is your responsibility and you are in charge of putting systems in place to prevent another episode. You may not be successful at first, but instead of looking at the episode as a failure, examine it as much as possible while it is happening and more extensively after the symptoms disappear. This will help you learn how to address early warning signs or the next episode even more effectively. Rather than looking at the depression as totally out of your control, look for ways you can make yourself feel better and get well more quickly. You may find a strategy that will work for you from reading about the successes of those in the study.

Here are some strategies people have used.

One person said, "I think my way through, rather than getting overwhelmed and succumbing to depression."

Realizing that poor dietary habits might be making her depression worse, a study volunteer shared this information with a supporter. The supporter agreed to do some shopping for her, and bought some easy-to-prepare healthy foods such as whole grain cereals, breads, and healthy frozen dinners to replace the snack foods that had become the mainstay of her diet. Her mood lifted somewhat.

Another person noticed a positive change when she began spending just a few minutes each day outdoors. As she felt better, she increased the time spent outdoors. She began taking short walks, gradually increasing her walking time.

A man who had a hard time getting up in the morning learned that it was easier to get up and get going if he had something planned to look forward to. He bought himself a supply of instant decaffeinated cappucino mix and treated himself to an iced cappucino as soon as he got up. Others have found that an enjoyable activity upon arising such as a phone visit with a friend or a few minutes reading a good novel helps alleviate early morning depressions.

Use your journal to record helpful strategies that you discover. This way, the next time you feel low, you won't have to relearn these lessons.

Seize Your Chance To Get the Upper Hand

To effectively prevent or limit depressive episodes, use the window of opportunity between episodes to take actions that will improve your chances of successful intervention in the future. The following checklist can help you determine the action you need to take for yourself between episodes.

☐ Have a complete physical evaluation and address any possible issues that might be causing or aggravating depression, such as hypothyroidism or a vitamin deficiency.

Which health care treatments are necessary to control depression and ensure your wellness?

_____

_____

_____

☐ Consult with health care professionals who have expertise in treating depression. Ask them for advice on treatment scenarios. Explore these options thoroughly. Then, based on what you learn, begin whatever treatment you have decided is in your best interest. In some cases, certain treatments will only be initiated if your depression is severe. You may find that there are some treatments you would not want under any circumstances. See chapter 1 on "How To Advocate Effectively for Yourself," and the information at the end of this chapter for guidance in setting up a treatment preference document.

Which treatments have you decided to use? Why? For what purpose?

_____

_____

_____

Which treatments are you planning to ask others to initiate if your depression is severe and you cannot make decisions for yourself? Why? For what purposes?

_____

_____

_____

Which treatments are not to be used under any circumstance? Why do you choose not to use them?

_____

_____

_____

☐   With health care professionals, supporters, health care organizations, and other people who have experienced depression, explore possible facilities where you would be safe and could receive appropriate treatment if your depression is severe, if you have suicidal thoughts, if you feel unsafe, or if your condition needs to be closely monitored. If you have been hospitalized in the past, you may already have firsthand information.

Which facilities do you prefer and why?

_____

_____

_____

Which facilities are unacceptable? Why?

_____

_____

_____

Develop an action plan supporters can undertake on your behalf when you cannot take action or make decisions for yourself. Once you have considered your options, you can make these decisions in advance. For instance, you can determine the kinds of treatment that are acceptable, the conditions under which acceptable treatments may be used, the health care professionals that can be included in the decision-making process, and the health care facilities you prefer. A trusted person (or people) can be given durable power of attorney to make decisions for you. A legal document can be drawn up defining the conditions under which the person or people who have durable power of attorney have the right to make decisions for you and carry out your wishes.

☐   Define your early warning signs of depression, set up a charting system to monitor these early warning signs and take preventive action early.

Take a conservative approach, remembering that you don't know how wide the window of opportunity is. You need to take action early even when you are not sure you are getting depressed.

☐ Develop and educate a support team that includes health care professionals and trusted family members and friends. These people will help you monitor your symptoms, support and advise you as necessary, make decisions for you when you cannot make them for yourself, and enrich your life. See chapter 2 on "Creating a Support Network" for information on how to set up a support team.

☐ Work on changing habits or implementing strategies that contribute to overall wellness. For more information, refer to chapter 5 on, "Developing a Lifestyle That Enhances Wellness."

Check off the strategies below that you intend to use.

☐ Identify early warning signs of depression and chart them.

☐ Adjust your diet .

☐ Get enough light.

☐ Exercise regularly.

☐ Seek counseling.

☐ Write in your journal.

☐ Do peer counseling.

☐ Do focusing.

☐ Make career changes.

☐ Begin a cognitive therapy program.

☐ Attend a support group.

Make a commitment to yourself that you will do whatever you have to do to prevent depression. Take a proactive role on your own behalf.

Plan To Avoid Depression

The following is my plan for preventing depression. It includes action I want taken on my behalf if my symptoms get worse. Be aware that I am listing my personal warning signs and that your own are likely to be different.

How do you plan to use the strategies you have selected?

_____

_____

_____

Plan To Avoid Depression and Depression Treatment Preference Document

I, *Mary Ellen Copeland*, never, under any circumstances, want to get depressed again. Therefore, when I become aware of the following early warning signs of depression, including:

I do not look both ways when I cross the street; I stuff myself with sweets; I have difficulty relaxing; I wake up at 3:00 a.m. and am not able to get back to sleep; I feel very tired; I avoid friends; I experience overwhelming difficulty with even the simplest tasks

I will take the following preventive actions:

Let a supporter know how I am feeling and what I am going to do about it; have an assessment of my thyroid condition and take action based on the findings; visit my naturopathic physician for recommendations; increase my relaxation sessions to five times a day; do focusing exercises at least three times a day; have daily peer counseling sessions; get outside and get light; take a walk with a friend; eliminate junk food and sugar from my diet; focus my diet on high carbohydrate foods; include activities I enjoy in my daily routine, such as watching a light video, reading a good book, drawing, or sewing.

If the depression continues to worsen, which means:

My activity level is markedly decreased; I am not able to do my work; I am not able to take appropriate care of myself; I am very despondent; I am having suicidal thoughts; I am agitated

I give the following people:

Iva Wood, Thomas Smith, Nancy Smith, Patti Smith, and Jerry Smith

authority to confer with my health care professionals:

My counselor, Karen Kamenetsky; my physician, Dr. John Glick; and my naturopathic physician, Dr. Connie Hernandez

and, based on their professional recommendations, authority to take any of the following preventive or protective actions they feel necessary:

Any action agreed upon by at least three of my children and one of my health care professionals.

I am willing to take the following medications:

Serotonin reuptake or blocker antidepressants, which have worked well in the past; an increase in B vitamins, which has helped in the past.

The following medications are unacceptable:

Tricyclic antidepressants, which have not worked in the past and have intolerable side-effects; MAO inhibitors, which have not worked in the past.

I prefer to be admitted to the following facility:

Dartmouth Medical Center, which can best meet my medical and psychiatric care needs.

I am willing to be admitted to the following facilities (in order of preference):

Vermont Medical Center, because others have said it is good, and Brattleboro Retreat or Cheshire Medical Center, which both have convenient, appropriate services.

My attorney: *Jean Giddings*

Signature: *Mary Ellen Copeland*　　　　　　　　　　　　Date: *March 28, 1994*

Plan To Avoid Depression and
Depression Treatment Preference Document

I, _____ , never, under any circumstances, want to get depressed again. Therefore, when I become aware of the following early warning signs of depression, including:

_____

_____

_____

_____

I will take the following preventive actions:

_____

_____

_____

_____

If the depression continues to worsen, which means:

_____

_____

_____

I give the following people:

_____

_____

_____

authority to confer with my health care professionals:

_____

_____

_____

and, based on their professional recommendations, authority to take any of the following preventive or protective actions they feel necessary:

_____

_____

_____

I am willing to take the following medications:

_____

_____

_____

The following medications are unacceptable:

_____

_____

_____

I prefer to be admitted to the following facility:

_____

I am willing to be admitted to the following facilities (in order of preference):

_____

_____

_____

My attorney: _____

Signature: _____ Date: _____

References

American Psychiatric Association (1987) *Diagnostic and Statistical Manual of Mental Disorders.* Washington DC: American Psychiatric Association.

> *This is a reference manual of symptoms that an extensive panel of medical practitioners have determined to be descriptive of various mental disorders.*

Copeland, M. (1992) *The Depression Workbook: A Guide for Living With Depression and Manic Depression.* Oakland, CA: New Harbinger Publications.

> *A workbook style compilation of self-help coping strategies and ideas from 120 people who experience either depressive or manic depressive symptoms.*

Audio Tape

Copeland, M. E. (1993) *Living With Depression and Manic Depression.* Oakland, CA: New Harbinger Publications.

> *A summary of self-help techniques to use as a reminder, or when reading is not an option.*

Video Tape

Copeland, M. E., and W. Hood (1993) *Coping With Depression.* Oakland, CA: New Harbinger Publications.

> *This video will assist you in implementing suggested self-help strategies in your life.*

16

Responding to
Symptoms of Depression

*I chart my moods by writing in a journal and from this my therapist and I
can locate the patterns and use the therapeutic plan we have negotiated.*

Responding early to symptoms of depression and aggressively implementing self-help strategies
to keep these symptoms at bay can prevent your depression from turning into a deep depressive
episode. This chapter describes the strategies and techniques used successfully by those who
have gotten well and stayed well for long periods of time. Many of these strategies are similar,
or the same as, those used to reduce early warning signs of mania.

A man who has had episodes of severe depression for many years and manages them
with a wide variety of self-help techniques and medications said:

> When I find myself moderately to severely impacted by depression, I have found
> it helpful to try to "liberate" myself from this oppressive beast as much as
> possible. At these times I notice sadness, hopelessness, and ominous feelings, as
> well as obsessive thoughts.
>
> Although these feelings are most unpleasant and at times nearly unbear-
> able, I can get used to them after a few days. I try to see them simply as symptoms,
> nothing else, and I do not have to take them seriously. It's like having a bad
> toothache, but I know it's false pain, because that tooth was pulled years ago. In
> this way, although sometimes greatly impaired, I can keep going.

Responding to Triggers

Most of the people in my study can identify a specific event or series of events that have triggered
early warning signs of depression or manic episodes. It is not always easy to identify such
triggers, but education and awareness help.

A common characteristic of a trigger is to feel stressed and overwhelmed by your current circumstances. Don't assume these triggers always lead to depression. As you learn to handle the triggers better, you can keep them from causing an episode.

Triggers may include:

- *A sudden unexpected change in your circumstances* such as the loss of a loved one, rejection, a house fire, loss of a job, a business failure, or a new relationship. For instance, one study volunteer began noticing signs of depression after he learned that his diabetes would curtail his activities and need lifetime management.

- *Real or perceived rejection or invalidation.* One woman noticed early warning signs of depression after her supervisor criticized her performance. She felt she had been doing very well.

- *Embarrassment or guilt about an event.* Another study volunteer realized that guilt over betraying an intimate relationship during a prolonged period of hypomania was triggering feelings of depression.

- *Having too much to do* such as completing college course work, meeting an unreasonable deadline, preparing for a wedding, moving, or feeling that you are not capable of doing what needs to be done. One woman in the study noticed that when her house got very messy and the thought of cleaning it felt overwhelming, feelings of depression began.

- *Having to do something you don't want to do* such as getting divorced or spending time away from a loved one. Many people have noted that an unexpected divorce action brought on the beginning of depression that deepened rapidly.

- *Anniversaries or reminders of traumatic events.* Another study volunteer has symptoms of depression on the days surrounding the anniversary of her brother's suicide.

- *A change in daily routine* that interrupts eating, sleeping, and activity patterns. On a recent business trip to Alaska, for example, I was stranded in a remote fishing village for five days, while waiting for a winter storm to subside so a small plane could fly me out. As soon as I realized I was not going to be able to leave as planned, that I was going to miss many scheduled appointments and that no one could predict when I would get out, I started experiencing early warning signs of depression.

- *A change of seasons.* Some people notice that symptoms of depression occur seasonally. They often begin in the fall as the days get shorter and continue through the winter months. You may also notice that you begin to feel depressed on a cloudy day or during a series of cloudy days or stormy weather.

What events, situations or circumstances do you feel may have triggered feelings of depression?

_____

_____

_____

How To Avoid an Episode

1. Be aware that such events have the potential for triggering depression.

2. With the assistance of a supporter, or by yourself if necessary, try to get a handle on what is happening. Ask yourself:

   - What action do I need to take to protect myself?

   - What is the worst thing that can happen?

   - Is there anything I can do to improve the situation?

   - What will make me feel better?

Letting out all your emotions and frustrations in a safe, supported place helps. Is there a place you can go with a trusted supporter and scream, cry, swear, yell—whatever you feel like doing for as long as you need to?

One man who has experienced many episodes of severe depression told me what he did to avert an episode. Attending a conference meeting at which a controversial subject was being discussed, he found that he was getting more and more angry as he listened to a number of heated arguments. He knew that an uncontrolled outburst would escalate the situation and might lead to a manic episode. He left the room and went to his car, where he could safely vent all his emotion. He then determined that nothing would be solved at such a meeting and it was not in his best interest to go back. Instead, he spent some time in the hot tub at the hotel.

When I was stranded in Alaska, I reviewed the situation with my daughter who was traveling with me. From that talk, I came to see that there was really nothing I could do about the situation. It was out of my hands. I was safe and had good lodging. The worst thing that could happen was that I wouldn't get out for a long time and would miss engagements. I improved the situation by getting in touch with a friend at home who postponed some appointments and let others know of my situation so they could be prepared if I could not meet my commitments. Then I knew that I would feel better if I had something to do. I went to the school library and got a supply of books to read. I borrowed a lap top computer from the school so I could do some of my work and had some leisurely visits with people in the community. It was a hard time, but all of that helped. I did my relaxation exercises regularly and had several emotional peer counseling sessions with my daughter.

Many people find that charting, relaxation, exercises, journaling, focusing, and peer counseling help to make them aware of triggers, and to respond to them in ways that prevent episodes.

What strategies are you going to use to make yourself aware of events and activities that are triggering episodes?

When you realize an episode has been triggered, take the following steps:

☐ Return your routine to normal as soon as possible.

☐ Take very good care of yourself.

☐ Use your support network to get an accurate view of your situation and to develop alternative strategies and solutions.

☐ Do relaxation and stress reduction exercises, focusing, peer counseling, and journaling.

A study volunteer said:

When I feel overwhelmed, I break the problem down into smaller "do-able" units. When this is done, I may find I suddenly *do* have the means and energy to accomplish what I want to do. Sometimes I turn the list of tasks to do into a kind of game, with rewards as I complete each unit. My main approach to these problems is to try to lighten up on myself and not take things so seriously. Certainly, in times of depression, my overall output is less than normal, but so what? I am alive, and I know that all I have to do is endure and eventually I will feel better.

What else do you think would help you avoid an episode when you are triggered?

_____

_____

_____

Monitor Symptoms

People who have experienced depression and achieved long-term wellness recognize their early warning signs of depression. This is done through reflection with trusted supporters or on their own. They know that these early warning signs are different for everyone.

Use the following list of common early warning signs to help you discover your own. This list includes my own early warning signs and those that were reported to me by people who took part in my study.

☐ feelings of hopelessness   ☐ feelings of uselessness

☐ feelings of worthlessness   ☐ apathy

☐ feeling unresponsive   ☐ extreme fatigue

☐ lack of motivation   ☐ slow movement

☐ low energy level   ☐ dark, bleak attitude

☐ loneliness   ☐ isolating behaviors

☐ excessive sleep   ☐ insomnia

☐ poor appetite   ☐ excessive eating

☐ chronic sadness   ☐ feeling dead inside

☐ anxiety   ☐ irritability

☐ lack of affect   ☐ low self-esteem

☐ disorganization   ☐ inability to make decisions

☐ chronic aches and pains   ☐ excessive feelings of guilt, embarrassment, or shame

What other feelings or behaviors are depression warning signs for you?

_____

_____

_____

It is very helpful to develop a chart to monitor early warning signs of depression. This allows you to take action before depression worsens and provides a daily record of how you feel. Use the list you have compiled to develop one for yourself. If a symptom or several symptoms recur over several days, respond immediately.

The chart on the next page is a sample composite of the many charting systems that I have reviewed as part of my research. If you feel that this format may also meet your needs, you'll find a blank chart for you to copy at the end of this chapter. Make an ample supply of copies for weekly use and then fill in your own early warning signs.

You may also want to use your chart to keep track of other daily events, such as:

• Days when you ate well (high carbohydrate, low protein and fat)

• Days when you exercised

• Days when you took good care of yourself

• Days when you spent time with supportive people

• Days when you did light therapy

• Days when you checked in with your support system

• Medications that you took

• Other necessary actions that you performed

Over time, I have found that keeping charts helps me to see the cyclical aspects of my depression and depression triggers. You may find that keeping records of your own will offer similar insights. If the format of the sample chart provided doesn't work for you, I urge you to find and use a system that does.

Do you think that using a chart to monitor your moods will be helpful? Why? Or why not?

_____

_____

_____

☐ *I am going to try using a charting system to monitor my early warning signs of depression.*

Take Action

If you note that you are experiencing signs of depression, take action early, before the depression worsens and it becomes harder to prevent. Your symptoms must be taken seriously, especially if they continue for more than several days or occur at regular intervals. Your symptoms can interfere with your personal, family, and work responsibilities, enjoyment of life, and the attainment of life goals. The life-threatening aspect of this condition argues strongly for serious, early intervention. You should also know that 10 percent of people who experience depression end their lives by suicide.

To short-circuit the depression, include activities in your daily schedule that make you feel better. Try one or more of the following:

- taking a walk with a friend
- swimming
- working with clay
- gardening
- dancing

- eating out with a friend
- reading a good book
- listening to favorite music
- journal writing
- playing a musical instrument

Keep your own list of mood-brightening activities posted in a convenient place (such as on the refrigerator). This can help you recall them when you are feeling low. Can you think of any other activities that you enjoy but haven't done for a while?

What activities help you feel better?

_____

_____

_____

Ask for Support

When you start noticing early warning signs of depression, tell your support team members. You may not be able to reach all of them, but be in touch with several at least. Let them know how you feel and what you are doing about it. Ask for their advice. Set up a time when you can get together and talk or share an activity.

Often, after talking and expressing emotion for a half hour or more, the symptoms subside and you are able to return to normal activities. If I notice early warning signs of depression, and a relaxation session or two does not calm me down, I contact a supporter and set up a listening or peer counseling session. I feel much better after venting.

Have your list of support team members and their phone numbers posted in prominent places.

☐ *When I start to notice warning signs of depression, I am going to tell several members of my support team and set up a time when we can talk or share an activity.*

Daily Warning Signs Chart

Warning signs	Mon	Tues	Wed	Thu	Fri	Sat	Sun
Overeating							
Lack of appetite							
Lethargy							
Difficulty exercising							
Fatigue							
Unwillingness to ask for things							
Low self-esteem							
Low self-confidence							
Procrastination							
Avoiding crowds							
Irritability							
Impatience							
Negative attitude							
Insecurity							
Difficulty getting up							
Insomnia							
Poor judgement							
Obsessive thoughts							
Repeating things							
Inability to concentrate							
Destructive risk taking							
Suicidal thoughts							
Paranoia							
Inability to feel pleasure							

Use Self-Help Strategies

Peer counseling. Many people successfully use peer counseling to lessen symptoms of depression. To increase its effectiveness when working to reduce symptoms, have regular peer counseling sessions. (See chapter 11 on "Peer Counseling.")

When you are having early warning signs of depression, include several peer counseling sessions in your daily plans. If your depression has progressed to a more serious stage and you have acute symptoms of depression, continue to peer counsel with supporters.

Relaxation and stress reduction techniques. Use your relaxation and stress reduction activities more often when you begin noticing symptoms of depression. For instance, if you do them after breakfast in the morning and before you go to bed, try to make mid-morning and mid-afternoon time for additional sessions.

Learn these exercises when you are stable, and practice them at least twice a day for ten to thirty minutes, every day. One good way to learn is to take classes at a hospital or health care agency. If such a course if not available, watch one of several instructional videos (many are available at libraries). There are many self-help books that give instructions for relaxation and stress reduction. *The Relaxation and Stress Reduction Workbook* (Davis, Eshelman, and McKay, 1988) is the best resource I have found. Many people use it to respond to early warning signs of depression.

There are also many audio tapes that will guide you through a relaxation exercise. These can be purchased at health food stores and book stores and through many mail order sources.

Alternatively, you can make these tapes for yourself by taping the following relaxation exercise, choosing one from another book, or developing an exercise that feels right for you. When you are beginning to feel signs of depression, you may find it easiest to relax by using an audio tape.

The following exercise will help you focus on body sensations and learn how relaxation feels by progressively relaxing your whole body. Make a tape recording of this exercise so you can use it when you need to. Be sure you leave yourself time on the tape to follow the directions. Do the reading in a relaxed manner. You may want to record some of your favorite music at the beginning and end of the tape.

> *To begin, lie down or sit up in a comfortable position. Make sure you are warm enough, but not too warm, and that you will not be interrupted by the phone, doorbell, or needs of others. Stare at a spot above your head on the ceiling. Then take a deep breath in to a count of eight, hold it for a count of four, let it out for a count of eight. Again—in to a count of eight, hold for a count of four, out for a count of eight. Again—in to a count of eight, hold for a count of four, out for a count of eight. Now close your eyes but keep them in the same position they were in when you were staring at the spot on the ceiling. Breathe in to a count of eight, hold for a count of four, out for a count of eight.*

> *Now focus on your toes. Let them completely relax. Now move the relaxation slowly up your legs, through your heels and calves to your knees. Now let the warm feeling of relaxation move up your thighs. Feel your whole lower body relaxing. Let the relaxation move very slowly through your buttocks, lower abdomen and lower back. Now feel it moving, very slowly, up your spine, one vertebra at a time and through your abdomen. Now feel the warm relaxation flowing into your chest and upper back.*

Let this relaxation flow from your shoulders, down your arms, through your elbows and wrists, out through your hands and fingers. Now let the relaxation go slowly through your throat, and up your neck, letting it all soften and relax. Let it now move up into your face. Feel the relaxation fill your jaw, cheek muscles, and around your eyes. Let it move up into your forehead. Now let your whole scalp relax and feel warm and comfortable. Your body is now completely relaxed with the warm feeling of relaxation filling every muscle and cell of your body.

Now picture yourself walking slowly through a beautiful meadow. It is spring. Birds are singing. The grass is filled with beautiful wildflowers in various shades of red, yellow, and blue. The sky is blue with soft white clouds moving along at a slow pace. You lie down on the grass. It cradles you. You feel warm, safe, secure, and happy.

As you lay here, you realize that you are perfectly and completely relaxed. You feel safe and at peace with the world. You know you have the power to make yourself feel happy any time you need to. You know that by completely relaxing you are giving your body the opportunity to stabilize itself, and that when you wake up you will feel calm, relaxed, happy, and able to get on with your tasks for the day.

Now, slowly wiggle your fingers and toes. Gradually open your eyes and resume your activities.

Have you tried relaxation and stress reduction exercises in the past? Did they help? Why or why not?

_____

_____

_____

☐ *I am going to learn relaxation and stress reduction techniques to help me relieve symptoms of depression.*

☐ *I am going to record relaxation tapes for myself.*

Focusing. Many people use focusing to alleviate symptoms of depression. It helps people understand the source of their feelings, separate themselves from these feelings, develop adequate responses, and create changes in the way they feel. Learn and practice focusing when you are well so you can use it when you are feeling low. (Focusing is described more fully in chapter 12.)

Have you tried focusing? In what ways was it helpful or unhelpful?

_____

_____

_____

☐ *I am going to read the focusing chapter and learn about focusing.*

☐ *I am going to try focusing.*

Journal writing. Many people use journal writing to help them figure out what their triggers are, to identify early warning signs, and to notice seasonal patterns of depressive episodes. Writing down your feelings and details of situations also helps release the surrounding tension and makes you feel better. (For a more complete description of the journaling process, see chapter 13 on "Using Your Journal for Release.")

A study participant said, "I chart my moods by writing in a journal, and from this my therapist and I can locate the patterns and use the therapeutic plan we have negotiated."

Have you tried journaling? In what ways has it been helpful or unhelpful?

_____

_____

_____

☐ *I am going to read the journaling chapter and learn about journaling.*

☐ *I am going to try journaling.*

Address issues related to trauma. A history of trauma or abuse, and the resulting fear and low self-esteem often cause feelings of depression from time to time. This often happens when you least expect it, such as when you are doing well or are very successful. To achieve long-term stability, you must resolve issues related to abuse and trauma. (Refer to chapter 9 on "Resolving Trauma" for more information.)

Do you think that old abuse or trauma issues may have something to do with your current feelings? Why?

_____

_____

_____

☐ *I am going to read the chapter on trauma.*

☐ *I am going to begin addressing my trauma and abuse issues.*

Take good care of yourself. Sometimes early warning signs appear because you are not taking good care of yourself. You need to ask yourself key questions about your personal care. If things are out of order, you need to take steps to rectify the situation. (These issues are addressed in chapter 5 on "Developing a Lifestyle That Enhances Wellness.")

Ask yourself these questions:

☐ Are you eating a diet focused on complex carbohydrates?

☐ Are you getting plenty of light?

☐ Are you getting plenty of exercise?

☐ Are you being exposed to too much electromagnetic radiation (such as too much close work at the computer)?

☐ Is your living space uncomfortable?

☐ Are there difficult issues at work that you need to address?

☐ Do you have health problems that need attention?

If you answered yes to any of these questions, what do you need to do to address these issues?

_____

_____

_____

What else do you need to do to take good care of yourself?

_____

_____

_____

Make copies of the checklist on the next page. When you are experiencing early warning signs of depression, check off each item as you do it. Keep extra copies on hand to use at other times.

Shift to the positive. People who have gotten well and stayed well know how to shift their focus away from negative thoughts and onto positive thoughts. Time spent obsessing about negative thoughts worsens symptoms of depression. Cognitive therapy can assist them in this process.

For instance, a close friend was supposed to call me and let me know what time we were meeting for breakfast. He didn't call when I expected to hear from him, and I started thinking such thoughts as, "He doesn't really care about me." The more I thought about it, the worse I felt. Then I realized that was really foolish. Instead, I called him. He had misunderstood the time I expected to hear from him. No big deal. But I was escalating it into a major production until my good sense, reinforced by cognitive therapy, intervened.

When you begin to feel depressed, you may fear that you will always feel this way. Consciously make it a habit to remind yourself over and over that these feelings will pass and you will feel good again.

Another negative thought that often occurs when you are starting to feel depressed is "No one wants to be bothered supporting me." This negative thought keeps you from reaching out to others when you most need to. Change this thought to "I have a list of people who are glad to support me." It helps to follow this change in thought with an action like "I will look at the list and give several of my supporters a call."

☐ *I am going to refer to the cognitive therapy resources listed at the end of this chapter.*

Daily Checklist

Today, to help maintain my stability, I will:

☐ Eat three healthy meals, focusing on foods that are high in complex carbohydrates.

☐ Avoid sugar, caffeine, alcohol, and junk foods.

☐ Exercise.

☐ Spend time out of doors.

☐ Increase my number of daily relaxation sessions to _____ times.

☐ Practice focusing, doing the exercises _____ times.

☐ Peer counsel for _____ sessions.

☐ Let the following members of my support team know how I am feeling:

_____

_____

_____

☐ Contact the following health care professionals:

_____

_____

_____

☐ Reduce the stress in my environment and avoid stressful situations.

☐ Develop and use a plan for the day.

☐ Do the following activities to make me feel better:

_____

_____

_____

_____

_____

_____

_____

☐ *I am going to learn to change my negative thoughts to positive ones.*

Simplify your day. When you notice early warning signs of depression avoid the following:

- Stressful people

- Stressful situations

- Starting new projects

- Working on difficult assignments

- Listening to sad music

- Reading sad books or articles in the newspaper

I avoid watching the news on television, sad or violent television shows, and reading about tragedies in the newspaper when I am beginning to feel depressed.

What activities should you avoid when you are having early warning signs of depression?

_____

_____

_____

Make a daily plan or a plan for that part of the day which is most difficult for you, such as the evening. You can do this alone or, preferably, with the help of a counselor or supporter. Write down what you plan to do and when. Don't expect too much of yourself. It will help you to stay focused, in control and in charge of your actions, and lessens symptoms.

For instance, you might be able to work from 9 a.m. to 5 p.m. However, if your early warning signs are worse in the morning, you may have to make special plans to get through that hard time. Try having some healthy muffins available for breakfast, or calling a friend first thing in the morning. You may be able to arrange going into work later and leaving later.

If your early warning signs are worse in the evening, be sure you have planned a pleasant activity and time together with supporters to get you through that hard time.

If you are not employed, the day's schedule could be a mix of daily chores and projects to help you feel that you are accomplishing something. Try mixing pleasant activities, such as writing, art or craft activities, and gardening, with self-help activities, such as sessions of relaxation and stress reduction, journaling, focusing, and peer counseling.

If you are employed, you will need to schedule wellness activities during breaks and before and after work.

A woman in the study said:

I alleviate symptoms of depression by keeping structure in my life. I go out to breakfast, lunch, and dinner with friends, I talk about the fact that I feel sad and what I am sad about. It usually is a pretty serious sadness that triggers depression for me.

These are sample plans for persons who are experiencing symptoms of depression.

Daily schedule for a person who is not working

6:30-7 a.m.	Relaxation exercises
7-8 a.m.	Get up, shower, eat (cereal with fruit, herb tea)
8-9 a.m.	Contact support system, arrange people for peer counseling, lunch, and therapy visit, take a walk
9-10 a.m.	Make beds, vacuum, do a load of wash
10-11 a.m.	Peer counseling with close friend
11-12 a.m.	Work on art project
12-1 noon	Lunch with close friend
1-2 p.m.	Walking
2-3 p.m.	Counseling appointment
3-4 p.m.	Errands (groceries, renew prescription at drug store, library, video store)
4-5 p.m.	Relaxation exercises
5-6 p.m.	Prepare dinner, eat
6-7 p.m.	Peer counseling
7-9 p.m.	Watch video with family member
9-10 p.m.	Read light novel

Daily schedule for a person who is working

6:30-7 a.m.	Relaxation exercises
7-8 a.m.	Get up, shower, dress, eat breakfast (bagel with cream cheese, herb tea)
8-8:45 a.m.	Contact supporters for lunch and evening
8:45-9 a.m.	Drive to work
9-10:15 a.m.	Work
10:15-10:30 a.m.	Break, relaxation techniques
10:30-12	Work
12-1 noon	Lunch and walk with member of support team
1-2:30 p.m.	Work
2:30-2:45 p.m.	Break, relaxation techniques
2:45-5 p.m.	Work

5-6 p.m.	Counseling appointment
6-8 p.m.	Dinner out with a member of support team followed by peer counseling
8-10 p.m.	Watch light video

If You Have an Episode

Despite your best efforts, you may become more deeply depressed. Don't consider this a failure. Don't be hard on yourself. Use the episode as a learning experience and keep track of those strategies that were and were not successful for future use. When you are feeling better, review problem areas and decide how you would address them differently at another time. Keep track of your episodes to see if the time between episodes is lengthening. Give yourself credit for your efforts, even if they were not totally successful. Give yourself credit for the times when you have maintained your stability, too. Don't allow yourself to get too discouraged. Focus on the positive instead of the negative.

Here are some ideas from study participants:

I take frequent naps or "little rests" during the day. These "time-outs" can also be spent listening to music and/or reading. This is a good way to pick up a little energy.

I watch myself carefully. If I get sad and sense that I am spiraling downward to depression, I fight to keep structure in my life. Depending on the event, I may give myself permission to be sad for a period of time. After that I have to come out of it. Usually I don't nap, but if I feel sad and feel I need one, I give myself permission to take a nap.

I try something like watching a funny video, riding in the car, getting more sleep, trying to pinpoint the cause, and reducing the stress in my life. If that doesn't work, I call my doctor.

I talk to my counselor if possible. I try to figure out if these feelings are situational or biochemical. I talk to my husband about feelings, I journal, and I stay as active as I can.

I reduce these symptoms by pushing myself every day. I keep doing one task at a time. I don't stay in bed. I get up and get going.

Resources

Copeland, M. E. (1992) *The Depression Workbook: A Guide for Living With Depression and Manic Depression.* Oakland, CA: New Harbinger Publications.
This book contains additional information on some of the self-help strategies described in this chapter including developing a support system, relaxation and stress reduction exercises, charting, diet, light, exercise, and changing negative thoughts to positive ones.

Davis, M., E. Eshelman, and M. McKay (1988) *The Relaxation & Stress Reduction Workbook.* 3rd ed. Oakland, CA: New Harbinger Publications.

This book is an excellent resource for learning stress reduction and relaxation techniques. It is popular with study participants.

Cognitive Therapy

Burns, D. (1980) *Feeling Good*. New York: W. Morrow.
This popular book has been used successfully by many study participants to effectively change negative thought patterns to positive ones.

Burns, D. (1989) *The Feeling Good Handbook*. New York: W. Morrow.
This book was written as a workbook-style follow-up to Burns' earlier work, Feeling Good.

McKay, M., M. Davis, and P. Fanning (1981) *Thoughts and Feelings: The Art of Cognitive Stress Intervention*. Oakland, CA: New Harbinger Publications.
This book is highly recommended as a starting point when beginning intensive work on changing negative thoughts to positive ones. It is widely used by support groups and individuals.

Audio Tape

Copeland, M. (1993) *Living With Depression and Manic Depression*. Oakland, CA: New Harbinger Publications.
A summary of self-help techniques as a reminder or for easy use when reading is not an option.

Preston, J. (1993) *Depression and Anxiety Management*. Oakland, CA: New Harbinger Publications.
A useful self-help tool for reducing symptoms of depression and accompanying anxiety.

Video Tape

Copeland, M., and W. Hood (1993) *Coping With Depression*. Oakland, CA: New Harbinger Publications.
This video will assist you in implementing suggested self-help strategies in your life.

Daily Warning Signs Chart

Warning signs	Mon	Tues	Wed	Thu	Fri	Sat	Sun
What to do everyday							
Medications taken							
Necessary actions							

17

Preventing Mania

I never want to be manic again—never.

Mania is at the opposite end of the mood swing pendulum from the depression that is experienced in what is commonly known as manic depression or bipolar disorder. Manic depression is characterized by recurring, alternating, but not usually predictable cycles of severe mania and depression. Although it is not common, occasionally people report that they experience episodes of mania without alternating episodes of depression.

This description was written by a person who experienced mania:

> I couldn't stop—moving, talking, doing, thinking. I wanted to rest but my body wouldn't let me. Firecrackers were going off in my brain. My bizarre actions—I didn't know they were bizarre—embarrassed my family and got me in serious trouble. I thought I could do anything. I spent money recklessly, money I didn't have. Everyone else seemed boring. I thought I knew everything. I felt so strong and creative. It seemed like fun then but now it seems like a horror story. I'm so ashamed, I can't face anyone.

The *Diagnostic and Statistical Manual of Mental Disorders* (DSM-III-R) describes a manic episode as:

> . . . a distinct period during which the predominant mood is either elevated, expansive, or irritable, and there are associated symptoms of the manic syndrome. The disturbance is sufficiently severe to cause marked impairment in occupational functioning or in usual social activities or relationships with others, or to require hospitalization to prevent harm to self or others. The associated symptoms include inflated self-esteem or grandiosity (which may be delusional), decreased need for sleep, pressure of speech, flight of ideas, distractibility, increased involvement in goal-directed activity, psychomotor agitation, and

excessive involvement in pleasurable activities which have a high potential for painful consequences that the person often does not recognize.

Symptoms of mania that are interfering with normal functioning need to be addressed and minimized safely and quickly. How to do this is the basis of the discussion in the next chapter, "Responding To Symptoms of Mania."

Most people who have experienced mania report that it can be enjoyable, especially in the early stages. This makes it difficult to use strategies known to keep the mania from building and getting out of control.

Mania tends to be an addictive phenomena for the following reasons:

1. In the early stages, it feels great!

2. You get things done and feel good (sometimes inappropriately) about the job you are doing.

3. You feel very powerful and superior to everyone else (for a change).

4. You may be coming out of a long, deep depression and are so relieved that you don't want to do anything that might interfere with recovery or cause a return to the depression.

5. You may be plagued by low self-esteem and lack of self-confidence when you are stable. These feelings tend to be even worse when you are depressed. Mania changes that. Finally you feel good about yourself and confident enough to do anything. That feels great and you don't want to interfere with that wonderful feeling.

As people who experience mania know, when you start getting higher and higher, you do whatever you can to increase those good feelings rather than putting on the brakes. It often gets out of control before you can do anything about it.

What difficulties have you had in intercepting or trying to stop your manic episodes?

_____

_____

_____

I am still picking up the pieces from a severe, prolonged manic episode six years ago, paying back bills and writing letters of apology as new information on that infamous episode comes to light. During that episode, I sent condemning letters to family members and bought antiques and clothes I didn't need and didn't even like. I confronted people inappropriately. I drove my car recklessly, endangering others and myself. I made bad decisions on my own behalf.

I have experienced extreme mania that included delusions, hallucinations, reckless behavior, violation of close relations, overspending, making a fool of myself in public, inappropriate outbursts, and the inability to sleep for long periods of time. The end result was physical debilitation and pain, emotional pain, confusion, severed relationships, embarrassment, guilt, loss of credibility, and depleted finances. I **never** want this to happen again.

I think it has been easier for me to put the brakes on mania because, as a child, I was witness to my mother's severe mania many times and for long periods of time. Her episodes, and the episodes of other people in the hospital with her, were terrifying to me. In their presence, I felt totally alone and unsafe. Their bizarre behavior embarrassed and humiliated me. I vowed that I would never behave that way, but I have.

The following is a list of reasons why people who have experienced mania **never** want to have another episode. Which ones are true for you?

- ☐ I make a fool of myself.
- ☐ I embarrass myself.
- ☐ I violate sacred relationships.
- ☐ I damage and end important relationships.
- ☐ I damage and destroy my credibility.
- ☐ I cause havoc for people, inappropriately interfering with their lives.
- ☐ I make it hard on my family and other people around me.
- ☐ People get sick of me.
- ☐ I risk my life and the lives of others.
- ☐ Others have to take over my responsibilities and care.
- ☐ I don't take good care of myself physically or emotionally.
- ☐ I cause damage to myself and others that, in some cases, can not be undone.
- ☐ My ideas are so outlandish, they cannot bear fruit.
- ☐ My thoughts and goals are inconsistent.
- ☐ I unknowingly become my own worst enemy.
- ☐ I spend money I don't have, buying lots of things I don't need or want, and have to pay it back later.
- ☐ I leave a trail of destruction and devastation in my wake.
- ☐ I don't want to spend my life this way.
- ☐ The psychosis is dangerous and scary.
- ☐ My public displays of inappropriate and bizarre behavior close doors of opportunity.
- ☐ Hospitalizations and use of extreme medical and control interventions become necessary for my protection or the protection of others.
- ☐ My behavior is obnoxious. I may be rude, argumentative, unreasonable, grandiose, inconsistent, and impatient.
- ☐ I become resistant to or avoid using strategies that might help reduce symptoms and become angry and defensive when confronted about behaviors that might indicate that I need help.

List other reasons you never want to get manic again.

_____

_____

_____

In order to stop the upward spiral, you have to make a serious commitment to yourself that no matter how good it makes you feel at the moment, you never want to get manic again. This is your personal responsibility. No one else can do it for you.

Fill in your name on the following statement. Then list the key reasons why you never want to get manic again. Make several copies. Post them in obvious places around your home. When you are tempted to let the mania take its course, these warning signs will remind you of your commitment to yourself.

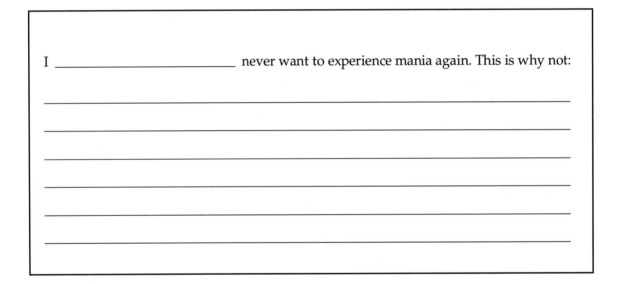

I _____ never want to experience mania again. This is why not:

Treating Each Episode as a Learning Experience

Now that you have decided that you never want to have another manic episode, you may find that you are not be able to intercept impending episodes. Don't give yourself a hard time. Do the best you can. A good first step is bringing yourself to an awareness of how you feel and taking whatever control you can, instead of just letting mania happen to you.

Look at each episode as a learning experience which contains information that will help you better avert or manage the next episode. If you can, write down anything that helps to stabilize you and anything that is making your condition worse. Learn from each episode about how to get more and more control. You will find that you will handle each episode better.

If you can't write things down during the episode, write down your recollections afterward.

☐   *If I have an episode, I will try to keep track of those strategies or activities that make me feel better and those that make my mania worse. If I can't write them down during the episode, I will write them down afterward.*

Notice the word "try." You may not always find it possible to follow through on this commitment. But writing and sharing your findings will improve your ability to recall these strategies and activities when you need to. Review what you have written from time to time so it will be easier to recall when you need to. Talk to your counselor and support people about what you have learned.

The record on the next page may help you with this. Make several copies so you will have them on hand in case you need them.

Prevention Involves Planning Ahead

When you have experienced one or more episodes of mania, it is essential to make plans and decisions about what action to take and what treatment to initiate if you have another episode and become unable to make decisions for yourself.

A woman who is trying to prevent future episodes of mania said, "Keeping on top of this feels like I have another job, constantly monitoring myself."

Steps to preventing mania:

☐   Define your early warning signs of mania and take preventive action early. (See chapter 18 on "Responding to Symptoms of Mania.")

☐   Take a conservative approach. Remember that there is often only a narrow window of opportunity when you can take action to avoid mania. Don't wait. Start protective intervention even if you are not sure you are getting manic.

☐   Develop a support team that includes trusted family members and friends and health care professionals who are responsible for giving you treatment information and advice for monitoring your condition and treating it. All these people will help you monitor your symptoms, support and advise you as necessary, make decisions for you when you cannot make them for yourself, and enrich your life experience. (See chapter 2 on "Creating a Support Network" for information on how to set up a support team.)

Who are the members of your support team?

_____

_____

_____

_____

_____

What I Learned From a Manic Episode

Dates of Episode: _____

Strategies and activities that helped reduce my manic symptoms:

_____
_____
_____
_____
_____
_____
_____
_____
_____
_____
_____

Strategies and activities that worsened my symptoms:

_____
_____
_____
_____
_____
_____
_____
_____
_____
_____
_____

☐ Have a complete physical examination to see if there are any physical problems that may be causing or aggravating the symptoms of mania. Review chapter 3 on "Eliminating the Physical Causes of Mood Disorders" and follow through with any necessary treatments.

What health care treatments are necessary to control your mania and ensure your wellness?

_____

_____

_____

☐ Consult with a health care professional who has expertise in treating mania and ask for advice on treatment scenarios. Explore these options thoroughly. Based on what you have learned, and with the assistance of health care professionals, begin whatever treatment you decide is in your best interest. You may find that certain treatments would only be initiated in the event that your mania is severe. You may find that there are some treatments you would not want under any circumstances. You have that right!

Which treatments have you decided to use? Why?

_____

_____

_____

_____

_____

Which treatments may be initiated if your mania is severe and you cannot make decisions for yourself? Why?

_____

_____

_____

Which treatments are not to be used under any circumstance? Why?

_____

_____

_____

☐ Explore with health care professionals, supporters, health care organizations, and other people who have experienced mania possible facilities where you would be safe and receive appropriate treatment if your symptoms of mania are out of control, you feel unsafe, or your condition needs to be monitored. If you have been hospitalized in the past, you may already have firsthand information.

Which facilities do you prefer and why?

_____

_____

_____

Which facilities are unacceptable? Why?

_____

_____

_____

☐ Develop a plan of action to be taken in your behalf when you cannot take action or make decisions in your own behalf.

Based on what you have learned through the educational process, decisions can be made in advance about such issues as the kinds of treatment that are and are not acceptable, under what conditions acceptable treatments may be used, health care professionals that can be included in the decision-making process, and health care facilities that are acceptable and those that are not. A trusted person or persons can be given durable power of attorney to make decisions. A legal document can be drawn up which defines the conditions under which the person or persons who have durable power of attorney have the right to make decisions and carry out wishes. Refer to chapter 1 on "How To Advocate Effectively for Yourself" and the end of this chapter for information on setting up such a document.

The key step is making a commitment to yourself that you will do whatever you have to do to prevent mania. This includes having, in writing, a clear plan of action you will take if you have signs of mania. It will spell out the actions you want others to take in your behalf if the mania gets out of control, who will make decisions, and under what circumstances they have your permission to make decisions for you.

Plan To Avoid Mania

The following is my plan for preventing mania. It includes action that I want taken on my behalf if my symptoms get worse. Be aware that I am listing my personal warning signs and that your own are likely to be different.

Plan To Avoid Mania and
Mania Treatment Preference Document

I, *Mary Ellen Copeland*, never, under any circumstances, want to get manic again. Therefore, when I become aware of the following early warning signs of mania, including:

> *I have racing thoughts; I move fast; I have difficulty relaxing; I feel overexuberant; I am inappropriately irritable; I feel confrontational; I sleep less than three hours a night*

I will take the following preventive actions:

> *let a supporter know how I am feeling and what I am going to do about it; increase my relaxation sessions to five times a day; do focusing exercises at least three times a day; avoid contra dancing and other strenuous exercise; avoid overstimulating activities, such as meetings or movies on controversial topics; avoid people whom I find irritating; avoid caffeine, sugar, and junk food; eat a complex carbohydrate snack before going to bed; go to bed at my usual time, even if I don't feel tired; avoid making any major decisions; stay home and get involved in quiet activity as much as possible; have a daily massage.*

If the mania continues to worsen, which means:

> *I am spending large amounts of money recklessly; I am inappropriately confronting and badgering people; I am driving carelessly and too fast; I am making a fool of myself; I am not sleeping; I am making rash decisions; my behavior is clearly bizarre*

I give the following people:

> *Iva Wood, Thomas Smith, Nancy Smith, Patti Smith, Jerry Smith, and John Smith*

authority to confer with my health care professionals:

> *My counselor, Karen Kamenetsky; my physician, Dr. John Glick; and my naturopathic physician, Dr. Connie Hernandez*

and, based on their professional recommendations, authority to take any of the following preventive or protective actions they feel necessary:

Any action agreed on by at least three of my children and one of my health care professionals, including confiscating my car keys and my car; confiscating my money, credit cards, and checkbook; and committing me to a major medical facility to begin treatment.

I am willing to take the following medications:

Tegretol, because I have used it in the past and it helped; or Valproate, which I have not used but I understand that it works well.

The following medications are unacceptable:

Lithium, because I have an allergic reaction to it; or neuroleptics, which have severe side effects.

I prefer to be admitted to the following facility:

Dartmouth Medical Center, which can best meet my medical and psychiatric care needs.

I am willing to be admitted to the following facilities (in order of preference):

Vermont Medical Center, because others have said it is good, and Brattleboro Retreat or Cheshire Medical Center, which both have convenient, appropriate services.

My attorney: *Jean Giddings*

Signature: *Mary Ellen Copeland*   Date: *March 28, 1994*

Plan To Prevent Mania and
Mania Treatment Preference Document

I, _____ , never, under any circumstances, want to get manic again. Therefore, when I become aware of the following early warning signs of mania, including:

_____

_____

_____

_____

I will take the following preventive actions:

_____

_____

_____

_____

If the mania continues to worsen, which means:

_____

_____

_____

I give the following people:

_____

_____

_____

authority to confer with my health care professionals:

_____

_____

_____

and, based on their professional recommendations, authority to take any of the following preventive or protective actions they feel necessary:

_____

_____

_____

I am willing to take the following medications:

_____

_____

_____

The following medications are unacceptable:

_____

_____

_____

I prefer to be admitted to the following facility:

_____

I am willing to be admitted to the following facilities (in order of preference):

_____

_____

_____

_____

My attorney: _____

Signature: _____ Date: _____

Resources

Copeland, M. (1992) *The Depression Workbook: A Guide for Living With Depression and Manic Depression.* Oakland, CA: New Harbinger Publications.
A workbook-style compilation of self-help coping strategies and ideas from 120 people who experience either depressive or manic-depressive symptoms.

Davis, M., E. R. Eshelman, and M. McKay (1988) *The Relaxation & Stress Reduction Workbook.* 3rd ed. Oakland, CA: New Harbinger Publications.

Audio Tape

Copeland, M. E. (1993) *Living With Depression and Manic Depression.* Oakland, CA: New Harbinger Publications.
A summary of self-help techniques. You can use these as a reminder or when reading is not an option.

Technical References

American Psychiatric Association, Williams, J., Ed. (1987) *Diagnostic and Statistical Manual of Mental Disorders.* Washington, DC: American Psychiatric Association.
This is a reference manual of symptoms that an extensive panel of medical practitioners have determined to be descriptive of various mental disorders.

Goodwin, F., and K. Jamison (1990) *Manic-Depressive Illness.* New York: Oxford University Press.
This book provides extensive information on every aspect of manic depression from a medical perspective.

18

Responding to Symptoms of Mania

I feel like I am always on guard. When I notice I am starting to have symptoms of mania, I know I have to take action right away.

Individuals who have experienced mania, and who have successfully maintained long-term stability, have learned how to respond to early symptoms of mania to keep the mania from escalating into a full-blown episode. This chapter describes those strategies and techniques used successfully by people who have gotten well and stayed well for long periods of time.

Responding to Triggers

Most of the people in my studies can identify a specific event or series of events that have triggered symptoms of mania or manic episodes. While it is not always easy to identify such triggers, education and awareness help.

It is common to feel very stressed and overwhelmed by your current circumstances. Some of these triggers are the same as those listed in chapter 16 on "Responding to Symptoms of Depression." You might assume that most of these triggers would lead to depression, but this is not always the case. Sometimes the body responds by going into persistent overdrive.

Mania triggers reported by study participants include:

- *A sudden unexpected change in your circumstance,* such as the loss of a loved one, rejection, a house fire, losing a job, a business failure, a new relationship. A man in the study was laid off when his company lost most of its business. He began talking incessantly to others, telling them that he had anticipated the layoff, and that it was a wonderful thing. As he became more and more hyperactive, he realized that the depression he had anticipated was not happening and that his symptoms of mania needed to be controlled.

- *Having too much to do.* Several people said that they had experienced their first episode of mania in college during examination periods, when they were responsible for an overwhelming amount of course work.

- *Excessive stimulation* such as traveling in an unfamiliar place, certain parties, spending time in bars, attending meetings where emotional and controversial topics are discussed, or working on a political campaign.

- *Unusual strenuous activity for an extended period,* especially in hot weather, such as spending the summer working on a fishing boat or harvesting crops.

- *Anniversaries or reminders of traumatic events.* This might include things such as seeing a car the same color as the one in which you had an accident, seeing a quilt that is the same as the one on the bed when you were abused, or the anniversary of the death of a parent.

- *A change in daily routine that interrupts eating, sleeping, and activity patterns,* such as being stranded in an unfamiliar place, having a new baby, or going away to school.

- *Seasonal change.* Some people in my study said they notice that there is a seasonal pattern to the symptoms of mania. Most often they occur in spring, with summer being second, and fall third. Only a few people said they had experienced mania in the winter. It is helpful to be more vigilant during high-risk seasons by increasing the use of wellness and self-help strategies.

- *Some antidepressant medications,* when these are taken in addition to a mood stabilizing medication. For this reason, be honest with health care professionals about previous episodes and family history so they can prescribe medications accordingly.

What events, situations, or circumstances do you feel may have triggered mania?

_____

_____

_____

How To Prevent an Episode of Mania

Many of the things you do to avoid mania are similar to, or the same as, the things you do to avoid depression. This may be difficult to understand, but the same events can trigger such different reactions. Here's how to respond:

1. Be aware of events that have the potential for triggering mania and your early warning signs.

2. With the assistance of a supporter, or by yourself if necessary, try to get a handle on what is happening. Ask yourself:

   - Is there anything I can do to improve the situation?

- What can I do about this situation?
- What action do I need to take to protect myself?
- What is the worst thing that can happen?
- What will make me feel better?

For example, in the aftermath of a natural disaster such as an earthquake, there may be more to do than you feel you can deal with. Sit down with someone else and plan carefully what you are going to do. If your home is unsafe, where can you live? Who should you contact about safe housing? What do you need to do to protect your belongings in the interim? The worst thing that could happen is that you could be hurt in an aftershock or lose a loved one. What can you do now to protect yourself and those you are responsible for? What will make you feel better? How about finding a place to take a shower, or getting a good meal at a crisis center, and then finding a place where you can safely let out all your emotions and frustrations?

Monitor Your Symptoms

If you experience mania, you must be vigilant about watching for early signs of mania, (although not so vigilant that your watching gets in the way of a normal life). You must also learn what your own early warning signs are. These differ for everyone.

Here are the early warning signs of mania reported to me by people who took part in my study. Which are early warning signs for you?

☐	insomnia	☐	sleeping much less than usual
☐	surges of energy	☐	others seem to be in slow motion
☐	flight of ideas	☐	speech or writing pressure
☐	making lots of plans	☐	irritability
☐	inappropriate anger	☐	spending too much money
☐	money losing its value	☐	making unnecessary phone calls
☐	restlessness	☐	hyperactivity
☐	loss of appetite	☐	increased appetite
☐	compulsive eating	☐	euphoria
☐	feeling superior	☐	obsessing
☐	over ambitiousness	☐	unusual bursts of enthusiasm
☐	taking on too much responsibility	☐	doing several things at once
☐	feeling nervous and wound up	☐	anxiousness
☐	inability to concentrate	☐	self-involvement
☐	outbursts of temper	☐	disorganization
☐	feeling of being unreal	☐	oversensitivity

☐ noises sound louder than usual ☐ experiencing bizarre ideas and thoughts

☐ inappropriate behavior ☐ poor judgment

☐ thrill-seeking ☐ oblivious to surroundings

☐ increased sexual activity ☐ increased alcohol or tobacco use

☐ negligent driving ☐ spotless, energetic housekeeping

☐ itching ☐ tingly feeling

☐ flushed and hot ☐ compulsiveness

☐ friends notice behavior change ☐ intense agitation

What other feelings or behaviors are mania warning signs for you?

_____

_____

_____

Caution: If you checked off insomnia or intense agitation, see a health care professional immediately.

Many people have developed charts to help them monitor early warning signs of an impending manic episode. This allows them to take action before the situation gets out of control and provides a daily record of how they feel. If a symptom recurs over several days, they know that evasive action is in order.

The chart on the next page is a sample composite of the many charting systems that I have reviewed as part of my research. If you feel that this format may also meet your needs, you'll find a blank chart for you to copy at the end of this chapter. Make an ample supply of copies for weekly use and then fill in your own early warning signs.

You may also want to use your chart to keep track of other daily events, such as:

- Days when you ate well (high carbohydrate, low protein and fat)

- Days when you exercised

- Days when you took good care of yourself

- Days when you spent time with supportive people

- Days when you checked in with your support system

- Medications that you took

- Appointments with health care professionals

- Other necessary actions that you performed

Over time, I have found that keeping charts provides a valuable record for me, my doctor, and my counselors in determining appropriate strategies and treatments. If the format of the sample chart provided doesn't work for you, I urge you to find and use a system that does.

Daily Warning Signs Chart

Warning signs	Mon	Tues	Wed	Thu	Fri	Sat	Sun
Insomnia							
Restlessness							
Hyperactivity							
Obsessiveness							
Irritability							
Tingly feeling							
Disorganization							
Poor judgment							
Loss of appetite							
Thrill seeking							
Overspending							
Pressured speech							
Racing thoughts							

Do you think that using a chart to monitor your moods will be helpful? Why? Or why not?

_____

_____

_____

☐ *I am going to try using a charting system to monitor my early warning signs of mania.*

Take Action

If you find yourself experiencing signs of mania that are rather intense for one day or milder over a period of several days, take action. Follow these steps:

- If you are not sleeping, are agitated, or are very uncomfortable with how you feel, insist on an emergency visit with a health care professional.

- Get in touch with health care providers and support team members. Let them know what is happening, ask for advice, and set up appointments and meetings.

Sometimes, just involving yourself in an activity that you have identified as calming will help. The following are activities that people, including myself, have used. Check off the ones that you think might work for you.

- doing mild exercise (any kind of exercise done slowly and thoughtfully)

- doing yoga

- reading for pleasure

- listening to classical or slow music

- taking long, slow, warm baths, hot tubs, or saunas

- gardening

- doing various crafts such as needlework, woodwork, pottery, drawing, or painting

- writing in a journal and other kinds of pleasurable writing

- relaxing in a meditative natural setting

- playing a musical instrument

What other activities help you feel more calm and relaxed?

_____

_____

_____

Post a list of the activities that make you feel calm in a convenient place, such as the refrigerator door. This can help you recall them when you are experiencing symptoms of mania.

Reach Out for Support

You need a strong, consistent support system comprised of at least five people who are knowledgeable about mood disorders to help you respond appropriately to symptoms of mania. These five (more, preferably) should be willing to work with you, monitor your symptoms, provide feedback, assist you in decision making, offer advice, and listen without judgment or criticism. Choose wisely. Your counselor may be able to help you with this. (Refer to chapter 2 on "Creating a Support Network" for more information.) Again, make a list of your supporters and their phone numbers and post it in a prominent place.

When you start noticing early warning signs of mania, tell your support team members. You may not be able to reach all of them, but be in touch with several at least. Let them know how you feel and what you are doing about the way you feel. Ask them if they have any advice. Set up a time when you can meet to talk or share an activity.

☐   *When I start to notice warning signs of mania, I am going to tell several members of my support team and set up a time when we can talk or share an activity.*

The most important thing your supporters can do for you is listen. It is not unusual, and in fact is quite understandable, for supporters to feel stymied, like there is nothing they can do to improve the situation. There is. Ask them simply to listen. It doesn't matter what you are saying. You don't have to make sense. You just need to get it all outside of yourself. Supporters can interject comments like "I'm sorry you feel that way" or "I hear what you are saying" to let you know they are paying attention. Tell them not to give any advice unless you ask for it. They should just let you spout off, without telling you that you are wrong.

Use Self-Help Strategies

Peer counseling. Let out all your feelings in a safe place. Is there someplace you can go with a trusted supporter and scream, cry, swear, yell—whatever you feel like doing for as long as you need? You may need to do this many times before you feel you have eliminated symptoms. (See chapter 11 on "Peer Counseling" for more information on this technique.) Peer counseling has been used successfully to lessen symptoms of mania and avoid episodes.

When you notice symptoms of mania, include several peer counseling sessions in your daily plans. If your mania has progressed to a more serious stage and you have acute symptoms of mania, continue to peer counsel with supporters who are not "put off" by your symptoms.

People who have contacted a supporter and done peer counseling when they were noticing early warning signs of mania found that after talking and expressing emotion for a half hour or more the symptoms subsided and they were able to return to their normal activities. If I am noticing early warning signs of mania and a relaxation session or two does not calm me down, I contact a supporter and set up a listening or peer counseling session. I feel much better after venting.

I was listening to a man whose symptoms of mania were beginning to escalate. I told him I had half an hour to listen. During that time, he talked, cried, and expressed anger. The more he expressed the anger, the calmer he became. At the end of the half-hour, he was calm enough to realize that his behavior was getting out of control (which would have been impossible for him at the beginning of the conversation) and he was able to make some good decisions about how he could help himself.

Relaxation and stress reduction techniques. Practicing relaxation and stress reduction techniques twice a day for ten to thirty minutes per session is part of the daily routine for people who have learned to keep mania at bay. Many have found that the exercises really do help interrupt and eliminate symptoms of mania. One man in my study told how relaxation exercises help him:

The thing that helps me when I am high is relaxation exercises. I need to control my high because what goes up must come down and I don't want to be depressed. When I am stressed out, I do relaxation exercises four or five times a day. Normally I do it twice a day.

When you first notice early warning signs of mania, increase the number of relaxation sessions you do in a day.

The time to learn these exercises is when you are feeling well. You cannot learn them when you are already experiencing symptoms.

Relaxation and stress reduction exercises can be learned at classes sponsored by health care professionals, agencies, or hospitals. Many of these courses are offered free of charge. If such a course is not available in your area, or if the cost is prohibitive, get an instructional video or audio tapes. (Many such tapes are available at libraries.) There are also many self-help books that include instructions for relaxation and stress reduction. *The Relaxation and Stress Reduction Workbook* (Davis, Eshelman, and McKay, 1988) is the best one I have found.

You can make relaxation tapes by taping the following relaxation exercise, or one from another resource book or by developing an exercise that feels right to you.

Many people notice that when they first begin to have symptoms of mania, it is difficult to do these exercises. An audio tape that guides you through the steps works well in these situations.

I have used the relaxation exercise below to reduce symptoms of mania. It can help you focus on body sensations and relax by systematically tensing and then relaxing muscle groups in your body. Make a tape recording of this exercise so you can use it when you need it. As you record it, be sure that you leave yourself enough time to tense and relax your muscles. Read the instructions very slowly. Before you begin, find a quiet space where you will not be disturbed. You may either lie on your back or sit in a chair, as long as you are comfortable. Then close your eyes.

Let yourself begin to relax completely . . . First, clench your right fist as tightly as you can . . . Be aware of the tension as you do so . . . Keep it clenched for a moment . . . Now relax . . . Feel the looseness in your right hand and compare it to the tension you felt previously . . . Tense your right fist again, then relax it and again, notice the difference . . . Now clench your left fist as tightly as you can . . . Be aware of the tension as you do so . . . Keep it clenched for a moment . . . Now relax . . . Feel the looseness in your left hand and compare it to the tension you felt previously . . . Tense your left fist again, relax it, and again notice the difference.

Bend your elbows and tense your biceps as hard as you can. Notice the feeling of tightness. Relax and straighten out your arms. Let the relaxation flow through your arms and compare it to the tightness you felt previously. Tense and relax your biceps again.

Wrinkle your forehead as tightly as you can. Now relax it and let it smooth out. Feel your forehead and scalp become relaxed. Now frown and notice the tension spreading through your forehead again. Relax and allow your forehead to become smooth.

Close your eyes now and squint them very tightly. Feel the tension. Now relax your eyes. Tense and relax your eyes again. Now let them remain gently closed. Now clench your jaw, bite hard and feel the tension through your jaw. Now relax your jaw. Your lips will part slightly. Notice the difference. Clench and relax again. Press your tongue against the roof of your mouth. Now relax. Do this again. Press and purse your lips together. Now relax them. Tense again and relax. Feel the relaxation throughout your forehead, scalp, eyes, jaw, tongue, and lips.

Hold your head back as far as it can comfortably go and observe the tightness in your neck. Roll it to the right and notice how the tension moves and changes. Roll your head to the left and notice how the tension moves and changes. Now straighten your head and bring it forward, pressing your chin against your chest. Notice the tension in your throat and the back of your neck. Now relax and allow your shoulders to return to a comfortable position. Allow yourself to feel more and more relaxed. Now shrug your shoulders and hunch your head down between them. Relax your shoulders. Allow them to drop back and feel the relaxation moving through your neck, throat, and shoulders; feel the lovely, very deep relaxation.

Give your whole body a chance to relax. Feel how comfortable and heavy it is.

Now breathe in and fill your lungs completely. Hold your breath and notice the tension. Now let your breath out and let your chest become loose. Continue relaxing, breathing gently in and out. Repeat this breathing several times and notice the tension draining out of your body. Tighten your stomach and hold the tightness. Feel the tension. Now relax your stomach. Now place your hand on your stomach. Breathe deeply into your stomach, pushing your hand up. Hold for a moment and then relax. Now arch your back without straining, keeping the rest of your body as relaxed as possible. Notice the tension in your lower back. Now relax deeper and deeper. Tighten your buttocks and thighs. Flex your thighs by pressing your heels down as hard as you can. Now relax and notice the difference. Do this again. Now curl your toes down, making your calves tense. Notice the tension. Now relax. Bend your toes toward your face, creating tension in your shins. Relax and notice the difference.

Feel the heaviness throughout your lower body as the relaxation gets deeper and deeper. Relax your feet, ankles, calves, shins, knees, thighs, and buttocks. Now let the relaxation spread to your stomach, lower back, and chest. Let go more and more. Experience deeper and deeper relaxation in your shoulders, arms, and hands. Let go at deeper and deeper levels. Notice the feeling of looseness and relaxation in your neck, jaws, and all your facial muscles.

Now picture yourself walking in the sand on the beach on a sunny day. As you stroll along, feel the warmth of the sun on your back. Lie down on the sand. Let it cradle you. Feel how warm and comfortable it is on your back. The sun warms your body. You hear the waves crashing against the shore in a steady rhythm. The sound of sea gulls calling overhead adds to your feeling of blissful contentment.

As you rest here, you realize that you are perfectly and completely relaxed. You feel safe and at peace with the world. You know you have the power to relax yourself completely at any time you need to. You know that by completely relaxing, you are giving your body the opportunity to stabilize itself, and that when you wake up, you will feel calm, relaxed, and able to get on with your daily activities in a calm, relaxed manner.

Enjoy the feeling of complete relaxation for a few minutes. (Extended pause.)

Now, slowly wiggle your fingers and toes. Gradually open your eyes and resume your activities.

Have you tried relaxation and stress reduction exercises in the past? Did they help? Why or why not?

_____

_____

_____

☐ *I am going to learn relaxation and stress reduction techniques to help me relieve symptoms of mania.*

☐ *I am going to record relaxation tapes for myself.*

Plan your day. If you make a plan for the day or that part of the day which is most difficult, it will help you to stay focused and in control. Let a supporter or counselor help you with this.

For instance, you may be able to work very effectively from 9:00 a.m. to 5:00 p.m. if your symptoms of mania tend to accelerate later in the day. From 5:00 p.m. to 6:00 p.m. you might take a walk with a family member or supporter. From 6:00 p.m. to 7:00 p.m. you could have dinner with another supporter, followed by a one-hour peer counseling session from 7:00 p.m. to 8:00 p.m. From 8:00 p.m. to 10:00 p.m. you might watch a video with a supporter. You could then follow this with a 30-minute session of relaxation exercises to help you get to sleep. If you are not working, the day's schedule could be filled with a variety of calming, low-key activities such as writing, art or craft activities, household chores, and gardening. Be sure to include stress reduction sessions, journaling, focusing, and peer counseling.

Deal with medication issues. Many people who have recurring episodes of mania use prescription mood stabilizing medications such as lithium (Lithane, Eskalith); carbamazepine (Tegretol); or valproic acid/valproate (Depakene/Depakote) to help avoid manic episodes.

Let counselors and supporters know what medications you are taking. The more they know about your medications and medication side effects, the more helpful they can be. Share the medication information sheet that you had your doctor fill out. Give them a copy for their file. This helps to assure that you will get appropriate treatment in case of a crisis.

What strategies are you going to use to make yourself aware of events and activities that are triggering episodes?

_____

_____

_____

What else do you think would help you avoid an episode when you are "triggered" unexpectedly?

_____

_____

_____

Make copies of the checklist on the next page. Use it when you are having symptoms of mania.

If You Have an Episode

If, despite your best efforts, you have a manic episode, don't be hard on yourself or give up. When you are feeling stable, review problem areas and rededicate yourself to avoiding mania. Keep track of your episodes to see if the time between episodes is lengthening and give yourself credit for your efforts, even if they are not totally successful. Give yourself credit for the times when you have maintained your stability. Don't allow yourself to get too discouraged. Focus on the positive instead of the negative.

Resources

Copeland, M.E. (1992) *The Depression Workbook: A Guide for Living With Depression and Manic Depression.* Oakland, CA: New Harbinger Publications.
   This book, based on my study of 120 people who live with depression or manic depression, contains useful information about many of the self-help strategies and techniques described in this chapter.

Davis, M., E. Eshelman, and M. McKay (1988) *The Relaxation & Stress Reduction Workbook.* 3rd ed. Oakland, CA: New Harbinger Publications.

Audio Tape

Copeland, M. E. (1993) *Living With Depression and Manic Depression.* Oakland, CA: New Harbinger Publications.
   A summary of self-help techniques to use as a reminder, for times when reading is not an option.

Daily Checklist

Today, to help maintain my stability, I will:

☐ Eat three healthy meals, focusing on foods that are high in complex carbohydrates.

☐ Avoid sugar, caffeine, alcohol, and junk foods.

☐ Get some mild exercise.

☐ Spend time out of doors.

☐ Increase my number of daily relaxation sessions to _____ times.

☐ Practice focusing, doing the exercises _____ times.

☐ Peer counsel for _____ sessions.

☐ Let the following members of my support team know how I am feeling:

_____

_____

_____

☐ Contact the following health care professional: _____

☐ Stay at home or in familiar surroundings.

☐ Stay away from stimulating environments such as bars or dances.

☐ Reduce the stress in my environment and avoid stressful people.

☐ Write a plan for the day and stick to it.

☐ Postpone major decisions.

☐ Avoid committing myself to extra activities.

☐ Avoid spending too much money.

☐ Sleep for _____ hours nightly.

☐ Quiet and soothe myself with the following activities:

_____

_____

_____

_____

_____

Daily Warning Signs Chart

Warning signs	Mon	Tues	Wed	Thu	Fri	Sat	Sun
What to do everyday							
Medications taken							
Necessary actions							

Some Other New Harbinger Self-Help Titles

Multiple Chemical Sensitivity: A Survival Guide, $16.95
Dancing Naked, $14.95
Why Are We Still Fighting, $15.95
From Sabotage to Success, $14.95
Parkinson's Disease and the Art of Moving, $15.95
A Survivor's Guide to Breast Cancer, $13.95
Men, Women, and Prostate Cancer, $15.95
Make Every Session Count: Getting the Most Out of Your Brief Therapy, $10.95
Virtual Addiction, $12.95
After the Breakup, $13.95
Why Can't I Be the Parent I Want to Be?, $12.95
The Secret Message of Shame, $13.95
The OCD Workbook, $18.95
Tapping Your Inner Strength, $13.95
Binge No More, $14.95
When to Forgive, $12.95
Practical Dreaming, $12.95
Healthy Baby, Toxic World, $15.95
Making Hope Happen, $14.95
I'll Take Care of You, $12.95
Survivor Guilt, $14.95
Children Changed by Trauma, $13.95
Understanding Your Child's Sexual Behavior, $12.95
The Self-Esteem Companion, $10.95
The Gay and Lesbian Self-Esteem Book, $13.95
Making the Big Move, $13.95
How to Survive and Thrive in an Empty Nest, $13.95
Living Well with a Hidden Disability, $15.95
Overcoming Repetitive Motion Injuries the Rossiter Way, $15.95
What to Tell the Kids About Your Divorce, $13.95
The Divorce Book, Second Edition, $15.95
Claiming Your Creative Self: True Stories from the Everyday Lives of Women, $15.95
Six Keys to Creating the Life You Desire, $19.95
Taking Control of TMJ, $13.95
What You Need to Know About Alzheimer's, $15.95
Winning Against Relapse: A Workbook of Action Plans for Recurring Health and Emotional Problems, $14.95
Facing 30: Women Talk About Constructing a Real Life and Other Scary Rites of Passage, $12.95
The Worry Control Workbook, $15.95
Wanting What You Have: A Self-Discovery Workbook, $18.95
When Perfect Isn't Good Enough: Strategies for Coping with Perfectionism, $13.95
Earning Your Own Respect: A Handbook of Personal Responsibility, $12.95
High on Stress: A Woman's Guide to Optimizing the Stress in Her Life, $13.95
Infidelity: A Survival Guide, $13.95
Stop Walking on Eggshells, $14.95
Consumer's Guide to Psychiatric Drugs, $16.95
The Fibromyalgia Advocate: Getting the Support You Need to Cope with Fibromyalgia and Myofascial Pain, $18.95
Healing Fear: New Approaches to Overcoming Anxiety, $16.95
Working Anger: Preventing and Resolving Conflict on the Job, $12.95
Sex Smart: How Your Childhood Shaped Your Sexual Life and What to Do About It, $14.95
You Can Free Yourself From Alcohol & Drugs, $13.95
Amongst Ourselves: A Self-Help Guide to Living with Dissociative Identity Disorder, $14.95
Healthy Living with Diabetes, $13.95
Dr. Carl Robinson's Basic Baby Care, $10.95
Better Boundaries: Owning and Treasuring Your Life, $13.95
Goodbye Good Girl, $12.95
Fibromyalgia & Chronic Myofascial Pain Syndrome, $19.95
The Depression Workbook: Living With Depression and Manic Depression, $17.95
Self-Esteem, Second Edition, $13.95
Angry All the Time: An Emergency Guide to Anger Control, $12.95
When Anger Hurts, $13.95
Perimenopause, $16.95
The Relaxation & Stress Reduction Workbook, Fourth Edition, $17.95
The Anxiety & Phobia Workbook, Second Edition, $18.95
I Can't Get Over It, A Handbook for Trauma Survivors, Second Edition, $16.95
Messages: The Communication Skills Workbook, Second Edition, $15.95
Thoughts & Feelings, Second Edition, $18.95
Depression: How It Happens, How It's Healed, $14.95
The Deadly Diet, Second Edition, $14.95
The Power of Two, $15.95
Living Without Depression & Manic Depression: A Workbook for Maintaining Mood Stability, $18.95
Couple Skills: Making Your Relationship Work, $14.95
Hypnosis for Change: A Manual of Proven Techniques, Third Edition, $15.95

More tools for change from Mary Ellen Copeland

THE WORRY CONTROL WORKBOOK
Helps you identify areas where specific types of worry are likely to reoccur and develop new skills for dealing with them.   **Item WCW $15.95**

WINNING AGAINST RELAPSE
Teaches anyone you how to monitor symptoms and respond to them in a way that reduces or eliminates the possibility of relapse.   **Item WIN $14.95**

LIVING WITHOUT DEPRESSION AND MANIC DEPRESSION
Covers self-advocacy, wellness lifestyle, dealing with sleep problems, finding a career that works, and much more.   **Item MOOD $18.95**

COPING WITH DEPRESSION
Condensed in this video 60-minute video are the fruits of years of research and hundreds of interviews with depressed persons. All the advice, sugestions, and techniques for self-help contained in her books are enriched with explanations and vivid examples presented to a live audience.   **Item 501 (VHS only) $39.95**

LIVING WITH DEPRESSION AND MANIC DEPRESSION
Inspires confidence that you can achieve real breakthroughs in coping with depression or manic depression. One cassette in a rigid plastic box.
Item 41 $11.95

——— Order Form ———

Complete this form and return it to New Harbinger Publications, Inc., 5674 Shattuck Avenue, Oakland, CA 94609, or phone us at (800) 748-6273, or fax this page to (510) 652-5472.

Please send _____ copies of the following items:
— *The Worry Control Workbook.* Item WCW $15.95 each
— *Winning Against Relapse.* Item WIN $14.95 each
— *Living Without Depression and Manic Depression.* Item MOOD $18.95 each
— *Coping With Depression.* Item 501 (VHS only) $39.95 each
— *Living With Depression & Manic Depression.* Item 41 $11.95 each

Your Name_____

Address_____

City, State, Zip_____

Telephone: Daytime, Mon.-Fri. (_____)_____
                          (In case we need to contact you about your order.)

Please include $3.80 shipping for one item and add $.75 for each additional item. California residents add appropriate tax.

Charge to   Visa   Mastercard   Expiration Date _____

Signature_____
Lifetime Guarantee: If not satisfied, return these products at any time for a full refund, less shipping and handling.